Photo credit: © Jerry Markatos

ABOUT THE AUTHOR

Frederick P. Brooks, Jr., is Kenan Professor of Computer Science at the University of North Carolina at Chapel Hill. He is best known as the "father of the IBM System/360," having served as project manager for its development and later as manager of the Operating System/360 software project during its design phase. For this work, he, Bob Evans, and Erich Bloch were awarded the National Medal of Technology in 1985. Earlier, he was an architect of the IBM Stretch and Harvest computers.

At Chapel Hill, Dr. Brooks founded the Department of Computer Science and chaired it from 1964 through 1984. He has served on the National Science Board and the Defense Science Board. His current teaching and research is in computer architecture, interactive computer graphics, and virtual environments.

The Design of Design

Essays from a Computer Scientist

Frederick P. Brooks, Jr.

University of North Carolina at Chapel Hill

✦Addison-Wesley

Upper Saddle River, NJ • Boston • Indianapolis • San Francisco
New York • Toronto • Montreal • London • Munich • Paris • Madrid
Capetown • Sydney • Tokyo • Singapore • Mexico City

Credits and permissions appear on page 421, which is a continuation of this copyright page.

Front Cover: John Constable's design (painting) for his view of Salisbury Cathedral, the design of Elias de Dereham and Nicholas of Ely. © Geoffrey Clements/ CORBIS. All rights reserved.

This material is based upon work supported by the National Science Foundation under Grant No. 0608665.

Any opinions, findings, and conclusions or recommendations expressed in this material are those of the author and do not necessarily reflect the views of the National Science Foundation.

Library of Congress Cataloging-in-Publication Data

Brooks, Frederick P. (Frederick Phillips)
  The design of design : essays from a computer scientist / Frederick P. Brooks, Jr.
     p.   cm.
  Includes bibliographical references and indexes.
  ISBN 978-0-201-36298-5 (pbk. : alk. paper) 1. Engineering design. 2. Software engineering. 3. Design—Case studies. I. Title.
  TA174.B752 2010
  620'.0042—dc22

                                                                2009045215

ISBN-13: 978-0-201-36298-5
ISBN-10:   0-201-36298-8

Text printed in the United States on recycled paper at Courier in Stoughton, Massachusetts.
First printing, March 2010

*To all who have shared in my
design adventures:*

Family,

Colleagues,

Friends, and

Construction professionals

Contents

Preface

I write to prod designers and design project managers into thinking hard about the *process* of designing things, especially complex systems. The viewpoint is that of an engineer, focused on utility and effectiveness but also on efficiency and elegance.[1]

Who Should Read This Book?

In *The Mythical Man-Month* I aimed at "professional programmers, professional managers, and especially professional managers of programmers." I argued the necessity, difficulty, and methods of achieving conceptual integrity when software is built by teams.

This book widens the scope considerably and adds lessons from 35 more years. Design experiences convince me that there are constants across design processes in a diverse range of design domains. Hence the target readers are:

1. Designers of many kinds. Systematic design excluding intuition yields pedestrian follow-ons and knock-offs; intuitive design without system yields flawed fancies. How to weld intuition and systematic approach? How to grow as a designer? How to function in a design team?

Whereas I aim for relevance to many domains, I expect an audience weighted toward computer software and hardware designers—to whom I am best positioned to speak concretely. Thus some of my examples in these areas will involve technical detail. Others should feel comfortable skipping them.

2. Design project managers. To avoid disaster, the project manager must blend both theory and lessons from hands-on experience as he designs his design process, rather than just replicating some oversimplified academic model, or jury-rigging a process without reference to either theory or the experience of others.

3. Design researchers. The study of design processes has matured; good, but not all good. Published studies increasingly address narrower and narrower topics, and the large issues are less often discussed. The desire for rigor and for "a science of design" perhaps discourages publication of anything other than scientific studies. I challenge design thinkers and researchers to address again the larger questions, even when social science methodology is of little help. I trust they will also challenge the generality of my observations and the validity of my opinions. I hope to serve their discipline by bringing some of their results to practitioners.

Why Another Book on Design?

Making things is a joy—immensely satisfying. J. R. R. Tolkien suggests that God gave us the gift of subcreation, as a gift, just for our joy.[2] After all, "The cattle on a thousand hills are mine. ... If I were hungry, I would not tell *you*."[3] Designing per se is fun.

The design process is not well understood either psychologically or practically. This is not for lack of study. Many designers have reflected on their own processes. One motivation for study is the wide gaps, in every design discipline, between best practice and average practice, and between average practice and semi-competent practice. Much of design cost, often as much as a third, is rework, the correction of mistakes. Mediocre design provably wastes the world's resources, corrupts the environment, affects international competitiveness. Design is important; teaching design is important.

So, it was reasoned, systematizing the design process would raise the level of average practice, and it has. German mechanical engineering designers were apparently the first to undertake this program.[4]

The study of the design process was immensely stimulated by the coming of computers and then of artificial intelligence. The initial hope, long delayed in realization and I think impossible, was that AI techniques could not only take over much of the drudgery of routine design but even produce brilliant designs lying outside the domains usually explored by humans.[5] A discipline of design studies arose, with dedicated conferences, journals, and many studies.

With so much careful study and systematic treatment already done, why another book?

First, the design process has evolved very rapidly since World War II, and the set of changes has rarely been discussed. Team design is increasingly the norm for complex artifacts. Teams are often geographically dispersed. Designers are increasingly divorced from both use and implementation—typically they no longer can build with their own hands the things they design. All kinds of designs are now captured in computer models instead of drawings. Formal design processes are increasingly taught, and they are often mandated by employers.

Second, much mystery remains. The gaps in our understanding become evident when we try to teach students how to design well. Nigel Cross, a pioneer in design research, traces four stages in the evolution of design process studies:

1. *Prescription* of an ideal design process
2. *Description* of the intrinsic nature of design problems
3. *Observation* of the reality of design activity
4. *Reflection* on the fundamental concepts of design[6]

I have designed in five media across six decades: computer architecture, software, houses, books, and organizations. In each I have had some roles as principal designer and some roles as collaborator in a team.[7] I have long been interested in the design process; my 1956 dissertation was "The analytic design of automatic data processing systems."[8] Perhaps now is the time for mature reflection.

What Kind of Book?

I am struck by how alike these processes have been! The mental processes, the human interactions, the iterations, the constraints, the labor—all have a great similarity. These essays reflect on what seems to be the underlying invariant process.

Whereas computer architecture and software architecture each have short histories and modest reflections about their design processes, building architecture and mechanical design have long and honorable traditions. In these fields design theories and design theorists abound.

I am a professional designer in those fields that have had only modest reflection, and an amateur designer in some long and deep fields. So I shall attempt to extract some lessons from the older design theories and to apply them to computers and software.

I believe "a science of design" to be an impossible and indeed misleading goal. This liberating skepticism gives license to speak from intuition and experience—including the experience of other designers who have graciously shared their insights with me.[9]

Thus I offer neither a text nor a monograph with a coherent argument, but a few opinionated essays. Even though I have tried to furnish helpful references and notes that explore intriguing side alleys, I recommend that one read each essay through, ignoring the notes and references, and then perhaps go back and explore the byways. So I have sequestered them at the end of each chapter.

Some case studies provide concrete examples to which the essays can refer. These are chosen not because of their importance, but because they sketch some of the experience base from which I conclude and opine. I have favored especially those about the functional design of houses—designers in any medium can relate to them.

I have done functional (detailed floor plan, lighting, electrical, and plumbing) design for three house projects as principal architect. Comparing and contrasting that process with the process of designing complex computer hardware and software has helped me postulate "essentials" of the design process, so I use these as some of my cases, describing those processes in some detail.

In retrospect, many of the case studies have a striking common attribute: *the boldest design decisions, whoever made them, have accounted for a high fraction of the goodness of the outcome.* These bold decisions were made due sometimes to vision, sometimes to desperation. They were always gambles, requiring extra investment in hopes of getting a much better result.

Acknowledgments

I have borrowed my title from a work of a generation ago by Gordon Glegg, an ingenious mechanical designer, a charming person, and a spellbinding Cambridge lecturer. It was my privilege to lunch with him in 1975 and to catch some of his passion for design. His title perfectly captures what I am attempting, so I reuse it with gratitude and respect.[10]

I appreciate the encouragement of Ivan Sutherland, who in 1997 suggested that I grow a lecture into a book and who more than a decade later sharply critiqued the draft, to its great improvement. My resulting intellectual journey has been very rewarding.

This work has been possible only because of three research leaves granted by UNC-Chapel Hill and my department chairmen, Stephen Weiss and Jan Prins. I was most graciously welcomed by Peter Robinson at Cambridge, Mel Slater at University College London, their department chairmen, and their colleagues.

The NSF Computer and Information Science and Engineering Directorate's Science of Design program, initiated by Assistant Director Peter A. Freeman, provided a most helpful grant for the completion of this book and the preparation of the associated Web site. That funding has enabled me to interview many designers and to concentrate my principal efforts for the past few years on these essays.

I am deeply indebted to the many real designers who have shared their insights with me. An acknowledgments table listing interviewees and referees is an end piece. Several books have been especially informative and influential; I list them in Chapter 28, "Recommended Reading."

My wife, Nancy, co-designer of some of the work herein, has been a constant source of support and encouragement, as have my children, Kenneth P. Brooks, Roger E. Brooks, and Barbara B. La Dine. Roger did an exceptional review of the manuscript, providing dozens of suggestions per chapter, from concepts to commas.

I've been blessed by strong administrative support at UNC from Timothy Quigg, Whitney Vaughan, Darlene Freedman, Audrey Rabelais, and David Lines. Peter Gordon, Publishing Partner at Addison-Wesley, has provided unusual encouragement. Julie Nahil, Full-Service Production Manager at Addison-Wesley, and Barbara Wood, Copy Editor, have provided exceptional professional skills and patience.

John H. Van Vleck, Nobel-laureate physicist, was Dean of Harvard's Division of Engineering and Applied Science when I was a graduate student there, in Aiken's lab. Van Vleck was very concerned that the practice of engineering be put on a firmer scientific basis. He led a vigorous shift of American engineering education away from design toward applied science. The pendulum swung too far; reaction set in; and the teaching of design has been contentious ever since. I am grateful that three of my Harvard teachers never lost sight of the importance of design and taught it: Philippe E. Le Corbeiller, Harry R. Mimno, and Howard H. Aiken, my adviser.

Thanks and praise to The Great Designer, who graciously grants us the means, the daily sustaining, and the joys of subcreation.

Chapel Hill, NC
November 2009

Endnotes

1. The caption for the book cover is based on Smethurst [1967], *The Pictorial History of Salisbury Cathedral*, who adds, "... Salisbury is thus the only English cathedral, except St. Paul's, of which the whole interior structure was built to the design of one man [or one two-person team] and completed without a break."

2. Tolkien [1964], "On Fairy Stories," in *Tree and Leaf*, 54.

3. Psalm 50:10,12. Emphasis added.

4. Pahl and Beitz [1984], in Section 1.2.2, trace this history, starting in 1928. Their own book, *Konstructionslehre*, through seven editions, is perhaps the most important systematization. I distinguish study of the *design process* from rules for design in any particular medium. These are millennia older.

5. The major monograph, tremendously influential, was Herbert Simon's *The Sciences of the Artificial* [1969, 1981, 1996].

6. Cross [1983], *Developments in Design Methodology*, x.

7. A table of the specific design experiences is included in the appendix materials on the Web site:
http://www.cs.unc.edu/~brooks/DesignofDesign.

8. Brooks [1956], "The analytic design of automatic data processing systems," PhD dissertation, Harvard University.

9. I thus do not contribute to the design methodologists' goal as stated in http://en.wikipedia.org/wiki/Design_methods (accessed on January 5, 2010):

> *The challenge is to transform individual experiences, frameworks and perspectives into a shared, understandable, and, most importantly, a transmittable area of knowledge. Victor Margolin states three reasons why this will prove difficult, [one of which is]:*
>
> *'… Individual explorations of design discourse focus too much on individual narratives, leading to personal point-of-view rather than a critical mass of shared values.'*

To this I must plead, "Guilty as charged."

10. Glegg [1969], *The Design of Design*.

I
Models of Designing

1

The Design Question

[New ideas would come about] by a connexion and
transferring of the observations of one Arte, to the uses
of another, when the experience of several misteries
shall fall under consideration of one mans minde.

SIR FRANCIS BACON [1605], *THE TWO
BOOKS OF THE PROFICIENCE AND
ADVANCEMENT OF LEARNING*, BOOK 2, 10

*Few engineers and composers ... can carry on a
mutually rewarding conversation about the content of
the other's professional work. What I am suggesting
is that they can carry on such a conversation about
design, . . . [and then] begin to share their experiences
of the creative professional design process.*

HERBERT SIMON [1969], *THE SCIENCES
OF THE ARTIFICIAL*, 82

Spiral staircase
Corbis

3

Is Bacon Right?

Sir Francis Bacon's hypothesis is our challenge. Are there invariant properties of the design process itself, properties that hold across a wide range of media of design? If so, it seems likely that designers in one medium would collectively grasp some of these principles more clearly than other designers, through struggles that are peculiarly difficult for that medium. Moreover, some media, such as buildings, have longer histories of both design and meta-design—"the design of design." If all this is true—and if Bacon's conclusion is true—designers in different media can expect to learn new things about their own several crafts by comparing their experiences and insights.

What Is Design?

The *Oxford English Dictionary* defines the verb *design* as

> *To form a plan or scheme of, to arrange or conceive in the mind . . . for later execution.*

The essentials of this definition are *plan*, *in the mind*, and *later execution*. Thus, a design (noun) is a created object, preliminary to and related to the thing being designed, but distinct from it. Dorothy Sayers, the English writer and dramatist, in her magnificent and thought-provoking book *The Mind of the Maker*, breaks the creative process out further into three distinct aspects. She calls them the Idea, the Energy (or Implementation), and the Interaction,[1] that is,

1. The formulation of the conceptual constructs
2. Implementation in real media
3. Interactivity with users in real uses

A book, in this conception, or a computer, or a program, comes into existence first as an ideal construct, built outside time and space, but complete in essence in the mind of the author. It is implemeted in time and space, by pen, ink, and paper; or by silicon and metal. The creation is complete when someone reads the book, uses the computer, or runs the program, thereby interacting with the mind of the maker.

In an earlier paper, I divided the tasks in building software into *essence* and *accident*.[2] (This Aristotelian language is not to denigrate the accidental parts of software construction. In modern language the terms would more understandably be *essential* and *incidental*.) The part of software building I called *essence* is the mental crafting of the conceptual construct; the part I called *accident* is its implementation process. *Interaction*, Sayers's third step, occurs when the software is used.

The design is thus the mental formulation, which Sayers calls "the Idea," and it can be complete before any realization is begun. Mozart's response to his father's inquiry about an opera due to the duke in three weeks both stuns us and clarifies the concept:

Everything has been composed, just not yet written down.

LETTER TO LEOPOLD MOZART [1780]

For most human makers of things, the incompletenesses and inconsistencies of our ideas become clear only during implementation. Thus it is that writing, experimentation, "working out," are essential disciplines for the theoretician.

The phases of Idea, Implementation, and Interaction operate recursively. Implementation creates a space in which another cycle of design must be done. Thus Mozart Implemented his opera Idea with pen on paper. The conductor, Interacting with Mozart's creation, conceived an Idea of an interpretation, Implemented it with orchestra and singers, and the Interaction with the audience completed the process.

A *design* is a created object; associated with it is a *design process*, which I shall call *design*, without any article. Then there is the verb *to design*. The three senses are intimately related; I believe context will resolve ambiguity.

What's Real? The Design Concept

If a number of individuals have a common name, we assume them to have also a corresponding idea or form:—do you understand me?

I do.

Let us take any common instance; there are beds and tables in the world—plenty of them, are there not?

Yes.

But there are only two ideas or forms of them—one the idea of a bed, the other of a table.

True.

And the maker of either of them makes a bed or he makes a table for our use, in accordance with the idea.

PLATO, *THE REPUBLIC* [360 BC], BOOK X

At the 2008 Design Thinking Research Symposium 7, each of the speakers presented analyses of the same four design team meetings.[3] Videos and transcripts had been distributed well in advance.

Rachael Luck of the University of Reading identified in the architectural conversations an entity that none of us had remarked but all then recognized: *the Design Concept*.[4]

Sure enough, both architect and client referred from time to time to this shared invisible entity. Speakers usually gestured vaguely toward the drawings when they spoke thus, but it was clear they were not referring to the drawings or any particular thing therein. Always, the concern was for the conceptual integrity of the developing design.

Luck's insight made the *Design Concept* a thing in its own right. This resonated strongly with my experience. When the IBM System/360 "mainframe" computer family's single architecture was being developed (1961–1963), such an entity was always present in the architecture group, although never named. Exploiting Gerry Blaauw's brilliant insight, we had explicitly separated the System/360 design activities into *architecture, implementation,* and *realization.*[5] The basic concept was a computer family with one face to the programmer—the architecture—and multiple concurrent implementations at various positions on the performance and price curves (Chapter 24).

The very simultaneity of multiple implementations, with their several engineering-manager champions, drove the common architecture toward generality and cleanliness and insulated it from small cost-saving compromises. These forces, however, were merely shields for the instincts and desires of the architects, who each wanted to make a clean machine.[6]

As the architecture design progressed, I observed what at first seemed quite strange. For the architecture team, the *real* System/360 was the Design Concept itself, a Platonic ideal computer. Those physical and electrical Model 50, Model 60, Model 70, and Model 90 things under construction out on the engineering floors were but Plato's shadows of the real System/360. The real System/360's most complete and faithful embodiment was not in silicon, copper, and steel, but in the prose and diagrams of *IBM System/360 Principles of Operation,* the programmer's machine-language manual.[7]

I had a similar experience with the View/360 beach house (Chapter 21). Its Design Concept came to be real long before any construction began. It persisted through many versions of drawings and cardboard models.

Interestingly enough, I never felt such a Design Concept entity of the Operating System/360 software family. Perhaps its architects did; perhaps I did not have an intimate enough acquaintance with its conceptual bones. Perhaps the Design Concept didn't emerge for me because OS/360 was in fact a fusion of four somewhat separate parts: a supervisor, a scheduler, an I/O control system, and a large package of compilers and utilities (Chapter 25).

What's the Value?

Is there positive value to recognizing an invisible Design Concept as a real entity in design conversations? I think so.

First, great designs have conceptual integrity—unity, economy, clarity. They not only work, they *delight*, as Vitruvius first articulated.[8] We use terms such as *elegant, clean, beautiful* to talk about bridges, sonatas, circuits, bicycles, computers, and iPhones. Recognizing the Design Concept as an entity helps us to seek its integrity in our own solo designs, to work together for it in team designs, and to teach it to our youth.

Second, talking frequently about the Design Concept as such vastly aids communication within a design team. Unity of concept is the goal; it is achieved only by much conversation.

> *The conversation is much more direct if the Design Concept per se, rather than derivative representations or partial details, is the focus.*

Thus, moviemakers use storyboards to keep their design conversations focused on the Design Concept, rather than on implementation details.

Detailing will of course surface conflicting versions of the Concept and force resolution. For instance, System/360 architecture needed a decimal datatype, as a bridging aid for thousands of existing users of IBM's decimal machines. Our developing architecture already had several datatypes, including a 32-bit fixed-point twos-complement integer and a variable-length character string.

The decimal datatype could be made similar to either one. Which choice better fit the Design Concept of System/360? Strong arguments were made each way; the strength of each depends on one's version of the Design Concept. Some of the architects had implicit Design Concepts reflecting earlier scientific computers; others' implicit concepts reflected earlier business computers. System/360 was explicitly intended to serve both kinds of applications well.

We chose to model the decimal datatype after the character-string one, the one more familiar to the largest particular user community of the decimal datatype, IBM 1401 users. I would decide that way again.

Thinking about the Design Process

Thinking about designs has a long history, going back at least to Vitruvius (died ca. 15 BC). His *De Architectura* is the important book about design from the Classical period. Major milestones are the *Notebooks* of Leonardo da Vinci (1452–1529) and the *Four Books of Architecture* by Andrea Palladio (1508–1580).

Thinking about the design process itself is much more recent. Pahl and Beitz trace German thought from Redtenbacher in 1852, stimulated by the rise of mechanization.[9] For me, major milestones have been Christopher Alexander's *Notes on the Synthesis of Form* (1962), Herbert Simon's *The Sciences of the Artificial* (1969), Pahl and Beitz's *Konstructionslehre* (1977), and the founding of the Design Research Society and the starting of the journal *Design Studies* (1979).

Margolin and Buchanan [1995] is an edited collection of some 23 essays from the journal *Design Issues*, primarily design criticism and theory, with "occasional ventures into philosophical issues that bear on the understanding of design" (p. xi).

My *The Mythical Man-Month* [1975, 1995] reflects on the design process for IBM's Operating System/360, later evolved to MVS and beyond. It emphasizes the human, the team, the management aspects of that design and development project. Of particular relevance to the present work are Chapters 4–6 of those essays, which address how to achieve conceptual integrity in a team design.

Blaauw and Brooks [1997]; *Computer Architecture: Concepts and Evolution*, includes extensive discussion of the design of the IBM System/360 (and System/370–390–z) architecture and the relationships of and rationales for dozens of design decisions. It doesn't treat the design process or human aspects of designing at all. But Section 1.4, which discusses criteria for goodness in computer architectural design, is indeed of particular relevance for this work.

Kinds of Design

System Design versus Artistic Design

This book is about the design of complex systems, and the viewpoint is that of the engineer, an engineer focused on utility and effectiveness but also on efficiency and elegance.

This contrasts with much of the design done by artists and writers, whose emphasis is on delight and the conveying of meaning. Architects and industrial designers, of course, fall into both camps.

Routine, Adaptive, Original Design

We often think of bridge design as one of the high arts of engineering, one where breakthroughs in concept or of technology have dramatic and highly visible cost, function, and esthetic consequences.

Well, a high fraction of all highway bridges are short, so cranking out a design for a 50-foot concrete bridge is a routine and automatable process. For short bridges, civil engineers know, and long ago codified into handbooks, the design decision tree, the constraints, and the desiderata. The same situation prevails for the design of compilers for established languages on new platforms. There are many areas of routine, automatable design.

The emphasis in this book is on original design, as opposed to the routine redesign of object after object with changed parameters, or even adaptive design, which is essentially the modification of a preceding design or object to serve new purposes.

Notes and References

1. Sayers [1941], *The Mind of the Maker.*

2. Brooks [1986], "No silver bullet."

3. McDonnell [2008], *About Designing.* This book is the edited Papers from the Design Thinking Research Symposium (DTRS7).

4. Luck [2009], "Does this compromise your design?" reprinted in McDonnell [2008], *About Designing.*

5. Blaauw and Brooks [1964], "Outline of the logical structure of System/360." Blaauw further divides Sayers's "Energy" into Implementation and Realization, a distinction I find immensely useful.

6. Janlert [1997], "The character of things," argues that designed things have character and discusses how one designs that character.

7. IBM Corp. [1964], *IBM System/360 Principles of Operation.*

8. Vitruvius [22 BC], *De Architectura.*

9. Pahl and Beitz [1984], *Engineering Design.*

- **Goal**
- **Desiderata**
- **Utility function**
- **Constraints, especially budget (perhaps not $ cost)**
- **Design tree of decisions**

  UNTIL ("good enough") or (time runs out)

   DO another design (to improve utility function)

    UNTIL design is complete

     WHILE design remains feasible,

      make another design decision

     END WHILE

     Backtrack up design tree

     Explore a path not searched before

    END UNTIL

   END DO

   Take best design

  END UNTIL

2

How Engineers Think of Design—The Rational Model

... [F]or the theory of design is that general theory of search ... through large combinatorial spaces.

HERBERT SIMON [1969], *THE SCIENCES OF THE ARTIFICIAL*, 54

A Rational Model of the design process

The Model

Engineers seem to have a clear, if usually implicit, model of the process of design. It is an orderly model of an orderly process as the engineer conceives it. I shall illustrate with an example of a beach house design (sketched in Chapter 21).

Goal. First one starts with a primary goal, or objective: "One wants to build a beach house to take advantage of wind and wave at an oceanfront lot."

Desiderata. Associated with the primary goal are a host of desiderata, or secondary objectives: "The beach house should be reinforced to withstand hurricane-force winds; it should sleep and seat at table at least 14 people; it should exploit the stunning views;" and so on.

Utility Function. One wants to optimize the design according to some utility or goodness function that weights the several desiderata as to their importance. So far as I can tell, most designers imagine the terms themselves to be linearly summed, but conceive of each goodness variable individually as not linear, but rather as curved asymptotically to saturation. For example, more window area is a desideratum, something desired in house design. But the utility added by each extra square foot of window diminishes. The same is true of electrical outlets. The utility of the windows and that of the outlets, however, seem simply to sum.

Constraints. Every design, and every optimization, is subject to constraints. Some of these are binary, either satisfied or not—"The house must be set back at least 10 feet from the lot's side lines." Others are more elastic, with steeply rising penalties as one approaches a limit, such as schedule constraints—one fiercely wants to have the beach house ready when warm weather comes.

Some constraints are simple, such as setback limits. Others blithely conceal terrifying complexity—"The house must satisfy all the building codes."

Resource Allocations, Budgets, and Crucial Budgets. Many constraints take the form of a fixed resource to be allocated among design elements. The most common is a total cost budget. But this is by no means the only such constraint, nor is it necessarily the one that most controls the designer's attention in a particular project. In the beach house floor plan, for example, the controlling commodity to be rationed was the feet (even inches) of ocean frontage. In the design of a computer architecture, the critical budget may be the bits in a control register or an instruction format, or the uses of the total memory bandwidth. When people were solving Year 2000 problems in software, working days on the schedule were the crucial allocable resource.

Design Trees.   Now, so the Rational Model goes, the designer makes a design decision. Then, within the design space narrowed by that decision, he makes another.[1] At each node he could have taken one or more other paths, so one can think of the process of design as the systematic exploration of a tree-structured design space.

In this model, design is conceptually (at least) very simple. One searches the tree-structured design space, testing each option against the constraints for feasibility and choosing so as to optimize the utility function. The search algorithms are well known and can be cleanly described.

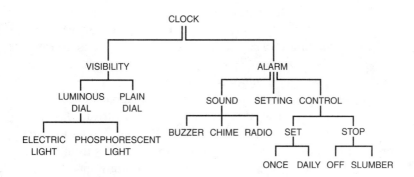

Figure 2-1   Portion of a design tree for an alarm clock
From Blaauw and Brooks [1997], *Computer Architecture,*
Figures 1-12, 1-14.

That cleanliness holds only for an exhaustive search of all paths, seeking a truly optimal solution. Designers commonly satisfice by searching only until a "good enough" solution is found.[2] Many engineers seem to approximate some sort of depth-first search strategy, choosing at each node the most promising or attractive option and exploring it to the end. At dead ends, one backtracks and takes another path. Hunches, experience, consistency, and esthetic taste guide each option selection.[3]

Whence Formulations of This Model?

The notion that the design process should be modeled as a systematic step-by-step process seems to have first developed in the German mechanical engineering community. Pahl and Beitz present the most widely used exposition in seven successive editions of their great work.[4] They observe the practice, but not the explicit statement, of systematic search of design alternatives in the *Notebooks* of Leonardo da Vinci (1452–1519).

Herbert Simon independently argues for design as a search process in *The Sciences of the Artificial* [1969, 1981, 1996]. His model and his discussion of it are much more sophisticated than those here. Simon, optimistic that the design process was a fit target for artificial intelligence (once adequate processing power became available), was motivated to lay out a strictly rational model of design precisely *because* such a model was a necessary precursor to automating design. His model remains influential even if today we recognize the "wicked problem"[5] of original design as one of the least promising candidates for AI.

In software engineering, Winston Royce, appalled at the failures of the "just write it" approach for large software systems, independently introduced a seven-step Waterfall Model to bring order to the process, as shown in the next chapter's frontispiece. In fact, Royce introduced his waterfall as a straw man that he then argued against, but many people have cited and followed the straw man rather than his more sophisticated models. I made that mistake myself in my younger days, and publicly repented of it later.[6] Even if ironically, Royce's seven-step model must be considered one of the foundational statements of the Rational Model of design.

As Royce emphasizes, his seven steps are distinctly different from one another and must be planned and staffed differently. Iteration is provided for but carefully limited in scope:

> *The ordering of steps is based on the following concept: that as each step progresses and the design is further detailed, there is an iteration with the [immediately] preceding and succeeding steps but rarely with the more remote steps in the sequence. ... What we have is an effective fallback position that tends to maximize the extent of early work that is salvageable and preserved.*[7]

The notion that a design space can be formulated as a tree is implied by Simon. It is described and illustrated by Gerry Blaauw and me in our *Computer Architecture*.[8] There we arrange the design choices for processor architecture strictly hierarchically in a giant tree, represented by 83 linked subtrees. A simple example of the design tree for the alarm of an alarm clock is shown in Figure 2-1. In it one observes two types of branches indicated by open and closed roots. The first, as shown for "Alarm," shows a subdivision; each branch is a different design attribute that must be specified. This is called an *attribute branch*. The *alternative branch*, shown for "Sound," enumerates alternatives of which one must be chosen.

What's Right with This Model?

Any systematization of the design process is a great step forward compared to "Let's just start coding, or building." It provides clear steps for planning a design project. It furnishes clearly definable milestones for planning a schedule and for judging progress. It suggests project organization and staffing. It helps communication within the design team, giving everyone a single vocabulary for the activities. It wonderfully helps communication between the team and its manager, and between the manager and other stakeholders. It is readily teachable to novices. It tells the novice facing his first design assignment where to begin.

The Rational Model in particular brings yet more advantages. The early explicit statement of goals, secondary desiderata, and constraints helps a team avoid wandering, and it breeds team unification on purposes. Planning the whole design process before starting coding or formal drawings avoids many troubles and much wasted effort. Casting the process as a systematic search of a design space broadens the horizon of the individual designers and lifts their eyes far beyond their previous personal experiences.

But the Rational Model is much too simplistic, even in Simon's richly developed version. Hence we must examine its faults.

Notes and References

1. Following Simon [1981], *The Sciences of the Artificial*, throughout this book I use *man* as a general noun, encompassing both genders, and *he*, *him*, and *his* as androgynous pronouns. I find it more gracious to continue the long tradition of including women and men equally in these general pronouns than to adopt more awkward, hence distracting, constructions.

2. To *satisfice* is to make good enough without necessarily optimizing (Simon [1969], *The Sciences of the Artificial*, 64).

3. But see Akin [2008], "Variants and invariants of design cognition," who finds evidence from the DTRS7 protocols that building architects tend to search laterally among several alternatives at every level, whereas engineering designers emphasize depth-first search based on an initial solution proposal.

4. Pahl and Beitz [1984ff.], *Engineering Design*.

5. Rittel and Webber [1973], "Dilemmas in a general theory of planning," define this term formally. It is well discussed in http://en.wikipedia.org/wiki/Wicked_problem.

6. Brooks [1995], *The Mythical Man-Month*, 265.

7. Royce [1970], "*Managing the development of large software systems*," 329.

8. Blaauw and Brooks [1997], *Computer Architecture*.

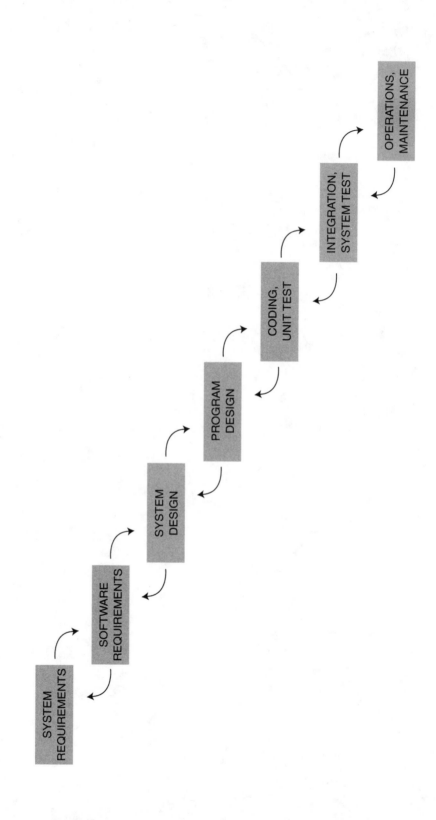

3
What's Wrong with This Model?

Sometimes the problem is to discover what the problem is.

GORDON GLEGG [1969], *THE DESIGN OF DESIGN*

A designer makes things. ... Typically his making process is complex. There are more variables—kinds of possible moves, norms, and interrelationships of these—than can be represented in a finite model.

DONALD A. SCHÖN [1984],
THE REFLECTIVE PRACTITIONER

Software's Waterfall Model

After Royce [1970], "Managing the development of large software systems," and Boehm [1988], "A spiral model of software development and enhancement." Royce © 1970 IEEE. Boehm © 1988 IEEE.

In fact, every designer will recognize the Rational Model as only an ideal. It somehow describes how we think the design process ought to work, but not how it works in real life.

Indeed, not every engineer will even admit to harboring so naive and idealistic a model in his heart. But I think most of us really do; I did for quite a long time. Therefore, let us take a hard critical look at the Rational Model of design, to identify precisely where it most departs from reality.

We Don't Really Know the Goal When We Start

The most serious model shortcoming is that the designer often has a vague, incompletely specified goal, or primary objective. In such cases:

The hardest part of design is deciding what to design.

As a student I spent one summer working at a large missile company, where I was once set to work designing and building a little database system for keeping track of the 10,000 drawings for a radar subsystem, and the updating status of each.

After a couple of weeks, I had a working version. I proudly presented a sample output report to my client.

"That's fine—it is what I asked for—but could you change it so that . . . ?"

Each morning for the next few weeks, I presented my client with the output report, revised yet again to accommodate the previous day's request. Each morning he studied the product report and asked for yet another system revision, using the same polite mantra.

It was a simple system (implemented on punched-card machines), and the revisions were conceptually simple. The most comprehensive change was to list the drawings sorted by, and indented to show, goes-into level, where level was represented by a single 0–9 digit in the card. Other refinements included multilevel subtotals, with exceptions of course, and the automatic marking of various noteworthy values with asterisks.

For a while, this frustrated me sorely: "Why can't he make up his mind as to what he wants? Why can't he tell me all at once, instead of one bit a day?"

Then, slowly, I came to realize that the most useful service I was performing for my client was helping him *decide* what he really wanted.

Well, today the software engineering discipline is much more sophisticated. We recognize that rapid prototyping is an essential tool for formulating precise requirements. Not only is the design process iterative; the design-goal-setting process is itself iterative.

This sophistication in software engineering does not forestall, or noticeably reduce, the numerous references in the literature to the "product requirements" as a normal given for a design process. But I will argue that knowing complete product requirements up front is a quite rare exception, not the norm:

> *A chief service of a designer is helping clients discover what they want designed.*

In software engineering, at least, the concept of rapid prototyping has a name and a recognized value, whereas it does not always have the same status in computer design and in building architecture. Nevertheless, I see the same goal iteration happening in these design fields. Increasingly, designers build simulators for computers and virtual-environment walk-throughs for buildings as rapid prototypes to drive goal convergence. Goal iteration must be considered an inherent part of the design process.

We Usually Don't Know the Design Tree—We Discover It as We Go

For the original design of complex structures, such as computers, operating systems, spacecraft, and buildings, each major design effort has enough novelty in the

- Goal
- Desiderata, and the utility function
- Constraints
- Available fabrication technologies

that the designer can rarely sit down and a priori map out the design tree.

Moreover, in high-technology design, few designers can know enough to draw the basic decision tree for their domains. Design projects often last two years or more. And designers get promoted out of design. Consequently, few designers will work in any depth on as many as 100 projects over a working life. This means the individual designer has not begun to explore all the branches of the basic design tree for his discipline. For it is characteristic of engineering designers, as opposed to scientists, that they rarely explore alternatives that are not clearly on the way to a solution.[1]

Instead, designers discover the design tree as they work—making a decision, and then seeing the alternatives it opens and closes for the next consequent design decision.

The Nodes Are Really Not Design Decisions, but Tentative Complete Designs

In fact, the very decision tree is itself only a simplistic model of the tree-search process. As Figure 2-1 illustrates, there are parallel attribute branches, as well as alternative branches. The choices in one branch are linked to those in others—by exclusion, affinity, or trade-off. Our massive design tree in *Computer Architecture* is much too simple; the entire "Computer Zoo" in that work is necessary to elucidate the decision linkings.[2]

This means that at each node of a design tree, one faces not a simple alternative choice among options for one design *decision*, but an alternative choice among multiple tentative complete *designs*.

Moreover, the ordering of decisions laying out a design tree matters greatly, as Parnas expounds in his classic paper "Designing software for ease of extension and contraction."[3]

The explosive combinatorics of these complications to the tree model boggle the mind. (This situation is like that of move trees in chess.) This difficulty is explored further in Chapter 16.

The Goodness Function Cannot Be Evaluated Incrementally

The Rational Model assumes that design involves a search of the design tree, and that at every node, one can evaluate the goodness function of the several downward branches.

In fact, one cannot in general do this without exploring all the downward branches to all their leaves, for many goodness measures (for example, performance, cost) will depend heavily on the subsequent design detailing. So although the goodness evaluation is possible in principle, one encounters here again the combinatorial explosion of alternatives in practice.

So what is a designer to do? Estimate, of course, either formally or informally. One *must* trim the design tree as one goes down.

Experience.   Many aids help intuition in this process. One is experience, both direct and surrogate: "The designers of OS/360 exposed detailed formats of system-wide-shared Control Blocks in Operating System/360, and it proved a maintenance nightmare. We will encapsulate them as objects." "The Burroughs B5000 family long ago explored the descriptor-based computer architecture. The performance hit was inherently too great, so we won't explore that subtree." Of course, the technological trade-offs are no longer the same, but the experience lesson is illuminating anyway. The most potent reason to study design history is to learn what *doesn't work*, and *why*.

Simple Estimators.   Designers routinely use simple estimators early in the design tree exploration. A building architect, given a budget goal, applies a rough square-foot cost estimate, derives a square-foot goal, and uses that for subsequent pruning of the design tree. Computer architects use instruction mixes to do rough-cut early estimates of computer performance.

A danger, of course, is that the rough estimator may lop off design branches that are in fact feasible but appear infeasible because of the very approximation involved in the estimator. I have watched an architect quote high costs for pushing out a wall under an already specified roof structure, based purely on a routine square-foot estimator. In fact, most of the cost of the added space was in the roof, and that was already committed, so the marginal cost was very low.

One can often get something for nothing, if one has previously bought nothing for something.

The Desiderata and Their Weightings Keep Changing

Donald Schön, the late MIT professor of urban studies and education, and a design theorist, said:

> [As the designer] shapes the situation in accordance with his initial presentation of it, the situation "talks back" and he responds to the situation's back-talk.
>
> In a good process of design, this conversation with the situation is reflexive. In answer to the situation's back-talk, the designer reflects-in-action on the construction of the problem, the strategies of action, or the model of the phenomena, which have been implicit in his moves.[4]

In short, as one ponders the trade-offs, there comes a new understanding of the whole design problem as an intricately interlocked interplay of factors. With it comes a change in the weightings of the desiderata. The same thing happens as the client, if there is one, grows his understanding of what he will get and develops his detailed vision of how he will use it.

In our house-remodeling design, for example (Chapter 22), a simple question, overlooked in the original program, arose well along in design, as my wife and I applied use scenarios to preliminary designs: "Where will guests at meetings put their coats?" This seemingly low-weight desideratum in fact tipped the big scales, and occasioned moving the Master Bedroom from one end of the house to the other.

Moreover, for designs that must be separately fabricated, such as buildings and computers, the designer learns from the builders a growing understanding of the interactions between design and fabrication. So many desiderata and constraints shift and refine. The fabrication technology may evolve as well, an especially common occurrence during computer design.

Since many desiderata (such as speed) are weighted on a value/cost ratio, yet another phenomenon occurs. As design proceeds, one finds opportunities to add some particular goodness at a very low marginal cost. So something that had not entered the original desiderata list at all comes in, and it often takes on a value that may demand preserving in later design changes.

Only after UNC's Sitterson Hall was designed, built, and in use, for example, did the Computer Science Department, as user, learn that the suite of spaces consisting of the Lower Lobby, Upper Lobby, Faculty Conference Room, Lecture Halls, and Vestibules combined beautifully into a facility well suited for hosting conferences of up to 125 people, with minimal impact on the work in the rest of the building. This was serendipitous—no such function was contemplated in the original architectural program. Yet it is a high-value feature: any future revision of Sitterson would surely aim to preserve this capability.

The Constraints Keep Changing

Even if the goal were fixed and known, all the desiderata enumerated, the design tree known precisely, and the goodness function precisely defined, design would still be iterative, because the constraints keep changing.

Often the environment changes—the city council passes new shadow-casting setback requirements; the electrical code has an annual updating; a microchip one planned to use is withdrawn by the vendor. The world keeps changing around us, even while we design.

The constraints also change due to discovery during the design process, or during the fabrication—the builders hit solid rock; analysis shows that chip cooling has newly become a constraint.

Not all constraint changes are increases. Often constraints go away. When this is fortuitous instead of intentional, the skillful designer recognizes the new opportunity and, with his flexible design, leaps to exploit it.

Alas! Not all designs are flexible. More commonly, when we are deep into a design process, we do not recognize that a constraint has disappeared, nor do we remember which design alternatives it formerly foreclosed.

It is important to list the known constraints explicitly at the start of the design process, as part of what architects call the *design program*. The design program is a document, prepared with the client, that sets forth the goal, the desiderata, the constraints. An example is given in this book's Web site. The design program is *not* the same thing as a formal requirements statement, which usually has contractual force in defining acceptability of a design.

The explicit listing of constraints smokes them out early, avoiding unpleasant surprises. It also impresses them on the designer's mind, radically improving the chances that he will recognize when one goes away.

All of us have designed around constraints, a process that calls forth much invention and exploration of unconventional corners of the design space. This is part of the fun of design, and a big part of the challenge.

Changing Constraints Outside the Design Space. Sometimes, however, a design breakthrough is achieved by stepping completely outside the design space, and working there to remove the design constraint. In designing the house wing (Chapter 22), I wrestled a long time, unsuccessfully, with a shadow-casting setback requirement constraint and the Music Room's desiderata (hold two grand pianos, an organ, and a square space for a string octet plus a 1-foot teaching margin). Figure 3-1 shows one iteration of the design, and the constraints.

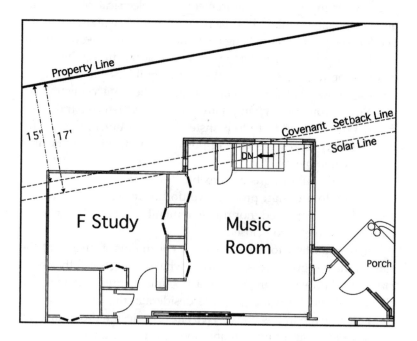

Figure 3-1   Design up against constraints

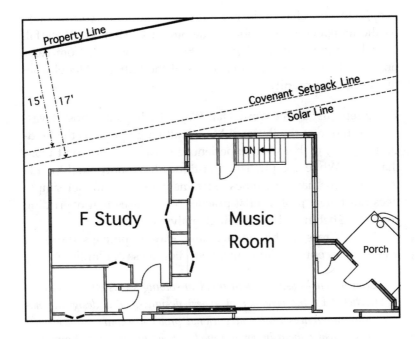

Figure 3-2   Constraint eased

The intractable design problem was finally solved completely outside the design space—I bought a 5-foot strip of land from my neighbor. This was probably cheaper and surely faster than attempting to get a setback variance from the city council, another outside-the-design-space approach. It also liberated other parts of the design, notably the placement of the northwest corner of F Study (Figure 3-2).

The explicit listing of known constraints in the design program helps here, too. The designer can periodically scan the list, asking, "Can this constraint now be removed because the world has changed? Can it be entirely circumvented by working outside the design space?"

Others' Critiques of the Rational Model

A Natural Model. The Rational Model as presented and criticized above may seem naive. But it is a very natural model for people to conceive. This naturalness is strongly corroborated by the independent creation of the Simon version, the Waterfall Model version, and the Pahl and Beitz version. Yet, from early on, there have been cogent critiques of the Rational Model from the design community.[5,6,7]

Designers Just Don't Work That Way.   Perhaps the most devastating critique of the Rational Model, although perhaps the hardest to prove, is that most experienced designers just don't work that way. While the published critiques have only rarely made the "emperor has no clothes" statement that the model simply does not reflect professional practice, one senses that overriding conviction behind all the detailed analyses.[8]

Nigel Cross, in his gentlemanly way, is perhaps the most articulate exception. Citing many studies, he says bluntly:

> *Conventional wisdom about problem-solving seems often to be contradicted by the behavior of expert designers. But designing has many differences from conventional problem-solving. ... we must be very wary about importing models of design behavior from other fields. Empirical studies of design activity have frequently found "intuitive" features of design ability to be the most effective and relevant to the intrinsic nature of design. Some aspects of design theory, however, have tried to develop counter-intuitive models and prescriptions for design behavior [emphasis added].[9]*

And,

> *The appositional nature of design reasoning has been neglected in most models of the design process. Consensus models of the design process, such as that promulgated by the Verein Deutscher Ingenieure [VDI, 1987] ... propose that designing should proceed in a sequence of stages. ... In practice, designing seems to proceed by oscillating between sub-solution and sub-problem areas, as well as by decomposing the problem and combining sub-solutions.[10]*

I find both the argument and the empirical evidence quite convincing. This oscillation has indeed characterized all my design experiences. The "where to put the coats?" requirement discovered deep into our house design process is typical.

Royce's Critique of the Waterfall Model.   Royce in his original paper describes the Waterfall Model so that he can point out its deficiencies.[11] Basically he argues that even with back-arrows describing counterflow between adjacent boxes in the waterfall, the model doesn't work. His prescription is, however, simply to augment the model with counterflow arrows that go back two boxes. A Band-Aid, not a cure.

Schön's Summary of the Critiques.

> *[Simon] has identified a gap between professional knowledge and the demands of real-world practice. ... Simon proposes to fill the gap ... with a science of design, his science can be applied only to well-formed problems already extracted from situations of practice.*

> *If the model of Technical Rationality ... fails to account for practical competence in "divergent" situations, so much the worse for the model. Let us search, instead, for an epistemology of practice implicit in the artistic, intuitive processes which some practitioners do bring to situations of uncertainty, instability, uniqueness, and value conflict.*[12]

But Despite All These Flaws and Critiques, the Rational Model Persists!

Often the original proponent of a theory or technique understands its promise, its liabilities, and its proper domain more clearly than his later disciples. Less gifted, more fervent, their very fervor leads to rigidity, misapplication, oversimplification.

So, unfortunately, are many applications today of the Rational Model. Writing as recently as 2006, design researcher Kees Dorst has to admit,

> *Although there have been many developments since then, the original work on problem solving and the nature of ill-structured problems, written by Herbert Simon, still looms large in the field of design methodology. The rational problem-solving paradigm, based on the conceptual framework that Simon introduced, is still a dominant paradigm in the field.*[13]

Indeed so! In the field of software engineering, we all too often still slavishly follow the Waterfall Model, our own embodiment of the Rational Model.

Verein Deutscher Ingenieure Standard VDI-2221. The Verein Deutscher Ingenieure in 1986 adopted the Rational Model, essentially as set forth by Pahl and Beitz, as an official standard for German mechanical engineering.[14] I have seen many rigidities in thinking engendered by this move. But Pahl himself has been at some pains to clarify that

> Procedures given in VDI-Richtlinie 2221-2223 and Pahl & Beitz (2004) are not of the "straight sequence" type, but should be utilized only as guides for basic purposeful action. A useful approach in actual situations might be to choose either an iterative approach (i.e. with "forward and back" steps) or by repetition using the next higher information level.[15]

DoD Standard 2167A. Similarly, the U.S. Department of Defense in 1985 enshrined the Waterfall Model in DoD Standard 2167A.[16] Only in 1994 did they, under the leadership of Barry Boehm, open up their acquisition by admitting other models.

So What? Does Our Design Process Model Matter?

Why all this fuss about the process model? Does the model we and others use to think about our design process really affect our designing itself? I believe it does.

Not Every Design Thinker Agrees with Me. Professor Ken Wallace of Cambridge, who translated three editions of Pahl and Beitz's work into English, believes the major step forward is to have some model that is readily understood and communicated. He points out how useful it is for beginning designers. The Pahl and Beitz model gives the novice a place to start work on a design, so he doesn't just wander. "I put up the Pahl and Beitz diagram [their Figure 1.6] and explain it. And then my very next slide says, 'But this is not the way real designers work.'"[17]

Hooray! But I am concerned whether younger teachers with less personal design experience always say that.

Suzanne and James Robertson, consultants who practice internationally and authors of excellent major works on requirements formulation, also feel that the deficiencies in the Rational Model don't really matter. "People who understand what design is, know better."[18]

Nevertheless, I believe our inadequate model and following it slavishly lead to fat, cumbersome, over-featured products and to schedule, budget, and performance disasters.

Right-Brained Designers. Designers are mostly right-brained people, visually and spatially oriented. Indeed, one of my curbstone tests for potential design talent is to ask, "Where is next November?" When my listener is puzzled, I elaborate, "Do you have a spatial mental model of the calendar? Many folks do. If you do, would you describe it for me?" The strong candidates almost always have one; the models themselves vary wildly.

Similarly, software design groups invariably scrawl diagrams, not words or code, on their shared whiteboards. Architects consider the broad-pen sketch on tracing paper an indispensable tool for communication, but even more for solo thinking.

Since we designers are spatial people, our process models live deep in our minds as diagrams, whether Pahl and Beitz's vertical rectangle, Simon's tree, or even the waterfall Royce draws and condemns. The diagrams subconsciously influence much of our thinking. Hence I believe a deficient process model hinders us in ways we cannot fully know and can barely suspect.

One obvious injury done by accepting the Rational Model is that we mis-educate our successors. We teach them modes of working that we ourselves do not follow. Hence we leave them unaided in arriving at their own real-world working modes.

I doubt if this is the case with more senior teachers, particularly those with industrial designing experience. We are keenly aware that models are intentional oversimplifications to help us with real-life problems that are frighteningly complicated. So we warn our students that "the map is *not* the terrain," the model is not a complete picture; it may even be inaccurate in what it does incorporate.

In software engineering practice, another kind of harm can readily be spotted—the Rational Model, in any of its forms, leads us to demand up-front statements of design requirements. It leads us to believe that such can be formulated. It leads us to make contracts with one another on the basis of this enshrined ignorance. A more realistic process model would make design work more efficient, obviating many arguments with clients and much rework. Chapters 4 and 5 elaborate on the requirements problem.

The Waterfall Model is wrong and harmful; we must outgrow it.

Notes and References

1. The engineer needs a satisficing solution; the scientist needs a discovery, and wider exploration often yields one.

2. Blaauw and Brooks [1997], *Computer Architecture*, 26–27, 79–80.

3. Parnas [1979], "Designing software for ease of extension and contraction," explicitly treats the design process as tree traversal. He argues strongly for making a design as flexible as possible. He urges that one do that by putting the decisions least apt to change nearest the tree root. Flexibility of a design is an important goal. In software engineering, both object-oriented design and agile development methodology have this as a fundamental aim.

4. Schön [1983], *The Reflective Practitioner*, 79.

5. Surprisingly, I found few critiques of the Pahl and Beitz formulation of the Rational Model and many of Simon's formulation. Pahl and Beitz themselves recognized the inadequacy of the model: in successive editions of their work, their model (Figures 3.3, 4.3 in the second and third English editions) includes more and more explicit iteration steps (Pahl and Beitz [1984, 1996, 2007], *Engineering Design*). Simon's three editions of *The Sciences of the Artificial* do not reflect any change in the model as proposed, although in personal conversation with me in November 2000 he said that his own understanding of the model had evolved, but that he had had no opportunity to rethink and rewrite accordingly.

    Visser [2006], *The Cognitive Artifacts of Designing*, has an excellent Section 9.2, "Simon's more nuanced positions in later work," which examines Simon's evolution as embodied in later papers. Visser shares my surprise that this evolution didn't get reflected in the later editions of *The Sciences of the Artificial*.

6. Holt [1985], "Design or problem solving":

> *There are two distinct interpretations of engineering design. The problem-solving approach, popular in many tertiary institutions and with an emphasis on solving structured, well defined problems using standardized techniques, may be traced to "hard" systems thinking. The creative design approach, on the other hand, combines analytical and systems thinking with human factors in engineering design to create and take advantage of opportunities to serve society. This paper discusses the limitations of the problem-solving approach in dealing with many real world tasks.*

7. Whereas Cross's critique is empirical, Schön criticizes the philosophy underlying the Rational Model. He says that the Rational Model, as enunciated by Simon, is a natural outgrowth of a much more pervasive philosophical mind-set, which he calls Technical Rationality and identifies as a heritage of now-discredited positivism. He finds the underlying philosophy itself totally inadequate for understanding design, even though it has been institutionalized into most professional design curricula:

> *From the perspective of Technical Rationality, professional practice is a process of problem solving. Problems ... are solved through the selection, from available means, of the one best suited to established ends. But with this emphasis on problem solving, we ignore problem setting, the process by which we define the decision to be made, the ends to be achieved, the means which may be chosen. In real-world practice, problems do not present themselves to the practitioner as givens. They must be constructed from the materials of problematic situations which are puzzling, troubling, and uncertain. ... a practitioner must do a certain kind of work. He must make sense of an uncertain situation that initially makes no sense. ... It is this sort of situation that professionals are coming increasingly to see as central to their practice. ... Technical Rationality depends on agreement about ends.*

8. A vivid example is Seymour Cray's 1995 quote: "I'm supposed to be a scientific person, but I use intuition more than logic in making basic decisions." http://www.cwhonors.org/archives/histories/Cray.pdf, accessed September 14, 2009.

9. Cross [2006], *Designerly Ways of Knowing*, 27.

10. Cross [2006], *Designerly Ways of Knowing*, 57. Dorst [1995], "Comparing paradigms for describing design activity," has an especially good discussion of Simon versus Schön. Their journal article is reprinted in Cross [1996a], *Analysing Design Activity*. Dorst also shows that for the Delft II protocols, Schön's model fits the observed designer behavior much more accurately.

11. Royce [1970], "Managing the development of large software systems."

12. Schön [1983], *The Reflective Practitioner*, 45–49.

13. Dorst [2006], "Design problems and design paradoxes."

14. VDI [1986], *VDI-2221: Systematic Approach to the Design of Technical Systems and Products*.

15. Pahl [2005], "VADEMECUM—recommendations for developing and applying design methodologies."

16. DoD-STD-2167A tried to fix this but unfortunately put a waterfall diagram in a prominent place and left things pretty much as they were. MIL-STD-498 superseded 2167A and addressed the model problem. DoD has since superseded 498 by adopting industry standards IEEE/EIA 12207.0, IEEE/EIA 12207.1, and IEEE/EIA 12207.2.

17. Personal communication [2008].

18. Personal communication [2008].

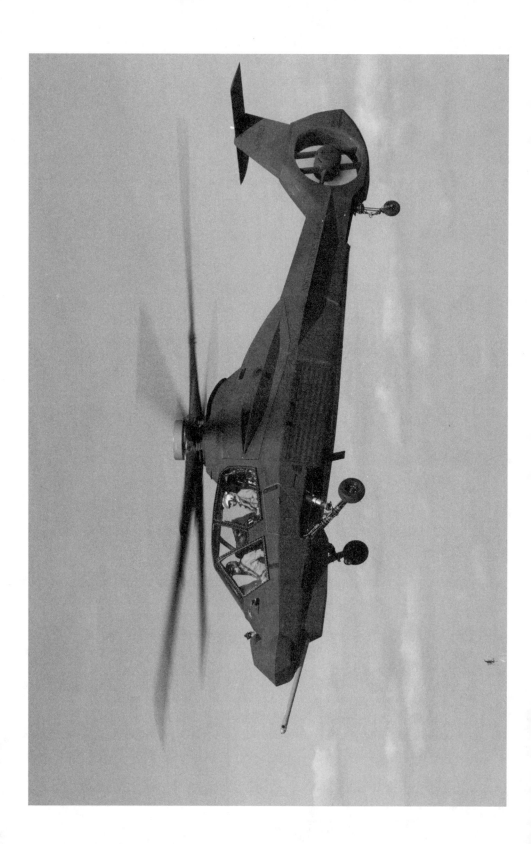

4

Requirements, Sin, and Contracts

*Any attempt to formulate all possible
requirements at the start of a project will fail
and would cause considerable delays.*

PAHL AND BEITZ [2007], *ENGINEERING DESIGN*

*The committee believes that getting to a state
of clear and complete system-level requirements
requires the interaction with potential contractors
that occurs between Milestones A and B.*

JAMES GARCIA, FOR THE AIR FORCE STUDIES
BOARD COMMITTEE ON PRE-MILESTONE A
AND EARLY-PHASE SYSTEMS ENGINEERING

Boeing-Sikorsky RAH-66 Comanche helicopter, originally the LHX
Sikorsky Aircraft/Richard Zellner/AP Wide World Photos

A Horror Story

The general had spent a career in Marine Corps aviation and knew helicopters. He and I had been dispatched into the depths of the Pentagon as a subcommittee of the Defense Science Board. We listened intently as a colonel briefed us on the in-progress design of the LHX (the Comanche), the next-generation light attack helicopter on which billions would be spent, and upon which soldiers' lives would depend. The helicopter was to be the successor to four different current helicopters, which had different missions.

The colonel outlined the requirements that had been developed by an inter-group committee representing the several using groups:

"Fly so fast, so far. Carry X armor; mount Y weapons; carry Z supply of ammunition; carry W fully equipped warriors, besides the crew.

"Fly close to the ground, under the radar cover. Even on a dark and stormy night, jump up to avoid obstacles. Pop up to shoot; pop back down to evade returned fire."

Then, without any change of inflection or expression, he said, "And it must ferry itself across the Atlantic [way beyond its normal operating range]."

The general and I were visibly shocked. The briefer quickly responded, "Oh, it will be designed to do that, by taking out all the ordnance and ammunition, and filling it with drums of gasoline." But our incredulity bore on rationale, not feasibility. Even I, a computer designer, knew in my gut that one *had* to pay for such a capability—not in dollars but in reduced capacity elsewhere.

"*Why* must it do that? Surely, it will have to do that only *twice*, if you're lucky."

"We don't have enough C-5 transport planes to carry them over."

"Why not take a bit of the program money for the LHX and buy more C-5s, instead of compromising the LHX design?"

"That's not possible."

Our shock at the extreme requirement was fully matched by our shock that its extremity didn't bother our briefer. Perhaps our instincts were wrong. Perhaps the marginal cost of the self-ferrying capability was indeed low. Perhaps knowledgeable designers had wrestled with that question.

But our ensuing conversation was not encouraging. If my recollection is accurate, the LHX Requirements Committee included neither an aircraft engineer nor a helicopter pilot—but rather mostly bureaucrats skilled at representing their groups in intergroup negotiations.[1]

Unfortunately, Not Unique

Many readers will have no trouble conjuring up a vision of a meeting of the LHX Requirements Committee; we have been to such meetings.

Each player has a wish list garnered from his constituents and weighted by his personal experiences. Each has both an ego and a reputation that depend on how well he gets his list adopted. Logrolling is endemic—an inevitable consequence of the incentive structure. "I won't naysay your wish, if you won't naysay mine."

Who advocates in the requirements process for the product itself—its conceptual integrity, its efficiency, its economy, its robustness? Often, no one. As often, an architect or engineer who can offer only opinion based on taste and instinct, unbuttressed as yet by facts.[2] For in a classical Waterfall Model product process, requirements are set before design is begun.

The result, of course, is a grossly obese set of requirements, the union of many wish lists, assembled without constraints.[3] Usually, the list is neither prioritized nor weighted. The social forces in the committee forbid the painful conflicts occasioned by even weighting, much less prioritizing.

Eventually, wish list and constraints must be reconciled. In practice, the product designers implicitly weight the official requirements using their own personal user models.[4] In many cases, the failure to provide weightings has decoupled the designers from deep user and application knowledge the several requirements setters do actually possess.

Generating requirements by committee, by the nature of the beast, tends to produce products that are too rich (Detroit cars, bloated software systems, unbuildable Internal Revenue and FBI systems). Perhaps committee specification is why large and super-ambitious software systems seem so prone to total disaster.

In the building of the IBM Operating System/360, require-ments were initially set by a large committee from the Marketing Division, following a process and producing a result just like that described. As Project Manager, I had to reject the requirements document as totally impractical and have a quite small team of architects, marketers, and implementers extract the essence.

Fighting Requirements Bloat and Creep

Requirements proliferation must be fought, by both birth control and infanticide. A very insightful report from the National Research Council's Air Force Studies Board addresses both attacks.[5]

The Committee on Pre-Milestone A and Early-Phase Systems Engineering starts with its own horror story. Major military sys-tems 30 years ago had a development time of around five years. Now times from program initiation to system deployment are two to three times longer, even while the pace of both technology and threat accelerates.

The dramatically successful programs of yore typically had *one or a few* clear overriding objectives and *schedule urgency*. These projects were begun with a few top-level requirements. As devel-opment proceeded, these were indeed broken down into more specific sub-requirements and key performance parameters, all under hard-driving, capable managers who continually balanced system *function* against *schedule* and *cost*.

As for requirements creep, whether pressed by users or by internal inventors, schedule urgency had been the best defense. (This has been my own best defense, as well, in system build-ing.) The committee perceives that Department of Defense acqui-sition has lost that permeating sense of urgency, replaced with ever-increasing layers of "oversight" mechanisms to avoid mis-takes. Such a progression is also not unknown within technical corporations.

The committee recommends that an organized systems engi-neering effort begin well before even the focused technology development for a new system is begun. But they recommend not the initial specification of requirements before Milestone A, but that the initial statement of detailed requirements be defined *during system development*, between Milestone A and Milestone B:

> *The definition of clear key performance parameters by Milestone A and clear requirements by Milestone B that can remain stable through Initial Operational Capability can be essential to an efficient development phase.*[6]

Requirements creep is addressed head-on in the most effective way. The committee's top-priority recommendation is: Appoint early-on strong, seasoned, domain-knowledgeable managers who can stay with the program through initial systems delivery. Then empower them to *"tailor standardized processes and procedures as they feel is necessary* [emphasis added]."[7]

They also urge the use of a Requirements Traceability Matrix to ensure that each requirement detailed, defined, and laid on is indeed derived from one or more of the initial overall requirements—that it didn't sneak in from a request by some user representative or a designer's desire to do something clever, novel, and putatively useful.[8]

Sin

Suppose:

- There is a client who is never greedy, but quite happy to pay his architect and builder fair prices for their expertise and labors (perhaps from enlightened self-interest, because he will want their help again).
- He has engaged an architect who always considers himself the client's agent, eager to use his talents and professional skills to best uncover and serve the client's true interests.
- He is contracting with a builder who sees and invariably performs his calling so as to produce high-quality products at the best possible value/cost ratio, within budget and on schedule.
- All the players are honest and truthful, and communication among them is excellent.

Then: I would argue that

- A cost-plus payment arrangement will give the client the most value per dollar.
- Design-build is the most rapid way to get a project built.
- An explicit Spiral Model process (next chapter) will yield the product best suited to the client's needs.

If this last is true, how can we explain the persistence of the Waterfall Model, when the greater fidelity of the Spiral and Co-Evolutionary models has been seen for more than a quarter century?

The one-word answer is *sin:* pride, greed, and sloth. We all recognize the suppositions above as ideals. The reader may have snorted on reading them: "Fat chance of all those conditions prevailing!" Because humans are fallen, we cannot trust each other's motivations. Because humans are fallen, we cannot communicate perfectly.

Contracts

For these reasons, "Get it in writing." We need written agreements for clarity of communication; we need enforceable contracts for protection from misdeeds by others and temptations for ourselves. We need detailed enforceable contracts even more when the players are multi-person organizations, not just individuals. Organizations often behave worse than any member would.

Clearly, it is the necessity for contracts, whether within an organization or between organizations, that forces the too-early binding of goals, requirements, constraints. Everyone recognizes the fact that these must later be changed. (This opens new opportunities for wrongdoing: "Low-ball on the contract; make it up on the change orders.") So it seems that the necessity for contracts best explains the persistence of the Waterfall Model for designing and building complex systems.

A Model for Contracting

The pressure for a complete and agreed-upon set of requirements comes ultimately from the desire—often, an institutional demand—for a fixed-price contract for a specific deliverable. Yet this demand runs head-on into the hard fact, argued in Chapter 3, that it is essentially impossible to specify a complete and accurate set of requirements for any complex system except in iterative interaction with the design process.

How have the centuries-old building design disciplines handled this perplexity? Fundamentally, by a quite different contracting model. Consider a normal building design process:

- The client develops a *program*, not a specification, for the building.
- He contracts with an *architect*, usually on an hourly or percentage basis, for *services*, not for a *specified product*.
- The architect *elicits* from the client, the users, and other stakeholders a *more complete program*, which does not pretend to be a rigid contractable product specification.
- The architect does a *conceptual design* that approximates the reconciliation of program and the constraints of budget, schedule, and code. This serves as a first *prototype*, to be *conceptually tested* by the stakeholders.
- After iteration, the architect performs *design development*, often producing more detailed drawings, a 3-D scale model, mock-ups, and so on. After stakeholder iteration, the architect produces *construction drawings and specifications*.
- The client uses these drawings and specifications to enter into a *fixed-price contract* for the product.

Notice how this long-evolved model separates the contract for design from the contract for construction. Even when both are performed by the same organization, this separation clarifies many things.

Of course, this model isn't fully sequential, either. As anyone ever involved in even a modest construction project knows, practical construction problems and late-stage client changes in either needs or design evaluation will occasion design changes, which in turn will necessitate contract change orders.

The classical architectural process sketched above has its own drawbacks, not least an extended schedule. Building projects with

- Close client-architect-contractor trust relationships,
- Well-understood design challenges, or
- A pressing hurry, justifying higher risks,

often conflate the normal process into a concurrent, pipelined design-build process. The architects organize their work so that the detailed construction drawings are produced first for the parts the contractor will need first: long-lead-time steel, site work, foundations.

System projects that meet the bulleted conditions should similarly be able to proceed on a design-build basis, too. Here the challenge is for the computer and software builders to identify the build order and the long-lead-time components.

Much hard thinking remains to be done here. I challenge the community to engage in this dialog.[9,10]

Notes and References

1. The Wikipedia [2002–2009] article on "RAH-66 Comanche" tells the history of the program. Its description of the helicopter's properties confirms my recollection of the stated requirements:

    The Comanche's very sophisticated detection and navigation systems were intended to allow it to operate at night and in bad weather. Its airframe was designed to fit more easily than the Apache into transport aircraft or onto transport ships, enabling it to be deployed to hot spots quickly. If transport assets were not available, the Comanche's ferry range of 1,260 nautical miles (2,330 km, 1,553 miles) would even allow it to fly to battlefields overseas on its own.

    In the event, the LHX evolved from a light attack helicopter to a reconnaissance helicopter, the Comanche pictured in the chapter frontispiece. Two were built; the program was scrapped because unmanned drones had taken over the reconnaissance function.

2. Squires [1986], *The Tender Ship*, studied government acquisition of innovative technology. "A theme running through the book is that the key to success is allowing the designers to be faithful to the engineering integrity of the product" (Mary Shaw, reviewer's comment). Squires urges designers to have a passion for the product's integrity:

    An applied scientist or engineer shall display utter probity toward the engineered object from the moment of its conception through its commissioning for use.

3. An anonymous reviewer correctly points out that one stakeholder's frill is often another's necessity. The effect I see, however, is that particular features have ardent champions. On the other hand, although everyone wants speed, smallness, robustness, ease of use, these requirements have no ardent champions in the requirements process, largely because the effect of a particular feature on them can't be known so early.

4. Chapter 9 discusses designers' mental models of users.

5. Air Force Studies Board [2008], *Pre-Milestone A and Early-Phase Systems Engineering*.

6. Air Force Studies Board [2008], *Pre-Milestone A and Early-Phase Systems Engineering*, 4. But see page 50, which might be misinterpreted:

> One must clearly establish a complete and stable set of system-level requirements and products at Milestone A. While requirements creep is a real problem that must be addressed, some degree of requirements flexibility is also necessary as lessons involving feasibility and practicality are learned. ... Certainly control is necessary, but not an absolute freeze.

   By communication with me, both the chair of the committee, Dr. Paul Kaminsky, and the NRC staff member responsible, Mr. James Garcia, clarified that the committee's intent is as stated in the page 4 paragraph. Mr. Garcia says:

> It was the committee's intent to say that clear KPPs [key performance parameters] be developed by MS [milestone] A, and clear and complete requirements by MS B, as stated in the Summary and in Chapter 4. The committee believes that getting to a state of clear and complete system-level requirements requires the interaction with potential contractors that occurs between MS A and B.

7. John McManus, MBCS, is a leading practitioner in project management and software development methods. Dr. Trevor Wood-Harper is Professor of Systems Engineering at Salford University: "A project charter laying out the reasons and expectations for a new initiative, and a project manager's vision for the task ahead are vital starting points for IT projects" (McManus [2003], *Information Systems Project Management*).

8. Boehm [1984], "Prototyping versus specifying," describes a classroom experiment in which one team built from lovingly crafted design specifications and a second team essentially built straight from the requirements. The first team's system suffered from feature bloat because the designers kept putting in things to "complete" the design or make it consistent. So it's not just the wish-listers who cause bloat—designers themselves can do it. I've done it myself, on the IBM Stretch computer.

9. Jupp [2007] treats the novel contracting schemes that have been used in public-private partnerships for public works in the UK.

10. Muir Wood [2007], "Strategy for risk management," is a conference paper that proposes how tunneling clients and contractors should deal with unforeseen risk in their contracting.

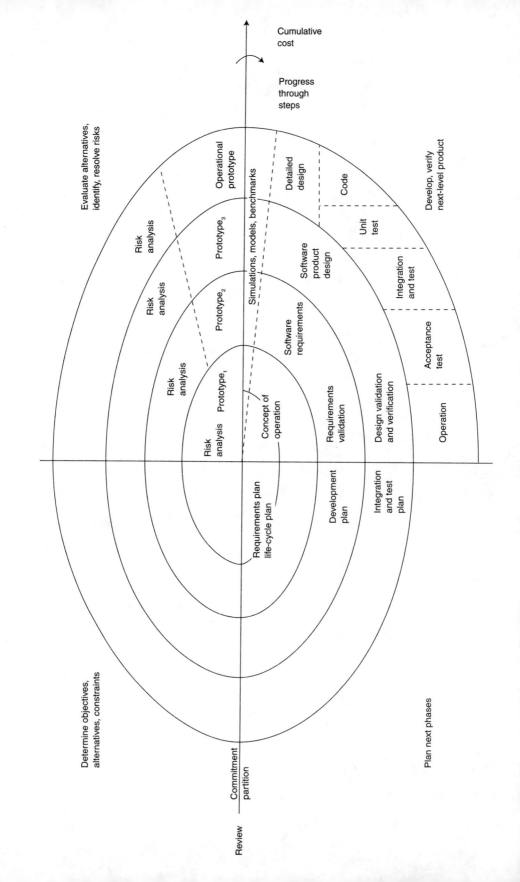

5

What Are Better Design Process Models?

It is widely accepted that creative design is not a matter of first fixing the problem and then searching for a satisfactory solution concept; instead it seems more to be a matter of developing and refining together both the formulation of the problem and ideas for its solution, with constant iteration of analysis, synthesis and evaluation processes between the two "spaces"—problem and solution.

NIGEL CROSS AND KEES DORST [1999],
"CO-EVOLUTION OF PROBLEM AND
SOLUTION SPACES IN CREATIVE DESIGN"

Boehm's Spiral Model
Boehm [1988]. Boehm © 1988 IEEE.

Why a Dominant Model?

Both practice and the education of designers now cry for answers:

- If the Rational Model is really wrong,
- If having a wrong model really matters, and
- If there are deep reasons for the long persistence of the wrong model,

then what are better models that

- Emphasize the progressive discovery and evolution of design requirements,
- Are memorably *visualized* so that they can be readily taught and readily understood by team and stakeholders, and
- Still facilitate contracting among fallen humans?

All models are by definition simplified abstractions of reality. Hence there can be many useful models of a design's life-cycle progression, each emphasizing some aspects and omitting others. Mike Pique made a video that dramatically highlighted this point by showing some 40 different computer graphics models of the protein bovine superoxide dismutase: stick models, ribbon models, solid models, action models, and others.[1]

One could therefore cogently argue that seeking a dominant model for the design process is a fool's errand. Why not let 100 models bloom? Each will add illumination.

I strongly disagree. The ubiquity of the Waterfall Model in software engineering, despite the many criticisms and the damage done by its oversimplification, convince me that the need to communicate and the nature of academic instruction mean that there *will* be a dominant model of the design process. Thus the pressing need is to *substitute* a less misleading model, not merely to augment present practice with a better model. Indeed, in the wider field of design, I see Simon's problem-solving model as having occasioned a lot of wasted effort in blind alleys by people trying to understand and improve design.

The Co-Evolution Model

Maher, Poon, and Boulanger proposed a formal model which I find helpful, the Co-Evolution Model.[2,3] Cross and Dorst describe this model as follows:

> *It seems that creative design is not a matter of first fixing the problem and then searching for a satisfactory solution concept. Creative design seems more to be a matter of developing and refining together both the formulation of a problem and ideas for a solution, with constant iteration of analysis, synthesis and evaluation processes between the two notional design 'spaces'—problem space and solution space. The model of creative design proposed by Maher et al. [1996] is based on such a 'co-evolution' of the problem space and the solution space in the design process: the problem space and the solution space co-evolve together, with interchange of information between the two spaces [Figure 5-1].[4]*

Evolution is used loosely here. The model is evolutionary in that both the understanding of the problem and the development of the solution are incrementally generated and incrementally evaluated.

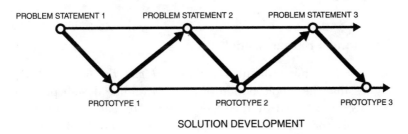

Figure 5-1   Maher, Poon, and Boulanger's Co-Evolution Model of design (Maher [1996])

Philosophers of technology have recently wrestled at length with the question of how well the process of human innovation is modeled by biological evolution. Ziman [2000], a work of many chapters by authors from many disciplines, gives a good summary of the state of thinking on the topic by philosophers and others as of 2000.[5] It sets forth arguments both that biological evolution is a good model, involving random generation and natural selection, and that it is not, because innovation is guided by purposeful design (the authors presume that evolution is not).

The Co-Evolution Model certainly emphasizes the progressive discovery and formulation of requirements. Its visual representation is memorable. It isn't very comprehensive: it doesn't pretend to include all aspects of the design-build-test-field-maintain-extend process. Moreover, the geometric image does not suggest a convergent process. So far as I can tell, the model has not yet had a lot of subsequent development and, as originally formulated, contained no milestones and contracting points. Although the model is attractive and better than the Rational Model, I don't think it is sufficient.

Whirligig Model. Yet it is important not to go overboard. Some of the proposed models, though rich, are so complex as to defy understanding, much less memorization and facile use in discussion. An example is Hickling's Whirligig Model, with cycles and epicycles.[6]

Raymond's Bazaar Model

Raymond in his brilliant *The Cathedral and the Bazaar* [2001] argues that the whole notion of a cathedral-like design process has been outmoded by the Open Source, "bazaar," process that has richly and effectively led to the development of Linux, a marvelously functional and robust operating system. His arguments are powerful and crisply formulated. He argues that the Open Source process can be the most effective way to develop all sorts of application programs, as well as operating systems. He illustrates with Fetchmail, his own creation.[7]

How It Works

As Raymond describes the bazaar process, a member of the using/ creating community sees a need, develops a module to meet it, and offers it to his peers as a gift. Integration of the module is, in the Linux community, greatly facilitated by the modularity of the Linux structure, especially its pipes and filters mechanisms. The same process works for the repair of bugs. Someone detects a bug in a module he is using, finds it, fixes it so he can get his own work done, and then offers the fix as a gift to the community.

Clearly people write new modules and fix bugs so they can do their own work. Why do they *give* away the results, when the necessary testing, documentation, and publication demand substantial extra work?[8] Raymond's answer, which rings true to me, is that the incentive and the reward is prestige.[9]

Often multiple modules or multiple fixes for the same bug are offered to the community. Raymond argues that a market mechanism (even among free goods) is at work. The better tool, the better fix, wins the more widespread acceptance, and its author proportionately wins more prestige.

So the bazaar is populated with many "vendors" offering their digital wares electronically. Many buyers, with their votes, pay recompense in a prestige communicated electronically throughout a worldwide community.

Strengths

What a wonder is this gift-prestige culture! How unlike crass work-for-money, claim-my-intellectual-property-rights! What a new model for other societal activities!

Moreover, Raymond cogently argues, the system products produced by the bazaar process are in general technically superior to those produced by the cathedral process. First, the market mechanism selects, in evolutionary fashion, the best-designed modules. Second, subjecting a new module simultaneously to hundreds of testers smokes out the bugs sooner, yielding a more robust product. Third, bugs are fixed better, because of market selection among fixes.

Thus the bazaar process is put forward as a totally new model both for product creation and for collaboration among electronically coupled, asynchronously communicating, mutually unacquainted teams.

I strongly urge all of my readers to read Raymond—not just the widely circulated title essay, but the other chapters in the book. There is much truth, much insight, and much wisdom there.

When Does the Bazaar Work?

Nevertheless, I would make six independent short observations about the Open Source process. This is in lieu of a protracted discussion, since I have no personal experience using it.

- The Bazaar *is* indeed an evolutionary model. The larger system is grown by adding components, each of which meets a need (a requirement, if you will) discovered by the user-designer.
- The gift-prestige economy works for people who are being otherwise fed; that is, the software gifts to the community are by-products of other work products that produce the revenue to pay the builders-donors.
- Since many of the products so made are indeed by-products, there have been more tools than applications. The results are not always quite polished or quite debugged—they only have to be good enough for the purpose of the builder. The "market" selection is in fact the quality control.
- Despite much that has been written about the "openness" and the "freedom" of the Open Source process, the total Linux edifice is hardly a random pile of idiosyncratic pieces—Linus Torvalds has been an overarching intellectual force for conceptual integrity. Moreover, for Linux a functional specification already existed: UNIX. Of equal importance, an overall system design existed.
- A key to all design processes is the discovery of the users' needs, wants, and criteria. The conspicuous success of the bazaar process in the Linux community seems to me to derive directly from the fact that *the builders are also the users*. Their requirements flow from themselves and their work. Their

desiderata, criteria, and taste come unbidden from their own experience. The whole requirements determination is implicit, hence finessed. I strongly doubt if Open Source works as well when the builders are not themselves users and have only secondhand knowledge of the users' needs.

- Hence there is still a need for cathedral processes, carefully architected, tightly controlled, and meticulously tested. Would you use the Open Source process to build the new national air-traffic control system?[10]

Boehm's Spiral Model

Barry Boehm proposed in 1988 the Spiral Model for the building of software.[11] The chapter frontispiece shows the model as originally proposed. The spiral shape certainly suggests progress. It associates successive repetitions of the same activity. The geometric shape is easily understood and memorable. The model emphasizes prototyping, starting with user-interface prototypes and user testing long before an operational prototype is possible.

The model has had wide acceptance; it is even permitted as a substitute for the Waterfall Model in U.S. Department of Defense procurements.[12] It has also had some development.

Denning and Dargan [1996] have criticized the Spiral Model: "[It is an improvement], but it is still designer and product centered, rather than user and action centered."[13] They go on to propose a rather informal *action-centered* design process which properly gives increased attention to the users and the use models. I recommend their thoughtful paper.

Nevertheless, since a development model is principally used by developers, I believe having it designer-centered is entirely appropriate. Moreover, their process approach does not address the need for a memorable geometric model or for a basis for arriving at contracts. With Boehm and against Denning and Dargan, I advocate *frequent* but not *continuous* interaction with representative users, with successive prototypes as the vehicles.

As originally proposed, the Spiral Model accommodated, but did not emphasize, the progressive discovery of requirements, nor did it emphasize contracting points.

I strongly believe the way forward is to embrace and develop the Spiral Model. I would suggest punctuating the spiral with explicit contracting points, augmented with clear specification of what can be contracted, with what certainties, and with what explicit distribution of risk. Risk management is the focus of much of Boehm's later work.[14]

Design Process Models: The Summary Argument of Chapters 2–5

- A formal design process model is needed, to help organize design work, to aid communication in and about projects, and for teaching.
- Having a visual, geometric representation of a design process model is crucial, for designers are spatial thinkers. They will most easily learn, think about, share, and talk in terms of a model with a clear geometric picture.
- The Rational Model of design occurs naturally to engineers. Indeed, it has been independently and formally set forth several times: for example, by Simon, by Pahl and Beitz, and by Royce.
- The linear, step-by-step Rational Model is highly misleading. It does not accurately reflect what real designers do, or what the best design thinkers identify as the essence of the design process.
- The bad model matters. It has led to the too-early binding of requirements, leading in turn to bloated products and schedule/budget/performance disasters.
- The Rational Model has persisted in practice despite its inadequacies and plenty of cogent critiques. This is because of its seductive logical simplicity, and because builders and clients need "contracts."
- Several alternative process models have been proposed. I find Boehm's Spiral Model the most promising. We need to keep developing it.

Notes and References

1. Pique [1982], *What Does a Protein Look Like?*

2. Maher [1996], "Formalising design exploration as co-evolution."

3. Maher [2003], "Co-evolution as a computational and cognitive model of design."

4. Cross and Dorst [1999], "Co-evolution of problem and solution spaces in creative design"; Dorst and Cross [2001], "Creativity in the design process."

5. Ziman [2000], *Technological Innovation as an Evolutionary Process.*

6. Hickling [1982], "Beyond a linear iterative process?"

7. Raymond [2001], *The Cathedral and the Bazaar.* I suspect the "cathedral" he has in mind is suggested by the frontispiece of Chapter 4 of *The Mythical Man-Month.*

8. Brooks [1975], *The Mythical Man-Month*, Chapter 2.

9. Raymond [2001], "The golden cauldron."

10. Richard P. Case wisely remarks,

    > *Maybe we should distinguish the "anybody can change it" and "any-body can see it" aspects of open-source design. If anybody can change it, nobody can do a confident analysis when something (even fatal) goes wrong, or give any kind of assurance that it has been fixed so that it won't happen again. Secrecy is a different matter. If only a few minds have access to the actual design, it is less likely that flaws will be discovered early and that alternate concepts will be developed and evaluated* (personal communication [2009]).

11. Boehm [1988], "A spiral model of software development and enhancement."

12. The Department of Defense has since wisely adopted industry software development standards IEEE/EIA 12207.0, IEEE/EIA 12207.1, and IEEE/EIA 12207.2. These permit spiral models.

13. Denning and Dargan [1996], "Action-centered design," 110.

14. Selby [2007], *Software Engineering: Barry W. Boehm's Lifetime Contributions to Software Development, Management, and Research*, collects Boehm's most important papers on risk into Chapter 5.

II

Collaboration and Telecollaboration

6

Collaboration in Design

A meeting is a refuge from "the dreariness of labor and the loneliness of thought."

BERNARD BARUCH, IN RISEN [1970],
"A THEORY ON MEETINGS"

Menn's Sunniberg Bridge, 1998
Christian Menn, ETH Zürich, ChristianMennPartners AG

Is Collaboration Good Per Se?

Two big changes in design have taken place since 1900:

- Design is now done mostly by teams, rather than individuals.
- Design teams now often collaborate by using telecommunications, rather than by being collocated.

As a consequence of these big shifts, the design community is abuzz with hot topics:

- Telecollaboration
- "Virtual teams" of designers
- "Virtual design studios"

All of these are enabled by telephony, networking, computers, graphic displays, and videoconferencing.

If we are to understand telecollaboration, we must first understand the role of collaboration in modern professional design.

It is generally assumed that collaboration is, in and of itself, a "good thing." "Plays well with others" is high praise from kindergarten onward. "All of us are smarter than any of us." "The more participation in design, the better." Now, these attractive propositions are far from self-evident. I will argue that they surely are not *universally* true.

Most great works of the human mind have been made by one mind, or two working closely. This is true of most of the great engineering feats of the 19th and early 20th centuries. But now, team design has become the modern standard, for good reasons. The danger is the loss of conceptual integrity in the product, a very grave loss indeed. So the challenge is how to achieve conceptual integrity while doing team design, and at the same time to achieve the very real benefits of collaboration.

Team Design as the Modern Standard

Team design is standard for modern products, both those mass-produced and one-offs such as buildings or software. This is indeed a big change since the nineteenth century. We *know the names* of the leading 18th- and 19th-century engineering design-ers: Cartwright, Watt, Stephenson, Brunel, Edison, Ford, the Wright Brothers. Consider, on the other hand, the *Nautilus* nuclear submarine (Figure 6-1). We know Rickover as the champion, the Will who made it happen, but which of us can name the chief designer? It is the product of a skilled team.

Consider great designers, and think of their works:

- Homer, Dante, Shakespeare
- Bach, Mozart, Gilbert and Sullivan
- Brunelleschi, Michelangelo
- Leonardo, Rembrandt, Velázquez
- Phidias, Rodin

Most great works have been made by one mind. The excep-tions have been made by two minds. And *two* is indeed a magic number for collaborations; marriage was a brilliant invention and has a lot to be said for it.

Figure 6-1   The *Nautilus* nuclear submarine
U.S. Navy Arctic Submarine Laboratory/Wikimedia Commons

Why Has Engineering Design Shifted from Solo to Teams?

Technological Sophistication.   The most obvious driver toward team design is the increasing sophistication of every aspect of engineering. Contrast the first iron bridge (Figure 6-2) with its splendid descendant (chapter frontispiece).

The first had to be wrought very conservatively, that is, heavily and wastefully, even though elegantly. Both the properties of the iron and the distribution of static and dynamic stresses were understood imperfectly (though remarkably well!).

Menn's bridge, on the other hand, soars incredibly but confidently, the fruit of years of analysis and modeling.

I am impressed that there are no naive technologies left in modern practice. It was my privilege to tour Unilever's research laboratory at Port Sunlight, Merseyside, UK. I was astonished to find a PhD applied mathematician doing computational fluid dynamics (CFD) on a supercomputer, so as to get the mixing of shampoo right! He explained that the shampoo is a three-layer emulsion of aqueous and oily components, and mixing without tearing is crucial.

Figure 6-2   Pritchard and Darby's Iron Bridge, 1779 (Shropshire, UK)
iStockphoto

The designers of a John Deere cotton-picking machine used CFD to structure the airflow carrying the cotton bolls. A modern farmer spends not only hours on the tractor, but also hours on the computer, matching fertilizer, protective chemicals, seed variety, soil analysis, and crop rotation history.[2] The master cook at Sara Lee adjusts the cake recipe continually to match the chemical properties of the flour coming in; the boss in the paper mill similarly adjusts for the varying pulpwood properties.

Mastering explosive sophistication in any branch of engineering forces specialization. When I went to graduate school in 1953, one could keep up with *all* of computer science. There were two annual conferences and two quarterly journals. My whole intellectual life has been one of throwing passionate subfield interests overboard as they have exploded beyond my ability to follow them: mathematical linguistics, databases, operating systems, scientific computing, software engineering, even computer architecture—my first love. This sort of splintering has happened in all the creative sciences, so the designer of today's state-of-the-art artifact needs help from masters of various crafts.

The explosion in the need for detailed know-how of many technologies has been partially offset by the stunning explosion in the ready availability of such detailed know-how—in documents, in skilled people, in analysis software, and in search engines that find the documents and plausible candidates for collaborators.

Hurry to Market. A second major force driving design to teams is hurry to get a new design, a new product, to market. A rule of thumb is that the first to market a new kind of product can reasonably expect a long-run market share of 40 percent, with the remainder split among multiple smaller competitors. Moreover, the pioneer can harvest a profit bubble while the competition builds up. In the biggest wins, the pioneer continues to dominate. These realities press design schedules hard. Team design becomes a necessity when it can accelerate delivery of a new product in a competitive environment.[3]

Why is this competitive time pressure more intense than before? Global communications and global markets mean that any great idea anywhere propagates more quickly now.

Costs of Collaboration

"Many hands make **light** *work"—Often*
But many hands make **more** *work—Always*

We all know the first adage. And it is true for tasks that are partition-able. The burden on each worker is lighter, hence the time to completion is shorter. But no design tasks are perfectly partitionable, and few are highly partitionable.[4] So collaboration brings extra costs.

Partitioning Cost.   Partitioning a design task is itself an added task. The crisp and precise definition of the interfaces between subtasks is a lot of work, slighted at peril. As the design proceeds, the interfaces will need continually to be interpreted, no matter how precisely delineated. There will be gaps. There will be inconsistencies in definition and conflicts in interpretation; these must be reconciled.

To simplify manufacture, there must be standardization of common elements across all the components; some commonality of design style must be established.

And then the separate pieces must be integrated—the ultimate test of interface consistency. It is not just in shipyards where the reality of integration is "Cut to plan; bang to fit."[5]

Learning/Teaching Cost.   If n people collaborate on a design, each must come up to speed on the goals, desiderata, constraints, utility function. The group must share a common vision of all of these things—of what is to be designed. To a first approximation, if a one-person design job consists of two parts—learning l and designing d—the total work when the job is shared out n ways is no longer

$$work = l + d$$

but now at least

$$work = n\, l + d$$

Moreover, someone with the vision and knowledge must do the teaching, hence will not be designing. One hopes that the efficiencies of specialization will buy back some of these costs.

Communication Cost during Design.   During the design process, the collaborating designers must be sure their pieces will fit together. This requires structured communication among them.

Change Control.   A mechanism for change control must be put into place so that each designer makes only those changes that (1) affect only his part or (2) have been negotiated with the designers of the affected parts. Since much of the cost of design is indeed change and rework, the cost of change control is substantial. The cost of *not* having formal change control is much greater.[6]

The Challenge Is Conceptual Integrity!

Much of what we consider elegance in a design is the integrity, the consistency of its concepts. Consider Wren's masterpiece, St. Paul's Cathedral (Figure 6-3).

Figure 6-3   Wren's St. Paul's Cathedral
iStockphoto

Such design coherence in a tool not only delights, it also yields ease of learning and ease of use. The tool does *what one expects* it to do. I argued in *The Mythical Man-Month* that conceptual integrity is *the* most important consideration in system design.[7] Sometimes this virtue is called *coherence*, sometimes *consistency*, sometimes *uniformity of style*. Blaauw and I have elsewhere discussed conceptual integrity at some length, identifying as component principles *orthogonality*, *propriety*, and *generality*.[8] The solo designer or artist usually produces works with this integrity subconsciously; he tends to make each microdecision the same way each time he encounters it (barring strong reasons). If he fails to produce such integrity, we consider the work flawed, not great.

Many great engineering designs are still today principally the work of one mind, or two. Consider Menn's bridges.[9] Consider the computers of Seymour Cray. The genius of his designs flowed from his total personal mastery over the whole design, ranging from architecture to circuits, packaging, and cooling, and his consequent freedom in making trades across all design domains.[10] He took the time to do designs he could master, even though he used and supervised a team. Cray exerted a powerful counterforce against those corporate and external pressures that would have steered his own attention away from design to other matters. He repeatedly took his design team away from the laboratories created by his earlier successes, considering solitude more valuable than interaction. He was proud of having developed the CDC 6600 with a team of 35, "including the janitor."[11]

One sees this pattern—physical isolation, small teams, intense concentration, and leadership by one mind—repeated again and again in the design of truly innovative, as opposed to follow-on, products: for example, the Spitfire team under Joe Mitchell, off at Hursley House, a stately home in Hampshire, UK; Lockheed's Skunk Works under Kelly Johnson, from which the U-2 spy plane and F-117 stealth fighter came; IBM's closed laboratory in Boca Raton, Florida, home of IBM's successful effort to catch up with Apple on the PC.

Dissent

Not everyone agrees with the thesis I have been arguing. Some argue the social justice of participatory design—that it is *right* for users to have a significant role in the design of objects for their use.[12] Whereas this participation is feasible (and prudent as well as fair) for buildings, user participation in the design of mass-market products is inherently limited to a small sample of prospective users. Such a voice must be conditioned by the representativeness of the sampling, and the vision of the designer.

Others argue that my facts are wrong, that team design has in fact always been the norm.[13] The reader will have to judge for himself.

How to Get Conceptual Integrity with Team Design?

Any product so big, so technically complex, or so urgent as to require the design effort of many minds must nevertheless be conceptually coherent to the single mind of the user.[14] Whereas such coherence is usually a natural consequence of solo design, achieving it in collaborative design is a management feat, requiring a great deal of attention. So, how does one organize design efforts to achieve conceptual integrity?

Modern Design as an Interdisciplinary Negotiation?

Many (mostly academic) writers conclude from the high degree of today's specialization that the nature of design has changed: design today must be done as an "interdisciplinary negotiation" (among the team). The clear implication, though not explicit, is that the team members are peers, and each must be satisfied. *NO!* If conceptual integrity is the final goal, negotiation among peers is the classic recipe for bloated products! The result is design by committee, where none dare say "No" to another's suggestion.[15]

A System Architect

The most important single way to ensure conceptual integrity in a team design is to empower a single system architect. This person must be competent in the relevant technologies, of course. He must be experienced in the sort of system being designed. Most of all, he must have a clear vision of and for the system and must really *care* about its conceptual integrity.

The architect serves during the entire design process as the agent, approver, and advocate for the *user*, as well as for all the other stakeholders. The real user is often not the purchaser. This is evidently true with military acquisitions, where the purchaser (and even the specifier) is far removed from the user. Indeed, the same system may have multiple users, wielding it at strategic, battalion, and personal levels. The purchaser is represented at the design table by marketers. The engineers are represented. The manufacturers are represented. Only the architect represents the users. And, for complex systems as well as for simple residences, it is the architect who must bring professional technology mastery to bear for the users' overall, long-run interest. The role is challenging.[16] I have discussed it in considerable detail in Chapters 4–7 of *The Mythical Man-Month*.

One User-Interface Designer

A major system will require not only a chief architect, but indeed an architectural team. So the conceptual-integrity challenge recurses. Even architecture work must be partitioned, controlled, and hence reintegrated. Here again, conceptual integrity requires special effort.

The user interface, the user's crucial system component, must be tightly controlled by one mind. In some teams, the chief architect can do this detailed work. Consider MacDraw and MacPaint, early Mac tools that were in fact built by their designers. In large architecture teams, the chief architect's scope is too large for him to do the interface himself. Nevertheless, *one* person must do it. If one architect can't master it, one user can't either. At Google, for example, one vice president, Marissa Mayer, maintains personal control over the page format and the home page.[17]

Such an interface designer not only needs lots of using experience and listening skills, he above all needs *taste*. I once asked Kenneth Iverson, Turing Award winner and inventor of the APL programming language, "Why is APL so easy to use?" His answer spoke volumes: "It does what you expect it to do." APL epitomizes consistency, illustrating in detail orthogonality, propriety, and generality. It also epitomizes parsimony, providing many functions with few concepts.

I once was engaged to review the architecture of a very ambitious new computer family, the Future Series (FS) intended by IBM's developers to be a successor to the S/360 family. The architectural team was brilliant, experienced, and inventive. I listened with delight as the grand vision unfolded. So many fine ideas! For an hour, one of the architects explained the powerful addressing and indexing facilities. Another hour, another architect set forth the instruction sequencing, looping, branching capabilities. Another described the rich operations set, including powerful new operators for data structures. Another told of the comprehensive I/O system.

Finally, swamped, I asked, "Can you please let me talk to the architect who understands it all, so I can get an overview?"

"There isn't one. No one person understands it all."

I knew then that the project was doomed—the system would collapse of its own weight. Being handed the 800-page user manual confirmed in my mind the system's fate. How could any user master such a programming interface?[18]

When Collaboration Helps

In some aspects of design the very plurality of designers per se adds value.

Determining Needs and Desiderata from Stakeholders

If deciding *what* to design is the hardest part of the design task, is this a part where collaboration helps? Indeed so! A small team is much better than an individual at studying either an unmet need or an existing system to be replaced. Typically, several minds think of many different questions and kinds of questions. Many questions mean many unexpected answers. The collaborating team must ensure that each member gets full opportunity to explore his trains of inquisitiveness.

Establishing Objectives. Under any design process, the designer begins by conversing with the several stakeholders. These conversations are about the objectives and constraints for the design. The hard task is to flush out the *implicit* objectives and constraints, the ones the stakeholders don't even recognize that they have. Indeed, from these conversations—what is said, how it is said, what is unsaid—comes the designer's first estimate of the utility function.

A crucial part of this phase is observation of how the user does the job today, with today's tools and circumstances. It often helps to videotape these observations, and to view them over and over.

Having collaborating designers participate is extremely useful for this phase. Extra minds

- Ask different questions
- Pick up different things that are not said
- Have independent and perhaps contradictory opinions of how things are said
- Observe different aspects of working
- Stimulate the discussion of the videotapes

Conceptual Exploration—Radical Alternatives

Early in the design process, designers begin exploring solutions—the earlier the better (as long as no one gets wedded to any solution), for the concreteness of postulated solutions usually elicits hitherto unspoken user desiderata or constraints.

Brainstorming. This is the time for brainstorming. Severally, each member of the design team sketches multiple individual schemes. Collectively, the team members prod each other into radical, even wild, ideas. The standard rules for this stage include "Focus on quantity," "No criticism," "Encourage wild ideas," "Combine and improve ideas," and "Sketch all of them where all can see."[19] More minds mean more ideas. More minds stimulating each other yield lots more ideas.

The ideas are not necessarily better. Dornburg [2007] reports a controlled industrial-scale experiment at Sandia Labs:

> Individuals perform at least as well as groups in producing quantity of electronic ideas, regardless of brainstorming duration. However, when judged with respect to quality along three dimensions (originality, feasibility, and effectiveness), the individuals significantly ($p<0.05$) out performed the group working together.

Competition as an Alternative to Collaboration.   In the conceptual exploration phase, one can alternatively harness and stimulate the creative powers of multiple designers by holding design competitions. These work best when the known constraints and objectives are concretely stated and shared, and when unnecessary constraints are carefully excised.

In architecture this practice has been routine for centuries. Brunelleschi established himself by winning the design competition for the dome of the Santa Maria del Fiore cathedral in Florence in 1419 (Figure 6-4). His radical concept, its feasibility made plausible by a scale model, opened new vistas, seen today in St. Paul's and the U.S. Capitol.

Figure 6-4   Brunelleschi's Dome, Santa Maria el Fiore
Anonymous, "View of Florence from the Boboli Gardens,"
19th Century, Watercolor, Museo di Firenze com'era, Florence, Italy/
Scala/Art Resource, New York.

In architecture and some major civil engineering works, there is a single client and multiple designers hoping to get the job. So a competition naturally suggests itself.

The situation is quite different in the normal product-development environment of a computer or software developer. There it is customary for a single team to be assigned to develop a particular product. There will always be competing ideas inside the team about different design decisions, and debates are routine. But only rarely does a management set up multiple teams to pursue a single objective competitively.

Occasionally, however, there will be a formal design competition within a corporate product-development setting. During System/360 architectural design we worked on a stack architecture for six months. Then came the first cost-estimating cycle. The results showed the approach to be valid for mid-range machines and up, but a poor cost-performer at the low end of the seven-model family.

So we had a design competition. The architecture team self-selected into some 13 little (one- to three-person) teamlets, and each did an architectural sketch, against a fixed set of rules and deadlines. Two of the 13 designs were best in my opinion as judge. They were surprisingly alike, more surprising because the teams were rather cool toward each other and had not communicated.

The confluence of those designs set the pattern for the project. (Their big difference, 6-bit-byte versus 8-bit-byte, occasioned the sharpest, deepest, and longest debate of the whole design process.)

I reckon the design competition, originally suggested by Gene Amdahl, to have been immensely invigorating and fruitful. It put everyone hard to work again after a demoralizing cost estimate. It got each person deeply involved in all aspects of the design, which greatly helped morale and proved valuable in the later design development. It produced a consensus on many design decisions. And it produced a good design.[20]

Unplanned Design Competitions: Product Fights.   Not infrequently, it happens that design team B will so evolve its design that it begins to overlap the market objective of design team A. Then one has an ad hoc design competition, a product fight.

I've seen many product fights. They follow a standard script in five acts:

1. The two teams, who may not already know the details of each other's work, meet, compare products and intended markets, and conclude unanimously that there is no real overlap between their products. Both should proceed full speed.
2. Reality appears, in the form of a market forecast or a skeptical boss.
3. Each team changes the design of its product to encompass all of the other product's market, not just the overlapping part.
4. Each team begins wooing supporters among customers, marketing groups, and product forecasters.
5. There comes a shootout before some executive with the power to decide.

Scripts diverge at this point: team A wins; team B wins; both survive; neither survives the intense scrutiny engendered by the competition.

This scenario can and usually should be shortened by early action by a skeptical boss. Sometimes, however, it may be the best way to get a thorough (and impassioned) exploration of two quite different design approaches.

Design Review

The phase of design where collaboration is most valuable, even necessary, is design review. Multiple disciplines must review: other designers, users and/or surrogates, implementers, purchasers, manufacturers, maintainers, reliability experts, safety and environment watchdogs.

Each disciplinary specialist must review the design documents alone, for careful review takes time, reflection, and perhaps the study of references, archives, and other designs.[21] Each will bring a unique point of view; each will raise different issues and find different flaws. But joint, group review is also imperative.

Demand Multidisciplinary Group Review. Group review has the power of numbers, but special power comes from the viewpoints of multiple disciplines. The review team should be much larger than the design team. Those who will build the design, those who will maintain it, sample users, those who will market it—all must be included. Consider the review for a new submarine design. The supply officer sees a shortcoming; his spoken concern triggers a similar concern for the damage control specialist. The manufacturing tooling expert sees something hard to build; his suggested solution sets off alarms in the acoustic expert's mind.

Designers at the Electric Boat Division of General Dynamics told me of a review in which the shipyard foreman took one look at a semicylindrical storage tank and quickly suggested rolling a one-piece cylinder, cutting it in half, and roofing it with a flat plate. This was in place of some 20 pieces the engineer had specified. Said the foreman, "We submarine builders are good at rolling cylinders."

Similarly, a designer at Brown & Root in Leatherhead, England, told me of a design review for a deep-sea oil-drilling platform. The maintenance foreman pointed to a particular unit and said, "Better make that one out of heavy-gauge steel."

"Why?"

"Well, we can paint it in the workshop before it's installed, but where it goes, we'll never be able to paint it again."

The engineers redesigned the whole vicinity of the platform so the unit could be reached.

Use Graphical Representations. For design review, the most important aid is a common model of the product—a drawing, a full-scale wooden mock-up or virtual-reality simulation of a submarine, a prototype of a mechanical part, perhaps an architectural diagram of a computer.

A multidisciplinary design review often demands a richer variety of graphical representations of the design than the designers themselves have been using. Not everyone in the review will be able to visualize the end product from the engineering/architectural drawings. My observation from visiting various facilities is that such design reviews are probably the most fruitful applications of virtual-environment visualization technology.[22]

Sharing the product model and sharing each other's comments are both vital to effective design review; tools for simulating such sharing are the sine qua non of group design reviews where all the players cannot be physically present. Here telecollaboration comes into its own.

When Collaboration Doesn't Work—for Design Itself

The Fantasy Concept of Design Collaboration.   The computer-supported-collaborative-work literature is peppered with a fantasy version of collaborative design. This would be harmless, except that the fallacious concept focuses ever more elaborate academic research on ever less useful technological tools for collaboration.

In this fantasy, a design team really or virtually sees a model of the design object—whether a house, a mechanical part, a submarine, a whiteboard diagram of software, or a shared text. Any team member proposes changes, usually by effecting the change directly in the model. Others propose amendments, discussion proceeds, and bit by bit the design takes form.

Not How Collaborators Design.   But the fantasy concept doesn't fit how collaborators really do design, as opposed to design review.

In all the multi-person design teams I've seen, each part of a design has at any time one owner. That one person works alone preparing a proposal for the design of his part. Then he meets with his collaborators for what is in effect a micro-session of design review. Then he normally retires and works out the detailed consequences of the decisions and directions discussed collaboratively.

If alternate proposals are made in the session, and not accepted by the owner, the proposer will often withdraw and develop an alternate design. Then the session will convene again, to choose, fuse, or strike off in some third direction.

Where's Design Control?   The fantasy concept has no function for originating designs, only refining them. The fantasy concept is flawed as a model for collaborative design change, too. Schedule gain from collaboration implies concurrent activity; and concurrent activity requires *synchronization*, a step totally missing from solo design. Designer Jack owns the air ducts in an oceangoing tanker; Jill owns the steam pipes. As each fleshes out his design, and at every subsequent change, some mechanism of *design control* must monitor that they don't both use the same space. Some *resolution procedure* must be in place for settling conflicts. Some *version control* must be established so that each designs against a *single time-stamped version* of all the earlier design work.

In one instance of the fantasy concept I have actually seen proposed, the client admiral views the design model for a nuclear submarine, and he moves a bulkhead to give equipment repairers better access. (Making this possible is a technically challenging task in a virtual-reality interface to a CAD system. Many techniques for real-time visualization depend upon the static nature of most of the world-model.)

But the challenge is not worth accepting! The admiral may want to move the bulkhead to see how the space will look and feel, and he may be allowed to do that in a playpen version of the model. But before any such move becomes part of the standard design version, someone or some program must check the effects on the space on the other side of the bulkhead, the structural consequences, the acoustic consequences, the effects on piping and wiring. Imagine the horror of the responsible engineers to find that the bulkhead has been moved by the admiral, who cannot possibly have known the constraints and design compromises it embodied. By the time there is a design for the admiral to walk through virtually, it is far enough along to require formal change control.

The fantasy model of collaborative design reflects a monumental unconcern about conceptual integrity. Jill pats the design here; Jim nudges it there; Jack patches it yonder. It is spontaneous; it is collaborative; and it produces poor designs. Indeed, we know the process so well that we have a scornful name for it—*committee design*. If collaboration tools are designed so they encourage committee design, they will do more harm than good.

Conceptual Design, Especially, Must Not Be Collaborative

Once the exploratory stage is past and a basic theme is selected, it's time for conceptual integrity to rule. A design flows from a chief designer, *supported by* a design team, not *partitioned among* one.[23]

To be sure, the conceptual design thus pursued may run into a blind alley. Then a different basic scheme must be selected, and collaborative exploration is again in order until that new basic scheme is selected.

Two-Person Teams Are Magical

The foregoing discussion of design collaboration dealt with teams of more than two people. Two-person teams are a special case. Even in the conceptual design stage, when conceptual integrity is most imperiled, pairs of designers acting *uno animo* can be more fruitful than solo designers. The literature on pair programming shows this to be true during detailed design. Typical initial productivity runs less than two working separately, but error rates are radically reduced.[24] Since perhaps 40 percent of the effort on many designs is rework, net productivity is higher and products are more robust.

The world is full of two-person jobs. The carpenter needs someone to hold the other end of the beam. The electrician needs help when feeding wire through studs. Child raising is best done by two actively collaborating parents. "It is not good for man to be alone," while spoken in its truest sense about marriage,[25] might usefully be preached to lone-ranger designers.

The typical dynamics of two-person design collaboration seem different from those of multi-person design and solo design. Two people will interchange ideas rapidly and informally, with neither a protocol as to who has the floor nor domination by one partner. Each holds the floor for short bursts. The process switches rapidly among micro-sessions of proposal, review and critique, counterproposal, synthesis, and resolution. There is typically a *single thread* of idea development, without the maintenance of separate individual threads of thought as in multi-person discussions. Two pencils may move over the same paper with neither collision nor contradiction.

"As iron sharpens iron," each stimulates the other to more active thought than might occur in solo design. Perhaps the very need to articulate one's thinking—to state *why* as well as *what*—causes quicker perception of one's own fallacies and quicker recognition of other viable design alternatives.

A classic 1970 paper by Torrance showed that dyadic interaction produced twice as many original ideas, produced ideas of twice as much originality, increased enjoyment, and led subjects to attempt more difficult tasks.[26]

Pair-wise design sessions still need to be interspersed with solo ones—to detail, to document the creative fruit, and to prepare proposals for the next joint session.

So What, for Computer Scientists?

Much effort by academic computer scientists has gone into the design of tools for computer-assisted collaboration by workers in their own and other disciplines. Distressingly few of these ideas and tools have made it into everyday use. (Important tools that have succeeded are code control systems and "Track Changes" in Word.) Perhaps this is because it is especially easy for academic tool builders to overlook some crucial properties of real-world team design:

- Real design is always more complex than we tend to imagine.[27] This is especially true since we often start with textbook examples, which have perforce been oversimplified. Real design has more complex goals, more complex constraints to be satisfied, more complex measures of goodness to be satisficed. Real design always explodes into countless details.
- Real team design always requires a design-change control process, lest the left hand corrupt what the right hand has wrought.
- No amount of collaboration eliminates the need for the "dreariness of labor and the loneliness of thought."

For these reasons, I think we should be very leery about assigning graduate students with little or no real-world design experience dissertation topics in the field of collaborative design tools. Moreover, our journals should be very slow to accept such papers that are not based on real-world experience and/or real design applications.

Notes and References

1. This marvelous phrase was quoted by Bernard Baruch, who said his attorney said it to him.

2. *Economist* [2009], "Harvest moon."

3. The wise manager of a multi-project organization early launches a solo designer, or a pair, to start exploring designing for a technology foreseeable, but not yet buildable.

4. Brooks [1995], *The Mythical Man-Month,* Chapter 2.

5. Shipyard foreman at Electric Boat, Groton, CT (personal communication).

6. The most complete scientific study I have seen comparing solo and individual designers is Cross [1996a], *Analysing Design Activity.*

   The Delft protocols included a solo designer and a three-person team attacking the same problem, with both observed by video and the solo designer encouraged to think aloud. Twenty different chapters, each using its own analytical method, analyze the Delft video protocols. Most apply their authors' own predefined categories of activity to one or both of the protocols. Many of the chapters either compare the activities and performance of the two alternatives or else analyze the social behavior of the team. The most specific conclusion is that by Gabriela Goldschmidt [1995], "The designer as a team of one": "Detailed analysis leads to the conclusion that there are almost no differences between the individual and the team in the way they bring their work to fruition."

Charles Eastman [1997] reviews this book in *Design Studies* (475–476):

> *Together the studies offer a rich set of perspectives that allow a reader to understand both the fertileness and the idiosyncrasy of design processes. The video transcription obviously captured a rich characterization of design behavior, . . . The limitation of current methods of protocol analysis, however, are made readily apparent. Each study by itself provides only a small peephole into the overall design process. Only through the cumulative breadth of multiple studies does the sense of the full process emerge.*

> *This book clearly presents the current state of design protocol studies after thirty years of effort and relates them more generally to various theories of design.*

7. Brooks [1995], *The Mythical Man-Month*, Chapter 4, 42ff.

8. Blaauw and Brooks [1997], *Computer Architecture*, Section 1.4; Brooks [1995], *The Mythical Man-Month*, Chapters 4–7, 19.

9. Billington [2003], *The Art of Structural Design*, Chapter 6; Menn [1996], "The Place of Aesthetics in Bridge Design."

10. Blaauw and Brooks [1997], *Computer Architecture*, Chapter 14.

11. Murray [1997], *The Supermen*.

12. Greenbaum and Kyng [1991], *Design at Work*; Bødker [1987], "A Utopian Experience."

13. Weisberg [1986], *Creativity: Genius and Other Myths*; Stillinger [1991], *Multiple Authorship and the Myth of Solitary Genius*.

14. R. Joseph Mitchell, the designer of the Spitfire, warned one of his test pilots (the user!) about engineers: "If anybody ever tells you anything about an aeroplane which is so bloody complicated you can't understand it, take it from me: it's all balls."

15. Eoin Woods of Artechra says,

> *I'm not as pessimistic as you about joint design. I've worked in teams where we had spirited discussion to drive our designs and then agreed the solution among us (albeit sometimes with a benign dictator making final decisions). The designs remained coherent because it was one or two strong concepts of the design that won out and then drove all of the other decisions; we didn't design by committee and "horse-trade" the detailed decisions (personal communication [2009]).*

16. Brad Parkinson, now at Stanford, one of the two system architects/contracting officers for the GPS system, pointed out that the challenges of that task were substantially increased by having multiple contractors for the several system pieces (personal communication [2007]).

17. Holson [2009], "Putting a bolder face on Google."

18. Mary Shaw of Carnegie-Mellon asks, "What does this say about modern software development environments and their APIs?"

19. Osborn [1963], *Applied Imagination*.

20. Design competitions in organization design are yet different; the task is inherently political. The various competing forces usually do not even share the objective of getting the organization that works best. How well the organization will work is subordinated to who will have which levers of power.

21. Margaret Thatcher: "One wants documents [as opposed to viewgraph foils] so one can think through beforehand, and consult colleagues" (personal communication via Sir John Fairclough). American business all too often does reviews via PowerPoint presentations. Those vague bullets enable each participant to interpret the information as he pleases; they also facilitate the suppression of embarrassing but crucial details.

    Lou Gerstner, turnaround CEO of IBM, startled the whole culture early on ([2002], *Who Says Elephants Can't Dance?*, 43): "Nick was on his second foil when I stepped to the table and as politely as I could in front of his team, switched off the projector . . . it had a terribly powerful ripple effect . . . Talk about consternation. It was as if the President of the United States had banned the use of English at White House meetings."

22. Brooks [1999], "What's real about virtual reality?"

23. Harlan Mills's concept of a supported-chief-designer team, a "surgical" team, is detailed in Brooks [1995], *The Mythical Man-Month*, Chapter 3.

24. Williams [2000], "Strengthening the case for pair-programming"; Cockburn [2001], "The costs and benefits of pair programming."

25. Genesis 2:18.

26. Torrance [1970], "Dyadic interaction as a facilitator of gifted performance."

27. See, for example, the impressive PhD dissertations by Hales [1991], "An analysis of the engineering design process in an industrial context" (Cambridge), or Salton [1958], "An automatic data processing system for public utility revenue accounting" (Harvard), for detailed documentation of what is involved in an actual design.

7

Telecollaboration

The new electronic interdependence recreates the world in the image of a global village.

MARSHALL MCLUHAN [1967],
THE MEDIUM IS THE MESSAGE

Henry Fuchs's vision of the office of the future

Drawings by Andrei State, University of North Carolina

Why Telecollaboration?

At last we are positioned to examine telecollaboration. Why do design teams now harness communications technologies to enable collaborations among people who are not collocated?

Specialization

The super-specialization of skills now occasions much collaboration. But any particular specialized skill is not available in every hamlet—or even in every city. The ubiquitous village blacksmith has become the rare materials-scientist expert in titanium alloys; the town fireman has become the Red Adair, summoned to the corners of the Earth to snuff multimillion-dollar oil-well fires.[1]

Home

People have strong, even dominating, preferences as to where they live. For many, it is the call of the family, of clan, of culture. For others it is rural versus town versus city. For yet others it is climate or seacoast or mountains. People with highly specialized skills can often write their own tickets. Telecollaboration technology enables more and more such experts to live where they please and work elsewhere. Of my own former students, one has lived in Iceland, one in Brazil, while working "in" Silicon Valley.

Around the Clock

Rotation of the Earth enables work to be advanced around the clock by team members each working only day shift.

Cost

Wide disparities in both cost of living and standard of living make common high-tech skills available at radically lower cost via outsourcing. Of course, dredging a (telecommunications) channel between disparate economies begins a torrent of leveling, surely the healthiest form of "foreign" aid.

Politics

Large international ventures with government support inevitably involve the partitioning of jobs among nations, hence among locations. Consider the Airbus 380, a bold work of engineering (Figure 7-1). Not only the manufacturing but also the development was partitioned among France, Germany, Britain, and Spain.

Jeffrey Jupp, then Technical Director of Airbus UK in England, explained to me how Airbus wings were designed in Bristol to lift and fit the fuselage designed in Toulouse:

- Full telecommunications capabilities were used.
- Bristol had some of its own engineers on-site in Toulouse as ambassadors.
- Every day a company plane flew from Britain to Toulouse and back, carrying live people both ways.

In my experience, none of these collaboration aids could be omitted. Alas, the Airbus 380 also illustrates a special pitfall, one perhaps more hazardous for politically occasioned distributions. The French and British teams used Release 5 of CATIA CAD

Figure 7-1   Airbus 380
iStockphoto

software. The German and Spanish teams used Release 4. Lo and behold, in part because of differences between these releases, the wiring harnesses designed by one team required larger radii than those provided by the other team's conduits. These and other initial delivery delays, some 22 months, have been very painful.[2]

Been There, Done That—Distributed Development of the IBM System/360 Computer Family, 1961–1965

The initial seven IBM System/360 computers were concurrently developed in four locations across three countries: Poughkeepsie and Endicott, New York; Hursley, UK; Böblingen, Germany. These computers, the first upward-downward strictly binary-compatible family, pioneered the industry switch from 6-bit to 8-bit bytes. I was Project Manager. Chapter 24 is a case study of the architecture design for System/360. (The Model 20 wasn't downward-compatible—a mistake in the mind of architect William Wright, and in my view.)

Over 40 new 8-bit input-output devices had to be concurrently developed, each exploiting the specialized skills and experience of still more separate and separated laboratories: La Gaude, France; Lidingö, Sweden; Uithoorn, the Netherlands; San Jose, California; Boulder, Colorado; Lexington, Kentucky; and Endicott, New York. A technical innovation radically aided the coordination of these efforts—the meticulous definition of a standard logical, electrical, and mechanical interface for attaching any I/O device to any computer.[3] Even so, managing the distributed development of these devices was a major task. Software development was even more widely partitioned.

For computers, software, and I/O devices, we used the same management techniques as those described above for BAE. Our telecommunications facilities were far more primitive: I leased IBM's first full-time transatlantic phone line. We didn't run a company plane back and forth, but we bought a lot of airline tickets. The British lab maintained a resident participant in Amdahl's Poughkeepsie architecture group; we maintained resident participants from Poughkeepsie on the processor implementation teams in Britain and Germany.

Besides thousands of phone calls and documents, many pairwise face-to-face meetings coupled the laboratories. Annual two-week-long whole-team meetings settled hanging conflicts and challenges—some 200 of them at one session.

Our distributed development effort was occasioned by the same forces as usual:

- Distributed technology specializations
- Immovable talent pools
- Interdivisional politics and distribution of work

The effort was highly successful.[4] Make no mistake, however: distributed development of a unified product is *work!* Moreover, the distribution per se creates a lot of *extra* work! We sorely underestimated the immense importance of the informal communication channels at work within collocated teams, until we experienced their absence. Space barriers are real![5] Time-zone barriers are real, sometimes more so than space barriers! And cultural barriers are very real and must be taken into account![6]

Making Telecollaboration Work

Distributed design will only increase. Telecommunications technology continues to explode. How shall designers and design managers harness it to make telecollaboration work?

Face-to-Face Time Is Crucial!

Consider your own telephone conversations. Do you experience a difference not only in comfort but also in effectiveness when talking to a stranger, as opposed to an acquaintance?

How far would you walk to avoid using each of {videoconferencing, telephone, email, written mail} to

- Make a lunch appointment?
- Seek a discount on a purchased service?
- Negotiate a complex business deal?
- Plan a family vacation?
- Fire your administrative assistant?

For some of these, you would prefer email or telephone over walking (and time synchronizing); for others, you would gladly walk quite a distance.

The most successful telecollaborations I have known have been built on extensive face-time histories, and even these have required some face time during the ongoing telecollaboration. Absent such histories, travel is worth what it costs in money and time.

Some of the most fruitful dollars I spent at IBM paid for a bus to take the S/360 project's administrative staff and secretaries 60 miles from Poughkeepsie to White Plains, New York. They spent the midday lunching and talking with their counterparts at division headquarters, familiar voices hitherto faceless. This lubrication was much more effective than just more pressure on cooperation.

I am told that Boeing brought its scores of distributed design teams for the 777 airplane to Everett, Washington, for weeks of together time, as the design was starting.

People instinctively know the value of face time. So, in spite of potent videoconferencing technology, airplanes still carry lots of business travelers.

Clean Interfaces

Defining clean interfaces among remotely designed components is a hard job. The job doesn't end with definition—continual question-and-answer interpretation of the definitions' semantics proves necessary. Changes must be made, controlled, and widely communicated.

Another important part of system architecture is not merely the definition of interfaces, but management's designing a predetermined mechanism for resolving differences of opinion or taste. There is no substitute for authority.

But the payoff from these costly labors is incredible! Clean interfaces make a big difference in the error rate of the design. Some have estimated that errors and rework, though affecting only a small fraction of a design, may account for half the design cost. Worse yet, errors due to vague or sloppy interfaces usually surface late, during system integration. Nastier to find, costlier to fix, they impact the whole system schedule.

Moreover, clean interfaces enhance the joy of the work. Designing is fun; ironing out misunderstandings with peers is usually not. When designing, one feels progress happening; when resolving interface misunderstandings, one feels slippage. Clean interfaces give multiple designers each the joy of ownership, of the privilege of signing a piece of work. They also facilitate sequential ownership, as small components flow together into recognizable larger subsystems.

Technologies for Telecollaboration

Decade after decade, technology pundits predict that designers' travel will be obviated by telecommunications. It hasn't happened yet.[7] Why? Will it? My guess is that more and more convenient and lifelike communications technologies will indeed successfully substitute for more and more face-to-face meetings.[8] Nevertheless, because of the endless nuance of human communication, being in the same room together from time to time will never cease to be very important for design collaborators.

Low Tech Often Suffices

The Document.   The most potent technology for telecollaboration is the document shared, whether by network or by post. Formal prose and formal drawings carry the precision that demands study, enables critique, stimulates interaction.

Gerry Blaauw and I found, when crafting our 1,200-page *Computer Architecture* [1997], that most of our transatlantic interaction was effectively done by mailed drafts. However, this effective remote cooperation was built upon nine years of daily face time; a resulting deep knowledge of each other's design style, sensitivities, and "collaboration manners"; and upon deeply shared convictions about computer architecture. Even with this foundation, iterations of remote exchanges of drafts had to be supplemented by quarterly telephone meetings and semiannual three-day face meetings.

These latter were always very instructive. Inherently, they focused on the tough nuts that had not yet been cracked. We found that when a text paragraph couldn't be made to work, it was always because we didn't know what we were talking about. Half-hour discussions usually ensued. We learned something new about computer architecture.

The modern equivalent of the red-marked draft is the Word document with changes tracked. Many critics can interact; each has his changes distinguished from all others. Word's Track Changes is a well-designed capability. Yet I find the red-marked document far easier to create and to study, largely because of its easy two-dimensional access. Our electronic technology isn't there yet. (Or I'm just a dinosaur.)

The Telephone.   Next to the document comes the telephone, an even bigger breakthrough than email. Email users know the hazards of extemporaneous writing with no attached vocal inflections and no instant give-and-take. Instant messaging is a poor substitute for telephony.

Telephone-Plus-Shared-Document.   Telephone-plus-shared-document becomes vastly more powerful than either alone. The combination adds real-time interactions, which save a lot of written explanation and head off much misunderstanding. Less obviously, the shared document adds much specificity and detail to a phone conversation. Having to agree word-by-word forces the collaborative facing of many issues that would otherwise be missed.

This combination is very powerful. In our laboratory, Kurtis Keller, our staff mechanical engineer, was collaborating with Sam Drake at the University of Utah on the design of a new head-mounted display. We were operating a quite effective real-time, high-bandwidth video teleconferencing system between UU and UNC. Our videoconferencing station was only 150 feet down the hall from Kurtis's office, a short walk. Yet we observed, well into the design process, that Kurtis was not investing even that minimal effort in the teleconferencing system. He was working in his office, by phone; both he and Drake had the drawing up on their workstations.

Videoconferencing

Once hyped as the "game-changing" tool for telecollaboration, videoconferencing has come into widespread use, but far more slowly and less extensively than originally expected.

Why so slowly? In the early days, low bandwidth led to low frame rates; the experience was quite artificial. Now that normal video rates are available, what technical advances will make the experience better?

- **Field of view.** Video is good for one-on-one conversations, but if one half of a committee is meeting with another, it's hard to see everyone and at the same time to really discern facial expressions.
- **Better sharing of documents and presentations.** One wants to view speaker and slide or document simultaneously, not alternatively. One wants to spread materials out on a table. One wants to make both private notes and shared markings. A symmetric shared whiteboard is really needed.
- **More resolution.** Resolution is still not good enough to enable one to share a full 8½ x 11 page of text, or to read faces well.
- **Better depth cues.** The lack of depth cues, although very rarely producing ambiguities, continually reminds the participant that he is in fact not there.

When Is Videoconferencing Most Valuable?   In spite of the current technical shortcomings, in some social situations videoconferencing is much better than telephony, although still poorer than face-to-face conferencing. These are situations when facial expressions and body language really matter:

- When screening stranger job applicants to select finalists
- When issues are vital to one or more participants
- When the participant at one end is quite insecure
- When organizational or national cultures are different

High-Tech Videoconferencing.   Considerable research has been done piloting maximum-realism teleconferencing systems. My colleague Henry Fuchs has enhanced videoconferencing with depth cues and demonstrated anecdotally that the enhancement substantially increases one's feeling of "being there." Each participant's head is tracked, so the powerful kinetic depth effect is harnessed—when one moves his head, the reconstructed objects on the screen shift according to their distance from the cameras. Moreover, multiple cameras yield a 3-D image, which is displayed in stereo via two projectors with polarized filters.[9]

Telecollaboration Technology—Pulled or Pushed? Much academic research has been invested in telecollaboration hardware and software. This has yielded many tools and systems, some commercially marketed, and a conference series[10] and a respected journal[11] that cover the subject (as well as collocated cooperation).

One is forced to the conclusion that most of those tools and systems spring from a technical idea rather than from an analysis of a collaboration pattern or need. Indeed, in a quick Web search for telecollaboration, 49 of the first 50 entries were on tools or education, not on collaboration in design. In a library shelf study, of 20 books, 19 were on tools, not on applications of the tools to accomplish tasks.

This inversion concerns me deeply. It is wasteful of a precious resource—PhD research efforts—and it mis-educates our ablest students. Effective toolsmithing always starts with the *user* and the *task*. In my experience, it is best done when the toolsmith has a *real* user with a *real* task that must be done. Buggy prototypes will not then satisfy; critical feedback will be immediate and blunt. I have written extensively on this elsewhere; those positions have not changed.[12]

Notes and References

1. Lohr [2009], "The crowd is wise (when it's focused)," reports on the concept of "collective intelligence" in which specialized teams coalesce via the internet for major technical projects:

    But a look at recent cases and new research suggests that open-innovation models succeed only when carefully designed for a particular task and when the incentives are tailored to attract the most effective collaborators. "There is this misconception that you can sprinkle crowd wisdom on something and things will turn out for the best," said Thomas W. Malone, director of the Center for Collective Intelligence at the Massachusetts Institute of Technology. "That's not true. It's not magic."

2. Clark [2006], "The Airbus saga," is an excellent newspaper account. See also http://en.wikipedia.org/wiki/Airbus_380, accessed on September 9, 2008.

3. This work required a small architecture team of its own.

4. Wise [1966], "I.B.M.'s $5,000,000,000 gamble," has a very competent, thorough, and fair discussion of the project and its troubles, as seen two years after announcement. As to collaborative design, he says, "The international engineering group was woven together with considerable effectiveness, giving I.B.M. the justifiable claim that the 360 computer was probably the first product of truly international design" (p. 142).

   Peter Fagg, the System/360 project's Engineering Manager, did a phenomenal job of managing the interdivisional, international development of the dozens of new input-output devices, without line authority over any of those teams.

5. Herbsleb [2000], "Distances, dependencies, and delay in a global collaboration," and Teasley [2000], "How does radical collocation help a team succeed?" document the disadvantages of distributed work. Hinds [2002], *Distributed Work*, presents a set of reports of various aspects of distributed work.

6. Ghemawat [2007], *Redefining Global Strategy*.

7. Garner [2001], "Comparing graphic actions between remote and proximal design teams," reports an interesting study comparing collocated and remote collaborations on a design project:

   This paper outlines the conduct and findings of a research project which compared the sketching activity and sketched output of pairs of design students collaborating face-to-face to other pairs linked by computer-mediated tools. . . . Sketch Graphic Acts are used to illuminate the phenomenon of shared sketches and the importance of "thumbnail" sketches—which were commonly exploited in laboratory studies of face-to-face collaboratively working but were significantly impoverished in studies of computer-mediated remote collaborative working.

On the other hand, Sonnenwald et al. [2003], "Evaluating a scientific collaboratory," not only observed no differences, but also discovered that scientists *found advantages and disadvantages to each mode of working:*

> *The evaluation of scientific collaboratories has lagged behind their development. Do the capabilities afforded by collaboratories outweigh their disadvantages? To evaluate a scientific collaboratory system, we conducted a repeated-measures controlled experiment that compared the outcomes and process of scientific work completed by 20 pairs of participants (upper level undergraduate sciences students) working face-to-face and remotely.*

> *We collected scientific outcomes (graded lab reports) to investigate the quality of scientific work, post-questionnaire data to measure the adoptability of the system, and post-interviews to understand the participants' views of doing science under both conditions. We hypothesized that study participants would be less effective, report more difficulty, and be less favorably inclined to adopt the system when collaborating remotely.*

> *Contrary to expectations, the quantitative data showed no statistically significant differences with respect to effectiveness and adoption. The qualitative data helped explain this null result: participants reported advantages and disadvantages working under both conditions and developed work-arounds to cope with the perceived disadvantages of collaborating remotely. While the data analysis produced null results, considered as a whole, the analysis leads us to conclude there is positive potential for the development and adoption of scientific collaboratory systems.*

8. An anonymous writer in Economist.com [2009] speculates that "the cyclical downturn may be coinciding with a structural decline in business travel because of advances in information technology." Thus the downturn may accelerate the adoption of videoconferencing.

9. Raskar [1998], "The office of the future"; Towles [2002], " 3D telecollaboration over Internet2"; http://www.cs.unc.edu/Research/stc/inthenews/pdf/washingtonpost_2000_1128.pdf, accessed on August 28, 2009.

Virtual worlds such as Second Life are also being explored for telecollaboration. See for example, http://blog.irvingwb.com/blog/2008/12/serious-virtual-worlds-applications.html.

10. See http://www.cscw2008.org/.

11. *Computer Supported Cooperative Work (CSCW): The Journal of Collaborative Computing.* ISSN: 0925-9724 (print version); ISSN: 1573-7551 (electronic version).

12. Brooks [1977], "The computer 'scientist' as toolsmith"; Brooks [1996], "The computer scientist as toolsmith II."

III
Design
Perspectives

8

Rationalism versus Empiricism in Design

All Men are liable to Error; and most Men are, in many Points, by Passion or Interest, under Temptation to it.

JOHN LOCKE [1690], *AN ESSAY CONCERNING HUMAN UNDERSTANDING*

... the two operations of our understanding, intuition and deduction, on which alone we have said we must rely in the acquisition of knowledge.

RENÉ DESCARTES [1628], *RULES FOR THE DIRECTION OF THE MIND*

John Locke (1632–1704), British empiricist philosopher
Wikimedia Commons (commons.wikimedia.org)

Rationalism versus Empiricism

Can I, by sufficient thought alone, design a complex object correctly? This question, particularized to design, represents a crux between two long-established philosophical systems, rationalism and empiricism. Rationalists believe I can; empiricists believe I cannot.[1]

The crux goes much deeper than first meets the eye. The philosophical issue is fundamentally one's view of the nature of man as creator.

The rationalist believes that man is inherently sound (and good), subject to mistakes, and perfectible by education. After *right education, maturing experience,* and *sufficient careful-enough thought,* a designer can make a flawless design. The design methodology task, therefore, is to learn how to reason a design into flawlessness.

The empiricist believes that man is inherently flawed, and subject repeatedly to temptation and error. Anything he makes will be flawed. The design methodology task, therefore, is to learn how to determine the flaws by experiment, so that one can iterate on the design.

Examples abound. Aristotle believed he could discover science deductively by reasoning; hence heavier objects would fall faster than light ones. Galileo believed that experiment was necessary and had the temerity to challenge Aristotle's ancient authority.

René Descartes (1596–1650) perhaps most directly enunciated the rationalist view. John Locke (1632–1704) clearly set forth the empiricist one.

To this day, French science excels in beautiful logical structures, from Fourier's analysis of heat flow, through Carnot's thermodynamics, to the mathematical edifices of the Bourbaki group. Meanwhile, British science has gone from strength to strength within the empirical tradition—Watt, Faraday, Heaviside, the Braggs all leap to mind.

Software Design

Is a computer program a mathematical object to be fashioned in abstraction and made correct by proof? So the rationalists would

contend, led by Edsger Dijkstra.[2] It is all a matter of proper careful thinking. One can, and should, design software to be correct
and then prove the design is correct. And that will suffice.[3]

Now, granted, a program is a pure mathematical object and
in principle can be designed perfectly by correct thought. The
difficulty is not with the design medium but with designers.
Empiricists believe that humans will inevitably make mistakes: in
defining objectives, in software architecture, in implementation
in objects (algorithms and data structures), and in realization in
code itself. This firm faith in fallibility prescribes a design methodology that includes design, early prototypes, early user testing,
iterative incremental implementation, testing on a rich bank of
test cases, and regression testing after changes.

I Am a Dyed-in-the-Wool Empiricist

I became so first from experience. Only twice in my life have I
written a program that ran correctly the first time and did exactly
what I needed it to do. One of those times was my very first substantial program. In graduate school at Harvard in 1953–1954, we
had programming term projects. The mode of use of the Harvard
Mark IV was hands-on, but each team of two students got two
one-hour shots in which to debug and run their semester projects.
William V. (Bill) Wright, a super-able peer, and I desk-checked
our modest 1,500-line program meticulously and ad nauseam. It
ran right the first time.

One might say that this experience is an existence proof for
the possibility of rational design for correctness. But we didn't
prove our program correct; we desk-tested it by simulated execution. Moreover, I doubt if anyone could maintain the state of
motivation and regularly repeat the level of meticulous checking
that we did. Yes, in principle it is possible. With real people and
real-scale contemporary software, it is not sustainable.

What is the experience in designing programs to be correct?
People have used formal proof methods to prove that the kernels
of secure operating systems are correctly designed and implemented.[4] This is an exactly proper use of the technique. One
needs the high degree of assurance that a formal proof offers.

Even that assurance is not 100 percent, of course. Over the history of mathematics, many proofs, once accepted, have later been found fallacious.[5] Formal proof is not an error-free technique. Its advantage is that the reasoning in a formal proof is different in form from that of program design, so the odds are radically improved that the same mistake will not slip past both scrutinies.

The kernel is probably as far as the correctness proof technique should be applied. If kernels are secure and correct, the damage of error, loophole, or malice elsewhere in the program can be contained. The work of proving a program correct is substantial, on the order of the work of building the program. No proof can show that the original objectives for the program were right.[6]

Harlan Mills and his colleagues at IBM developed a variant of design correctness-proving that makes a lot of sense to me. In their "cleanroom" technique, Mills and team expose every aspect of a design to intense group scrutiny. The design group, in meeting assembled, hear the designer explain why the design is correct, as they challenge his arguments and their implicit assumptions.[7]

Formal proof of correctness is usually infeasible; abandoning all effort at systematic verification (the more common extreme) is dangerous: Mills's systematic but non-formal group scrutiny of logical argument seems to me a wise and practical balance.

Rationalism, Empiricism, and Correctness in Other Design Domains

So far as I can tell, in no design domain other than software engineering have designers even attempted to prove correctness by rigorous formal methods. Perhaps this is because software is, like mathematics, fashioned of pure thought-stuff, so rigorous proof is conceivable. Most other design domains result in physical implementations, and one cannot prove theorems about materials and their faults, or about spaces and their suitability.

Organization design is like software design in that no material is involved. I know of no attempt to prove correctness, or even workability, of a postulated organization. The authors of the *The Federalist Papers*, however, undertook to demonstrate the feasibility of the United States Constitution by closely reasoned logical arguments. Whereas much of their wisdom still impresses succeeding generations, the Civil War (a system crash of extreme severity) demonstrated the incompleteness of the demonstration.

Design domains other than software engineering may not undertake correctness-proving, but they make extensive use of design verification, using a myriad of analysis and simulation techniques.

People now do stress, vibration, acoustic analyses on mechanical parts. Real-time or videotaped walk-throughs enable architects and clients to run simulated use scenarios on designed buildings. Loading-stress analyses test against snow and hurricane. Earthquake analyses provide dynamic stress testing.

Computer hardware undergoes extensive simulation at the circuit level, the logical design level, and the program execution level. Even the operating system for a not-yet-built computer is extensively tested; it is executed (dead slow) on a computer simulator on an existing host.

An inevitable consequence of these extensive empirical analyses is greater iteration in the design process. The more sophisticated analysis means more precise measures of the degree to which desiderata have been satisfied and constraints obeyed. Hence verification of the design *against the goals specified* becomes a more straightforward and certain process. *But none of these analyses and simulations addresses the rightness of the goals or the validity of the assumptions about the environment.*

Can I, by sufficient thought alone, design a complex object correctly? No; testing and iteration are in practice necessary. But careful thought helps. The succeeding essays in Part III suggest some aspects of such thought.

Notes and References

1. Rationalism and empiricism are approaches to epistemology—how one can know something. The classic propounders of these positions

were far from polarized. Descartes advocated empirical science; Locke saw rationalism as the basis for mathematics.

This particularization from epistemology to design is my own; I am in deep water here and quite subject to error.

2. Dijkstra [1982], *Selected Writings on Computing*.

3. Dijkstra [1968], "A constructive approach to the problem of program correctness," 174–186.

4. Klein [2009a], "Operating system verification," and [2009b], "seL4: Formal verification of an OS kernel," gives a good overview and an impressive current achievement. The authors claim this as the first time that a nontrivial kernel's implementation has been completely functionally verified.

5. For example, there was a proof that a matrix multiplication requires n^3 scalar multiplications. The flaw was in the assumption that the operations would be on vectors. Strassen [1969], "Gaussian elimination is not optimal."

6. A famous and instructive case is the accident of Lufthansa Flight 2904, which went off the runway at Warsaw due to a failure of the computer-controlled stopping systems to engage. The code followed the specification, which was wrong for the unexpected circumstances. According to http://en.wikipedia.org/wiki/Luftansa_Flight_2904, referenced on July 16, 2009:

> To ensure that the thrust-reverse system and the spoilers are only activated in a landing situation, all of the following conditions have to be true for the software to deploy these systems:
>
> - there must be weight of over 12 tons on each main landing gear strut
> - the wheels of the plane must be turning faster than 72 knots
> - the thrust levers must be in the reverse thrust position
>
> In the case of the Warsaw accident neither of the first two conditions was fulfilled, so the most effective braking system was not activated. Point one was not fulfilled, because the plane landed inclined (to counteract the possible windshear). Thus the pressure of 12 tons on both landing gears required to trigger the sensor was not reached. Point two was also not fulfilled because of a hydroplaning effect on the wet runway.

7. Mills [1987], "Cleanroom software engineering."

   Wikipedia (referenced on October 30, 2008 at http://en.wikipedia.org/wiki/Cleanroom_Software_Engineering) provides a good summary of the whole approach:

   > *The basic principles of the Cleanroom process are*
   >
   > ### Software development based on formal methods
   >
   > *Cleanroom development makes use of the Box Structure Method to specify and design a software product. Verification that the design correctly implements the specification is performed through team review.*
   >
   > ### Incremental implementation under statistical quality control
   >
   > *Cleanroom development uses an iterative approach, in which the product is developed in increments that gradually increase the implemented functionality. The quality of each increment is measured against pre-established standards to verify that the development process is proceeding acceptably. A failure to meet quality standards results in the cessation of testing for the current increment, and a return to the design phase.*
   >
   > ### Statistically sound testing
   >
   > *Software testing in the Cleanroom process is carried out as a statistical experiment. Based on the formal specification, a representative subset of software input/output trajectories is selected and tested. This sample is then statistically analyzed to produce an estimate of the reliability of the software, and a level of confidence in that estimate.*

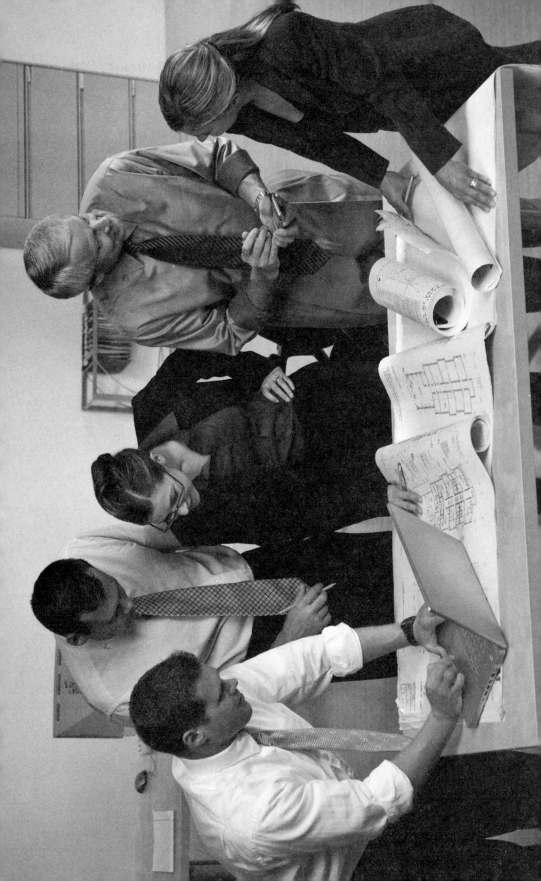

9

User Models—Better Wrong than Vague

. . . [T]ruth will sooner come out of error than from confusion.

SIR FRANCIS BACON [1620],
THE NEW ORGANON

An architecture team

Anderson Ross/Getty Images Inc.—Stockbyte

Explicit User and Use Models

Experienced designers often begin by writing down exactly what they know about the user, the user's purposes of use, and the modes of use. Wise designers also write down explicitly what they don't know but *assume* about the user and users.

Where there are multiple different applications or multiple different sets of users, they describe each, then define explicitly the weightings among them so as to define the use model.[1]

The more detailed and particularized these assumptions, the more occasion they offer for early detailed thinking. This thinking would have been required anyway later, as the design proceeds. Doing it early forfends mistakes.[2]

Really?

Who actually does all that extra work before starting on a design? The answer, of course, is that very few of us do. In my view, we need to define explicit use and user models in many more cases than we do. Doing so will improve design practice.

The need for explicit models of both applications and users follows directly from the peculiar characteristics of modern design: design by teams and the design of complex tools as opposed to simple ones.

Team Design

All designers in fact have user and use models consciously or subconsciously in mind as they work. Team design creates the all-new requirement that the entire team have the same user model, the same use model. This requires explicit models and assumptions.

This exercise is rare because the members of the team usually believe, without anyone saying so, that they share a common set of assumptions. After all, each one heard the enterprise leader charge and challenge the team. Each one has read the goal-defining document. All are expert.

Matters are not so simple. Each of us has in fact had a different experience using similar systems; my experience informs my picture of the typical user. Each of us has been exposed to a different set of applications; my exposure helps me define this application. If the team does not draft a common set of explicit assumptions, each designer will work with a distinct set of implicit ones. Microdecisions too minor ever to be discussed will be made differently, and conceptual integrity will be lost.

Differing use models inevitably yield design inconsistencies in a team design. Operating System/360 (now z/OS), for example, reflects in several parts two quite inconsistent debugging philosophies—one assuming batch use, the other assuming time-shared use from terminals. There was no conscious decision to cater to two use modes; it merely reflected subgroups holding differing use models.[3] The result was bloat and incoherence.

Complex Designs. As tool complexity grows, the need for explicit use models increases. Even for a shovel, it is important to be explicit as to whether it is for coal, dirt, grain, snow, or some mix; whether for child, woman, or man; whether for the casual user or the manual laborer. How much greater is the need for explicit use models for a truck, a spreadsheet, an academic building!

Moreover, the more complex the design, the less likely the designers are to be domain experts who could do the users' jobs. Implicitly assumed models are then much more dangerous.

What If the Facts Are Not Available?

As soon as the designer starts to make explicit use models, trouble strikes: he is rudely confronted with how much he doesn't know. The very effort forces him to ask questions he might not otherwise have asked until much later. This is an unmitigated good.

Suppose one is designing a program product to route and schedule school buses. Some careful fieldwork with two or three "representative" school systems will yield facts galore: time constraints, number of buses, number of drivers, geographic distribution of pupils. Yet, when one sets out to state a use model for a general routing and scheduling program, these facts just drive more questions.

To what degree are the sampled systems representative? Over the whole intended user set, what are the ranges of all those parameters? Their distributions?

What are the rates of change from scheduling period to scheduling period? What will the ranges be five years from now? Ten years?

As the questions get harder, the answers get vaguer. What is the designer to do if he has committed himself to making explicit use models?

Guess!

I am quite convinced that, once he has moved beyond questions that can be answered by reasonable inquiry, the designer should *guess* or, if you prefer, *postulate* a complete set of attributes and values, with guessed frequency distributions, in order to develop complete, explicit, and shared user and use models.

An articulated guess beats an unspoken assumption.

Many benefits flow from this "naive" procedure:

Guessing the values and frequencies forces the designer to think very carefully about the expected user set.

Writing down the values and frequencies exposes them to debate. It is easier to criticize something concrete than to create, so there will be more input from the whole team. The debate will inform all the participants and will surface the differences in user images that the several designers carry. It typically also will surface other unrecognized assumptions.[4]

Enumerating the values and frequencies explicitly helps everyone realize which decisions depend upon which user set properties.

More important, it raises these crucial questions: Which assumptions matter? How much? Even this sort of horseback sensitivity analysis is valuable. When it develops that important decisions are hinging on some particular guess, it is worth the cost to develop a better estimate.

In the end, however, many assumptions will remain debatable and unverifiable. The chief architect must own—and make known—the set the team goes with.

Better Wrong than Vague!

At this point the reader will object, "How can I know or even assume so much detail about uses and users?" The answer is, "You will in fact make those assumptions anyhow"; that is, each design decision will be guided, consciously or unconsciously, by the designer's assumptions about uses and users. What this often means in reality is that the vague designer substitutes *himself* for the user, designing for what he assumes he would want if he were the user. But he isn't.

Therefore, wrong explicit assumptions are much better than vague ones. Wrong ones will perhaps be questioned; vague ones won't.

Notes and References

1. A *use model* is a weighted collection of *use cases*. Robertson and Robertson [2005], *Requirements-Led Project Management*, treat use cases in considerable detail.

2. Cockburn [2000], *Writing Effective Use Cases*, is a thorough treatment.

3. Brooks [1995], *The Mythical Man-Month*, 56–57.

4. Students in my advanced computer architecture course have been required to do this for their term projects. When it has been done conscientiously, the effect on the designs has been very beneficial.

10

Inches, Ounces, Bits, Dollars—The Budgeted Resource

If a design, particularly a team design, is to have conceptual integrity, one should name the scarce resource explicitly, track it publicly, control it firmly.

Apollo **rocket**
iStockphoto

What's the Budgeted Resource?

Within any design, there is at least one scarce resource to be rationed or budgeted. Sometimes there are two or more to be jointly optimized; but most commonly, one is dominant, and others appear chiefly as desiderata or constraints. Economists call this the *limiting resource*; I prefer to emphasize the necessary designer action: conscious budgeting.[1]

Although designers often talk as if cost or some performance/cost ratio were the resource to be optimized, that is often not how they act in practice. It follows that if a design, particularly a team design, is to have conceptual integrity, one wants to *name the scarce resource explicitly, track it publicly, control it firmly*.

Often Not Dollars

Ponder some budgeted critical resources that are not dollars:

- Inches of oceanfront, in a beach house
- Ounces of payload, in a spacecraft—or in a backpack
- Memory bandwidth, in any von Neumann computer architecture
- Nanoseconds of timing tolerance, in a GPS system
- Calendar days, on an asteroid-interception project
- Resident kernel memory space, in OS/360 design
- Program hours, at a conference
- Pages, on a grant proposal or a journal paper
- Power (and stored energy) on a communications satellite
- Heat, in a high-performance chip
- Water, on western farmland
- Student learning hours, in a degree curriculum
- Political power, in an organization's constitution
- Seconds, even frames, in a film or video
- Hours of access to the track per day, in London Underground engineering and maintenance
- Format bits, in a computer architecture
- Hours or minutes, in a military assault plan

Even Dollars Have Flavors, and Surrogates

Even when cost is in fact to be the budgeted commodity for a design project, cost varieties must be considered. For personal computers, made by the hundreds of millions, manufacturing cost is dominant. For supercomputers, made by the dozens, development cost dominates.

Quite often, designers adopt surrogates for dollars as their budgeted resources. Building architects will do program development, and often schematic design, using square feet as the rationed resource. Computer architects used to use bits of register and of various cache levels as surrogates for chip area.

Surrogates have several advantages: They are usually simpler. One can design with them long before one knows the surrogate/dollar ratio. They are more stable. Using the same surrogate harnesses one's previous design experiences, even though the surrogate/dollar ratio may be different, or even varying. One knows how many square feet per occupant an auditorium needs.

Surrogates can also lead one astray; the temptation is to use them after they cease being appropriate. Chip designers often thought in terms of area well after wiring length or pin count became the important critical resource.

The Budgeted Resource Can Change

Shifts in technology sometimes change which resource is critical. Therein lie snares for the unwary. As chip densities went up, I/O pins displaced chip area as the limiter on function, hence became the rationed commodity. But power dissipation has now displaced pins as the rationed commodity on many chip designs. Seymour Cray once famously said, "Refrigeration is the key to supercomputer design."[2] Gene Amdahl told me, about the same time, that off-chip capacitance was the speed-limiting commodity in his designs.[3]

Some think that number of classes has replaced function points as the estimator for software complexity, hence for probable size. Experienced consultants Suzanne and James Robertson, however, say that they find function points still to be the most robust estimator.[4] Eoin Woods, an experienced developer, points out:

> *People want to measure two things: How much value is delivered and how much artefact needs to be produced to deliver it. Function points are good because they try to measure the former, whereas lines of code, number of classes, and so on, are very sensitive to style. One can reduce both of these while increasing delivered value quite easily* [reviewer's comment].

The budgeted resource can change in the middle of a design, just because we get smarter. Operating System/360 (1965) was designed to cover a 16-fold range of computer memory sizes, from 32K bytes (yes, K, not M) up to and beyond 512K. Clearly, some memory space had to be left for the application program, so the resident kernel of the operating system was sorely constrained—to 12K in the tightest case. We were sure that memory space was the constraining "budgeted resource." We were wrong.

OS/360 was one of the first operating systems that could assume a disk for storing the operating system. Earlier operating systems were tape- or even card-based. Having random-access systems resident wonderfully expanded the function one could build into limited space. "Just read in a chunk from disk." And everybody in the system design team did—with great frequency: chunks had to be small, to fit the 1K buffer area of the smallest configuration.

One of our wisest developers, Robert Ruthrauff, began early in the OS/360 project to build a performance simulator, and fortunately he got it running early. The first results were horrifying! On our second-fastest computer model (Model 65), our programming system would compile only five Fortran source statements a minute! That day, the project's budgeted resource switched from memory bytes to disk accesses.[5]

So What?

If thinking in terms of a budgeted resource is a healthy discipline for a design team, what actions follow as corollaries?

Identify Explicitly

A project manager naturally begins by enumerating all the objectives and constraints. Explicit identification of the budgeted resource should be next. Notice that as defined and discussed, this is usually a resource of the design, not of the design process. For example, skill allocation is always crucial to a design project, but it is not a property of the design itself.

Project schedule may be critical, but it is often the property of the project, not the resulting design. For example, in preparing a competitive proposal against a hard deadline, "We'll do the best design we can in the time we've got." On the other hand, if designing to divert the asteroid, schedule days become the budgeted resource. Similarly, in a race to be first to market with a totally new product, schedule may become the budgeted resource.

Track Publicly

The whole team needs to know, continually, the current budget for the critical resource. In particular, each sub-team, each team member, must know how many chip milliwatts or transaction-processing disk accesses their part of the design may use, how many they control.

Control Firmly

Whatever the critical resource, the team leader will keep a small personal kitty for late allocation, just as a general keeps some reserves for dispatch to the hottest part of the battle as it develops.[6]

It is imperative that only one person control budgeting and rebudgeting. Gerry Blaauw did this superbly with bits in the Program Status Word of the System/360 architecture. These were, along with memory bandwidth and bits in instruction formats, the budgeted resources the architects were allocating. His total system overview, his cautious stinginess, his inventiveness of alternatives within the existing architecture, all combined to make a highly efficient architecture.[7]

Ken Iverson, winner of the Turing Award for his APL language, desired conceptual integrity above all, so he made the number of distinct language concepts the budgeted resource. Countless proposals were made, both within the implementing team and from the using community, for new constructs embodying additional concepts. His total system overview, his cautious stinginess, his inventiveness of solutions within the existing language, all combined to make a highly elegant language.

Marissa Meyer today exerts the same total system overview, the same passion for consistency in design, and the same cautious stinginess in her role as the dragon guarding Google's look and feel.[8]

Notes and References

1. Simon [1996], *The Sciences of the Artificial*, also treats finding the limiting resource as crucial to the design process (143–144).

2. Murray [1997], *The Supermen.*

3. Personal communication [about 1972].

4. Personal communication [2008].

5. Digitek's elegant little Fortran compiler (1965) used a very dense, specialized representation for the compiler code itself, so that external storage was not needed. The time lost in decoding this representation interpretatively was gained back tenfold by entirely avoiding the budgeted constraint—disk accesses. Brooks [1969], *Automatic Data Processing*, Chapter 6.

6. A general planning a battle is a designer in a most serious sense, and one who perhaps more than any other must rapidly revise his design in the face of new facts and constraints.

7. Blaauw [1997], "IBM System/360," Section 12.4.

8. Holson [2009], "Putting a bolder face on Google."

11
Constraints Are Friends

Form is liberating.

ARTISTS' APHORISM

I need four walls around me, to hold my
life, and keep me from going astray.

JAMES TAYLOR, "BARTENDER'S BLUES"

A general-purpose product is harder to design
well than a special-purpose one.

Michelangelo's *David*, carved from an "abandoned" block of marble
iStockphoto

Constraints

Constraints may be burdens, but they also may be friends. Constraints shrink the designer's search space. By so doing, they focus and speed design. Many of us disliked "Write an essay on whatever you want" assignments in junior high, and we were on to something real: removing all constraints makes the task of "designing" the essay harder, not easier.

Bach understood this. Wolff says, "Bach, predisposed from the very beginning toward traversing conventional boundaries, nevertheless preferred to work within a given framework and accept the challenges it imposed."[1]

Constraints not only shrink the search space, they challenge the designer, often thereby stimulating a completely fresh creation. Consider Michelangelo's *David*. According to legend, the block of marble had been abandoned by Antonio Rossellino 25 years earlier as unusable, because of a crack. The result is a *concept* of David different from that in previous and contemporary art. One is piqued to study exactly how Michelangelo coped with the block's defects, and how this stimulated the different artistic concept.

Christopher Wren's London churches offer another vivid example. Commissioned to rebuild 50 Anglican churches destroyed by the Great Fire of 1666, Wren was sorely constrained. For each, he had to take as given the site, its environment, and often the previous foundation. Moreover, Anglican churches must be oriented with the altar to the east in symbolic anticipation of Christ's promised return as the "bright morning star."[2] It is great fun to go today to each of the 27 Wren churches that remain after the attrition of time and the World War II Blitz. Look at each site and its problems, consider the orientation constraint, and see how Wren invented different solutions.

The designers of a viaduct on the Blue Ridge Parkway in the North Carolina mountains had to touch ground as little as possible to minimize environmental damage. The result was quite elegant.[3]

Up to a Point

Artificial constraints for one's design task have the nice property that one is free to relax them. Ideally, they push one into an unexplored corner of a design space, stimulating creativity. But any constraint set may push the designer into an empty corner, where no conceivable design works.

Therefore, one must carefully distinguish

- Real constraints
- Obsolete once-real constraints
- Constraints misperceived as real
- Intentional artificial constraints

Obsolete Constraints. The experienced designer, like a lion accustomed to pace the confines of its cage, may find himself obeying by habit constraints made obsolete by technological advances. Chapter 9, "Ten pounds in a five-pound sack," in *The Mythical Man-Month* [1975], now reads like a joke. It teaches techniques for squeezing software into cramped memory spaces. Crucial in 1965, they were already less important in 1975, but many programmers still strained for small sizes. (Of course, memory size has always mattered for embedded computers, especially now for those stunningly rich systems we still call "cell phones.")

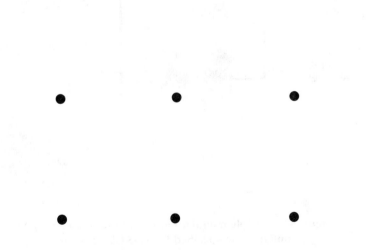

Figure 11-1   Misperceived constraint puzzle: Run a continuous line of no more than four straight segments through all nine dots.

Misperceived Constraints. These are more subtle. Figure 11-1 shows a classic example. (See Figure 11-5 for a solution.[4]) The boundary-line constraint described in Chapter 3 is another.

To multiply two 2 x 2 matrices in only seven multiplications instead of eight, one must discard the misperceived constraint that vector operations must be used.

The design of the IBM 9020 computer system for the Federal Aviation Administration (FAA) furnishes a painful example. System architects at MITRE Corporation, acting for the FAA, were properly aiming at a super-reliable system. They specified the configuration shown in Figure 11-2.

So far, so good. The IBM team responding to this request for bids discovered that the new System/360 semi-integrated

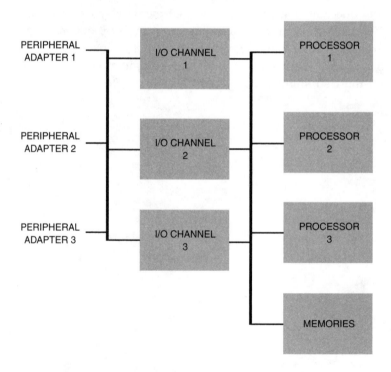

Figure 11-2   Triple modular redundant processor and I/O configuration specified for 1965 FAA system

circuit technology was very well suited for the unit-reliability demands.

The S/360 Model 50, a mid-range computer, more than met both the speed and reliability requirements for the processors. The same Model 50's I/O system, implemented with the same memory and datapaths as the processor, but with different microcoding, handsomely met the requirements for the I/O controller.

So the IBM engineers designed the system sketched in Figure 11-3.

Careful analysis showed that the Figure 11-3 configuration more than met all the system performance requirements and all the system reliability requirements. But it was rejected.

It did not have the specified configuration topology. The MITRE system architects had mistakenly insisted on the specified topology as an essential constraint—although what they were actually shopping for was function and reliability, not topology. So IBM bid, built, and delivered the configuration

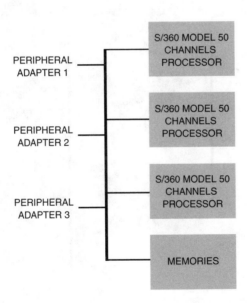

Figure 11-3   FAA system as first proposed with System/360 Model 50 computers

shown in Figure 11-4. Unchallenged reliability analyses showed this configuration to be in fact considerably *less* reliable than that in Figure 11-3, since there are twice as many components and many more connectors that can fail. But it met the specified constraints!

The pricing was magical for the taxpayers. Quite independently from cost, the government paid for system 11-4 just what it would have paid for system 11-3. IBM really wanted that contract! Of course, the lifetime costs for power, cooling, and maintenance would not have been at all equal.

When you specify something to be designed, tell what properties you need, not how they are to be achieved.

If implementation approaches are given as constraints, better solutions are cut off. For the sake of the artifact and the user, the designer confronted with false constraints should fight back!

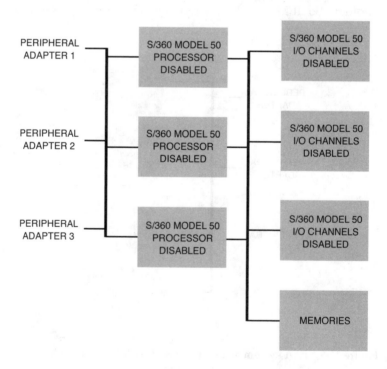

Figure 11-4   IBM 9020 FAA system as delivered

A Design Paradox: General-Purpose Artifacts Are Harder than Special-Purpose Ones

I have earlier argued that the hardest part of designing is deciding exactly *what to design*. Above, I argued that constraints are friends, that they make the design task easier, not harder. It follows that the more specialized the purpose, the easier the design task.

At first this seems wrong. One would offhand think it an easier assignment to "Design a 1,000-square-foot house" than to "Design a 1,000-square-foot house for a family with two children of opposite genders, located in Chapel Hill, North Carolina, facing north."

In one sense, of course, the former task is indeed easier—it is harder for the design to be criticized. If there are no constraints, there are no criteria for excellence. In general, it is easier to do a mediocre general-purpose design than to do a mediocre special-purpose design.

Nevertheless, overall the latter job is easier if one wants an excellent design. Any design process begins with the designer elaborating and particularizing the objectives and constraints. The first task is to narrow the design space. The more constrained the assigned goal, the more of this task has already been accomplished.

Dashing Off a General-Purpose Design.   How can this be so? Consider the case of computer architecture. General-purpose computers are well understood. Over a hundred exemplar architectures have been built and sold. Everybody knows what they have to do. A good designer can sketch one out in a few days; the set of architectural decisions is clear:

- Instruction formats
- Addressing and memory management
- Datatypes and their representations
- Operation set
- Instruction sequencing
- Supervisory facilities
- Input-output

Designing the Special-Purpose Computer Architecture. On the other hand, designing a special-purpose computer clearly takes a lot of extra work up front. One must study the application. What makes it peculiar? What are the relative frequencies of operations? What are the weightings of desiderata for the clients: performance, cost, reliability, weight? Indeed, one has to develop an explicit characterization of the application.

Designing an Excellent General-Purpose Architecture. But one also needs an explicit user model to do proper design of a general-purpose architecture, and the user model is much harder to craft. In fact, one must study each of a whole set of applications, determining the peculiar needs and balances of each. Scientific computing emphasizes matrix algebra and partial differential equations; engineering computation emphasizes data reduction and formula evaluation; database query emphasizes optimum disk utilization. Each application must be understood.

Then they all have to be weighted:

- Across the entire application set
- Across the entire set of intended machine implementations
- Across the decades of lifetime that a new architecture must contemplate[5]

Likewise, as the design proceeds, the nascent result must be tested against the assumed characteristics of each user segment. When the design is complete and prototyped, the prototype must be tested by actual users from each segment.

So it is that I always assign my students in my advanced computer architecture course to do special-purpose architecture projects. They cannot offer gas and platitudes; the application and user analysis must be precise. And yet, they often do an excellent job of this, whereas they could not possibly devise an excellent unconstrained general-purpose architecture in the time available. The task is far easier than would be the in-depth analysis that a serious general-purpose design effort must make.

Software Design. The same paradox holds for software. Designing a special-purpose programming language is straightforward compared to the delicate balancing of expressive power, generality, and parsimony that one must seek in a general-purpose programming language. Restraint is so much easier to practice in the special-purpose design.

Spatial Design.   The paradox holds as well for building spaces. Designing a superb bedroom is easier than designing superb public living spaces, precisely because the public spaces have so many more functions, so many more scenarios to be studied, and so many more furnishing options.[6]

Similarly, designing a specialized laboratory is easier than designing the public lobby of a computer science building.

Net

Since constraints are the designer's friend, if the task originally seems unconstrained, first think harder about what is really desired, about the user and use models, and you will probably find some narrowing constraints, to the benefit of both designer and user.

Notes and References

1. Wolff [2000], *Johann Sebastian Bach*, 387. When not sufficiently constrained by commission or available performance talent, Bach would sometimes adopt quite artificial constraints to stimulate his creativity. An example is the repeated use of the BACH motif (the sequence of notes B-flat, A, C, B-natural). I don't recommend the adoption by engineering or software of artificial constraints to stimulate creativity.

2. Revelations 22:16.

3. http://www.blueridgeparkway.org/linncove.htm,   accessed   on July 18, 2009.

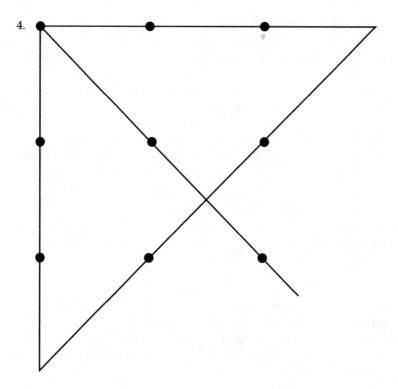

Figure 11-5   A solution to the nine-dots puzzle

5. We originally predicted that the System/360 architecture would have to live 25 years, through generations of implementations (Brooks [1965], "The future of computer architecture"). The forces for preserving programming languages, computer architectures, and operating system architectures are stronger than we then knew. IBM's z/90 still embodies System/360 architecture 45 years later, and the end is not yet in sight. Fortran (1956) use today is another good indicator of the strength of those persistence forces.

6. For the Kenwood House in Hampstead near London, Robert Adam (1728–1792) designed every detail of the furnishings, down to the doorknobs (*Kenwood Guidebook*).

12
Esthetics and Style in Technical Design

Firmitas, utilitas, venusitas
  (Firmness, usefulness, delight)

MARCUS VITRUVIUS [22 BC],
DE ARCHITECTURA

Style is the dress of thought, and a well-dressed thought,
like a well-dressed man, appears to great advantage.

LORD CHESTERFIELD [1774], LETTER CCXL, 361

Monticello: Jefferson's adaptation of Palladio's adaptation of Roman style
iStockphoto

Esthetics in Technical Design

Vitruvius famously asserted that a good building architecture achieves "firmness, usefulness, and delight."[1] Delight is equal with firmness and usefulness, although from a purely utilitarian point of view firmness and usefulness should quite suffice.

The whole human experience confirms him. We have always wanted our public and private structures to satisfy the soul's need for beauty, and we have almost always been willing to invest extra work toward that end.

The cave man painted on the walls of his cave; Native Americans decorated their hide tepees. Prehistoric Britons decorated their pottery with fingernail carvings. Moldings, carving, tiling, paneling, and painting have supplemented the firm structures and the convenience features of dwellings through the centuries. Standards of beauty have varied widely, from the ornate to the lean, by culture and by epoch, but visual beauty has always been a goal for building design.

What is the role of beauty, of esthetics, in technical design? Cars, airplanes, and ships have physical forms and therefore are capable of visual beauty. But this is not the whole story. We find ourselves talking about "elegant" and "ugly" programming languages. When we speak of a "clean" computer, we are referring not at all to the visual appearance of its industrial design, but to some property of its logical structure.

We rejoice as we behold and use some designs. Others with equivalent function and equal soundness fail this test, and we care. The delight may be visual, auditory, gustatory, or haptic. It may even be purely intellectual, as with a beautiful proof or a well-dressed thought. Our language captures this in many ways—we casually talk about an "elegant" program, and our hearers know what we mean.[2]

What Is Logical Beauty?

Parsimony

"Elegance" Requires Parsimony.   One definition of elegance in mathematics is "accomplishing a great deal with few elements."

This certainly applies to proofs. Alas, too many math textbook authors believe it applies as well to explication. Clearly sufficiency is not enough for good explication; clarity demands expansion and illustration with examples.

One is tempted to design programming languages with parsimony as the guiding principle. And computer design clearly must place a high value on parsimony, the use of few elements.[3]

Lisp, for example, has a tiny core, but elegant provisions for extensibility and composability give it power. Visual Basic, on the other hand, is considerably more complex, but much more difficult to extend.

Not the Whole Story.   Parsimony is not enough, however. Adding an "unnecessary" bit of componentry, such as index registers, to a computer can radically improve its performance and its performance/cost ratio. Common Lisp expands the basic language to make it easier for programmers to get about their business.

Van der Poel designed a computer with only one operation code.[4] Every instruction carried out the same operation. He demonstrated the sufficiency of his operation—his machine could do anything any other computer could do. And yet it was very difficult to program. Ironically, the delight that came from using it was similar to the delight from working out a crossword puzzle— a construct of intentional complexity and no intended utility.

In practice, the effective use of van der Poel's machine required mastery of a whole library of nonobvious idioms. Van der Poel coded up some subroutines and macro operations, and everybody else programmed in the somewhat higher-level language thus produced.

A similar story can be told of APL, a very elegant and powerful programming language. Many styles of programming can readily be expressed in APL—from the clear and straightforward to the convoluted and overcompacted. Although the operators have quite straightforward actions, nonobvious idiomatic combinations are sometimes used for high-frequency functions. Examples are given in *Computer Architecture*, Section A.6. Program A-41, "Force to even," halves a number, floors it, and doubles it (Blaauw and Brooks [1997]).

In some circles, it is even fashionable to see how much function can be packed into one line of APL, however convoluted and idiomatic. "One-liners" are traded about and published with glee and pride. But again, this is crossword puzzle sport, not elegant design. Programming languages exist to facilitate the writing—and the much more frequent reading—of programs, not to serve as puzzles.[5]

Structural Clarity

Parsimony Is Not Enough.   One also demands a certain straightforwardness in a language or a computer architecture. There should be a direct route from what one wants to say to how one says it.

Human natural language, which we may assume developed to meet a total combination of real needs, is far from parsimonious. Shannon [1949] showed that the redundancy of English is about 50 percent.[6] Even with this much redundancy, human languages develop idioms, just as programming languages do.

Structure.   "Elegance" in a technical design demands that the basic structural concept of the design be plainly evident and, if not logically straightforward, easily explained.

Metaphor.   Both "elegance" and comprehensibility are aided by the use of familiar and simple metaphors, especially in user interfaces to the designed object. The "Desktop" of the Macintosh operating system is a prime example. VisiCalc's "spreadsheet," now more familiarly embodied in Excel and Lotus, is another.

Consistency

Gerry Blaauw and I have studied the question "What is *good* computer architecture?" Perhaps a look at that small treatment can illuminate the much larger question, "What is lovely technical design?" In the next subsection, I summarize Section 1.4 from our *Computer Architecture* [1997].[7]

What Is Good Computer Architecture?

An architecture that fails to include needed functions is *erroneous*. But even if the needed functions are present, they may still be awkward. Or the whole may be so complex that it is hard to learn and remember the functions and their rules. An architecture that is straightforward to use is often called *clean*.

Blaauw and I believe that consistency underlies all principles of quality. A good architecture is *consistent* in the sense that, given a partial knowledge of the system, one can predict the remainder.[8]

For example, the mere decision to include a square-root operation in an operation set should almost fully define the operation. The data and instruction formats should be the same as those for other floating-point arithmetic operations. Precision, range, rounding, and significance should be handled as with other results. Even taking the square root of a negative number should have an exception treatment similar to that of division by zero.

Still, the truly consistent solution can be hard to identify. For computer architecture, some touchstones are brevity of description, simplicity of code generation, and suitability for many implementations.

Derived Principles.   From consistency flow three major design principles: *orthogonality, propriety*, and *generality*.

Orthogonality: Do Not Link What Is Independent.   A change in one orthogonal function has no observable effect on any other function in the set. For an alarm clock, for instance, a set of functions might include a lighted face and an alarm. Orthogonality would be violated if the alarm operated only when the face was lighted. We give many examples of the violation of orthogonality in computer architectures in our book.

Propriety: Do Not Introduce What Is Immaterial.   A function meeting an essential requirement is called *proper*. For a car, functions such as steering, speed control, lights, and windshield washer are proper to its purposes.

The opposite of propriety is *extraneousness*. An example is the automotive gearshift. Shifting gears is not proper to driving; the extraneous component of the user interface arises from the implementation of the car.

An example of propriety in computers is the unique representation of zero in twos-complement notation. In contrast, both signed-magnitude and ones-complement notations attach a sign to zero, a distinction that is extraneous. More rules have to be made as to how the signed zero behaves in arithmetic and zero-test operations; these often have unexpected effects in use.

Parsimony is a subset of propriety. Another is *transparency*, the property that a function's implementation produces no visible side effects. In a computer, the implementation of the datapath with a pipelined organization should be invisible to the programmer.

Generality: Do Not Restrict What Is Inherent.   *Generality* is the ability to use a function for many ends. It expresses the professional humility of the designer, his conviction that users will be inventive beyond his imagination and that needs may change beyond his ability to forecast. The designer should avoid limiting a function by his own notions about its use. When you don't know, grant freedom.

The Intel 8080A has an operation called Restart. It was indeed intended for restarting after an interruption. But it was designed with enough generality that its most frequent use is for return from a subroutine.

The major ways generality is achieved are open-endedness (space for future development), completeness of function sets, decomposition of functions into orthogonal components, and composability.

More Virtues of Consistency

Consistency is reinforcing and self-teaching, because it confirms and encourages our expectations. It also solves the conflict between ease of use and ease of learning. Ease of learning requires a simple architecture, as with fixed-point arithmetic. Ease of use requires a complex one, as with floating-point arithmetic. When the designer makes fixed-point a subset of floating-point, the user's comprehension of the architecture can grow naturally.

Style in Technical Design

On tuning in to the middle of a piece of classical music, a knowledgeable listener can usually guess the century and often the composer, even if he has never heard the particular work. On seeing an unfamiliar painting, we often can say, "Looks like a Rembrandt," or "Dutch Golden Age." British WRENs during World War II learned to recognize the characteristic Morse code "fists" of Axis broadcasters and were thereby able to identify military units as they moved. So it is with bridges, automobiles, airplanes, and computer architectures. A particular computer "looks as if" Seymour Cray designed it.

One of the drivers of delight is what we call *style* (definition attempted below). Two style components affect delight: the consistency with which a style is effected, and the intrinsic qualities of the style itself. In architecture, music, cuisine, or computers, no style will appeal to everyone; a mishmash of styles delights no one.[9]

I have earlier argued that conceptual integrity is the most important attribute of a design. Surely the most important integrity of a design is in the overall structure, the very bones of the design. But it is important to follow a uniform style in the details, the skin, as well.

A style consistently applied is a component, even if only the "dress," of the conceptual integrity of a product. It does more than delight—it aids the *comprehensibility* of the design. In turn, this begets ease of initial learning, ease of use, ease of recollection after disuse, ease of maintenance, ease of extension.

Style matters in all media of design, all genres.

What Is Style?

Precisely what is this characteristic way of working that confers designer recognizability on the products? This question is harder than it appears.

Definitions. *The Oxford English Dictionary* defines *style*, in the sense we are considering, as

> 14. *Those features of literary composition that belong to form or expression rather than to the substance of the thought or matter expressed.*

21. A particular mode or form of skilled construction, execution or production; the manner in which a work of art is executed, regarded as characteristic of the individual artist or of his time and place.

Webster's Revised Unabridged Dictionary (1913 edition):

4. Mode of presentation, especially in music or any of the fine arts; a characteristic or peculiar mode of developing an idea or accomplishing a result.

Akin [1988], "Expertise of the architect":

Style as an expression of the designer's personal and professional choices is a vehicle which helps limit the many degrees of freedom that design problems have.

A Characteristic of Detailing.   We observe that different works by the same artist are different in the subject painted, or the genre and themes of music composed, but alike in recognizable style. Similarly, the Oak Park church by Frank Lloyd Wright has certain resemblances of parts and arrangement to other architects' churches, but it has a close affinity of line, of detailing, of ornamentation, of palette, with Wright's residences. Whatever style is, it has more to do with details of design than with the main purpose or thrust.[10]

A Hypothesis: Minimization of Mental Effort.   All design, all creation, involves hundreds of microdecisions. Habits seem to be a mechanism by which humans economize on mental effort, by which we reduce the burden of decision making in everyday life. If this is indeed an inborn human trait, it surely carries over into our creative activities. Absent substantial reasons to do otherwise, we make the same microdecision the same way every time. The bundle of microdecisions, consistently made, characterizes our work and gives it the particularity, the distinctiveness, that yields recognizability.

Consistency across Microdecisions.   One would expect microdecisions to be consistent not only across time but also across sets of similar decisions. In related microdecisions, the same factors enter, and the same mind would naturally weight them in a consistent way.

A Frank Lloyd Wright will tend to use rectilinear elements instead of curved ones in all his decorations, and in his structures, too. A Seymour Cray will consistently opt for maximum performance over compatibility with his earlier computers.

Clarity of Style.   To the degree that a designer does indeed achieve consistency across a wide range of macro- and micro-decisions, we say that he has a *clear* style, meaning that it is possible to describe it economically. It follows that recognition is easier.

Even a baroque architecture can show clarity of style. Wright's architecture was spare as well as clear, but those aren't the same property.

When little consistency across design decisions is achieved, we call the style *opaque* or *muddled*. Somehow, consistency brings clarity, and clarity brings delight.[11]

My working definition:

> *Style is a set of different repeated microdecisions, each made the same way whenever it arises, even though the context may be different.*

Moreover, related microdecisions are resolved in related ways.

Style unquestionably exists. A few bars tell us that a work is Bach's, or Mozart's, or Schubert's. A famous exhibition brought together many Rembrandts, and many works once attributed to Rembrandt but now recognized as imitations. The experts agreed as to what was genuine; even laymen could tell surprisingly often.[12]

Reasonably knowledgeable people can readily tell a Seymour Cray computer from a Gerry Blaauw or Gordon Bell one.[13] The authors of the unsigned *Federalist Papers* have been conclusively identified by details of their prose styles.[14] Programmers can identify each other's code. C. S. Lewis argues that Jesus's miracles faithfully display the hallmarks of the Father's creative style.[15,16]

Properties of Styles

Regardless of the medium of design, styles share some common properties.

Specification Is Costly. First, making a style explicit takes a remarkable amount of specification. *The Chicago Manual of* [English prose] *Style* runs 984 pages. Fowler's *Modern English Usage* [1926ff.] invests some 2,800 words into defining the proper usage of *the*. Our implicit recognition of Bach's style uses a lot of stored information.

Specification Is Hierarchical. Second, any style specification (explicit or implicit) is inherently hierarchical. Consider English prose:

- Dialect and diction
- Person, tense, formality, vividity of color, warmth of tone
- Balance and rhythm—prosody
- Usage—for instance, gender pronouns
- Punctuation
- Compositional layout—font, spacing, and so on

The compositional styling for this book, shown on its Web page,[17] deals with book styling, chapter styling, headings, paragraphing, fonts, and other elements.

Styles Evolve. Third, styles evolve over time, even an individual's style. Cognoscenti can tell Turner's late pictures from his early ones.[18] Larger styles, such as Gothic architecture, evolved so much that we distinguish Early, Decorated, and Perpendicular. Moreover, fashions in style evolve even faster, whether in pop music, teenage jargon, or 17th-century English gardens.

To Get a Consistent Style—Document It!

A design style is defined by a set of microdecisions. A clear style reflects a consistent set. A clear style may not be a good style; a muddled one never is.[19]

The aspiring designer must therefore strive for consistency of style. A design team has to work even harder at it. A sole author writing a ten-page paper, all at once, will have a clear style. The same writer, producing a book, will find he needs to document some stylistic microdecisions as he goes along, to maintain consistency. Moreover, even the ten-page paper will need a style sheet (or a careful final editor) if sections have multiple authors.

In most design contexts, many stylistic decisions are given at the start. A technical paper has the journal's style manual; a book, the publisher's. An automobile designer assumes a mammoth set of SAE standards plus a company catalog of preferred springs, nuts, bolts. An operating system designer has a library of standard subroutines.

Nevertheless, each particular design occasions lots of unprescribed microdecisions. Gerry Blaauw and I found that our large joint *Computer Architecture* grew a 19-page Writing Style Sheet.[20] This of course supplemented both the overarching *Chicago Manual of Style* and Addison-Wesley's own house style document. Comprehensive as these were, they left many unanswered questions that we had to specify. For example, how were we to refer to a particular computer? Manufacturer plus model number? All this for each and every mention, for only first mention? Or first mention per chapter?

Of course, a design team must document the design proper, whether in engineering drawings, building blueprints, or a user manual. They also must say *why*, capturing the designers' intent so that the later maintainer will not in ignorance loose a vital stone from the edifice's arch. This is the final work product. The team must also, to preserve conceptual integrity during maintenance, document internally the myriad of microdecisions that govern and compose the visible design.

How to Achieve a Good Style

The prescription is simple; the methods, straightforward; the work, arduous.

Study Other Designers' Styles Intentionally.   Practice working in another's style. This will force close attention to detail and explicit thinking. It might also produce great works— consider Respighi's *Ancient Airs and Dances*, or Fritz Kreisler's

Classical Manuscripts or his *Praeludium and Allegro (in the style of Pugnani).*[21]

Make Conscious Judgments. Write opinions as to what styles you like and why, what aspects of a particular style and why.

Practice. Practice. Practice.

Revise. Look for stylistic inconsistencies.

Choose Designers Carefully. Seek for your products designers who have clear styles and good taste, as demonstrated by their previous works.

Notes and References

1. Vitruvius [22 BC], *De Architectura.*

2. Gelernter [1988], *Machine Beauty,* makes a powerful argument that a sense of beauty, not just analysis, should govern design.

3. Steve Wozniak [2006], *iWoz,* proudly claims that the Apple I used only two-thirds as many components as other equivalent machines.

4. van der Poel [1959], "ZEBRA, a simple binary computer." An accessible explanation of the machine is given in Blaauw and Brooks [1997], *Computer Architecture,* Section 13.1. See also van der Poel [1962], *The Logical Principles of Some Simple Computers.*

5. We commit a difficult APL one-liner in *Computer Architecture* in Program 9-8 on page 511 (Blaauw and Brooks [1997]).

6. Shannon [1949], *The Mathematical Theory of Communication.*

7. Blaauw and Brooks [1997], *Computer Architecture.*

8. Blaauw [1965], "Door de vingers zien"; Blaauw [1970], "Hardware requirements for the Fourth Generation."

9. C. S. Lewis [1961], *An Experiment in Criticism,* argues strongly that excellence and level of style ("highbrow" versus "lowbrow") are independent.

10. Alexander [1977], *A Pattern Language,* is an important architectural example.

11. Examples of clear styles that have particularly delighted me include some artificial and imitative ones:
    - The open-air Spanish architecture museum, El Poble Espanyol, at Barcelona
    - EPCOT at Walt Disney World, with its national pavilions
    - Duke University's Gothic campus
    - Jefferson's ten Pavilions on the Lawn at the University of Virginia, each illustrating a particular style
    - Sidney Smith's 18th-century prose
    - The Respighi and Kreisler works cited

12. One work came as an imitation and went home to the Art Institute of Chicago as genuine.

13. For example, see Chapters 14 (Cray) and 15 (Bell) and Section 12.4 (Blaauw style) in the "Computer zoo" section of Blaauw and Brooks [1997], *Computer Architecture*.

14. Mosteller [1964], *Inference and Disputed Authorship*.

15. Lewis [1947], *Miracles*, Chapter 15.

16. Chen [1997], "Form language and style description," is a serious review of What is style? and an attempt to quantify it.

17. http://www.cs.unc.edu/~brooks/DesignofDesign.

18. Most artists' styles evolve. The exhibition "Monet in Normandy" (2006–2007) at the North Carolina Museum of Art emphasized the striking evolution of his style over the years.

19. One may or may not like Gaudí's stunning Barcelona church, La Sagrada Familia, but there is no doubt about the conceptual integrity of the style.

20. Posted on this book's Web page: http://www.cs.unc.edu/~brooks/DesignofDesign.

21. Kreisler first published *Classical Manuscripts* in 1905, asserting that he had found them in an old convent in the South of France. He was embarrassed to have his own name appear too often as composer on his concert programs. In 1935, he admitted that he had composed them, and they were republished as pieces "in the style of."

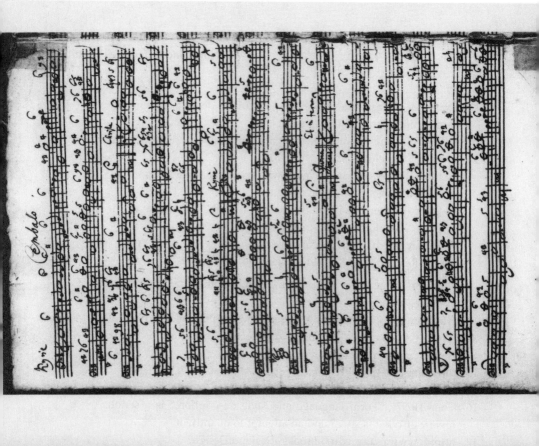

13

Exemplars in Design

. . . [T]he vast field of possibility can only be searched if you have some idea in advance of what you are looking for. Without prestructures of some kind, you cannot know where to look, or whether you have found what you are looking for. This again seems to justify architects in bringing past solutions and notions of style to bear on the search . . .

BILL HILLIER AND ALAN PENN
[1995], "CAN THERE BE A DOMAIN-
INDEPENDENT THEORY OF DESIGN?"

Pages from a Palestrina Mass copy in Bach's own hand

Staatsbibliothek of Berlin

Few Designs Are All-New

But These Surely Are Fun!   Rarely does one get to do a design that is entirely new. Imagine designing the first Earth-orbiting satellite, the first portable telephone, the first WIMP interface, the first air terminal, the first supercomputer!

The Common Lot. Usually, however, even novel designs derive from earlier artifacts intended for similar purposes and built with similar technology. The designer himself may have designed an earlier work; if not, he surely has seen, studied, and perhaps used some.

What then is the proper role of exemplars, precedents, in design? How should the designer study and use them? Should each design domain develop an accessible cumulative store of exemplars? How? Who?

The Roles of Exemplars

Exemplars provide safe models for new designs, implicit checklists of design tasks, warnings of potential mistakes, and launching pads for radical new designs.

Hence great designers have invested great efforts in studying their precedents. Palladio (1508–1580) not only studied Vitruvius [22 BC], he journeyed to Rome and measured and documented the surviving monuments, learning the most successful of the concepts and proportions evolved by the Romans of antiquity. From this tedious and unsung labor sprang not only his own original designs, but a design book that fathered a most enduring style of architecture.

Jefferson carefully studied not only Palladio's books, but the buildings around him in Paris.[1]

Bach took a six-month unpaid leave from his job and walked 250 miles to study the work and ideas of Buxtehude. (He lost his job for overstaying his leave.) Bach proved to be a much greater composer than Buxtehude, but his surpassing excellence came from comprehending and using the techniques of his predecessors, not ignoring them.[2]

I argue that great technical designers need to do likewise, but that the hurried pace of modern design has discouraged this practice.

Besides what individual designers do, technical design disciplines eager to produce great designs need to develop accessible bodies of exemplars and knowledgeable critiques of them.

What about Computer and Software Design?

What is the state of exemplar-based design in the computer and software fields? I think a fair answer is that we are rather behind older design disciplines. We are coming along rather well in developing the art and the resources for exemplar-informed design. But many of our curricula do not yet emphasize it, and penetration into design practice is not yet high.

What Exemplars Do You Use?

Amateur designers and trained professionals in the older design disciplines differ substantially in their use of exemplars.

The amateur uses those exemplars he happens to have encountered in his own experience. The trained professional has been exposed to a far wider range: whole libraries of exemplars representing different eras, different styles, different schools of thought. At best, he has had expert-guided tours through these libraries, with his teachers highlighting the noteworthy characteristics and explicating differences.

Much design in the computer and software fields suggests the use of only exemplars encountered in personal experience; even our trained professionals are not studying the exemplars available.

Computers. Computer architectures reveal the profound influence of the machine on which the architect first had substantial programming experience. Thus the early DEC minicomputers have a strong flavor of the MIT Whirlwind; IBM's System/360 is heavily flavored by the IBM 704 and 1401; the early microcomputers are clearly inspired by the DEC PDP-11.

One can also discern corporate memory—computers, unlike buildings, are designed by architects working within the implementing companies. They are more familiar, by explicit training and by informal culture, with their company's predecessor machines than with those of competitors. The Intel microprocessors strongly reflect a particular corporate style.

Design by adaptation is common in this field. Successful computers breed families of compatible siblings and successors, usually designed by adding function to the earlier models.

Mass-Product Software. Products such as Microsoft Word have followed the design pattern of computers, with successive generations created by progressively modifying function and implementation. This has been well studied and documented by Lehman and Belady.[3]

Custom Application Software and Operating Systems. Historically, most custom application software and operating systems reflect chiefly the experience of their designers, rather than that of the whole discipline.

More recently, the documentation and teaching of patterns has provided cross-fertilization for the field. Gamma [1995], *Design Patterns*, is strong on data structures and component-level patterns; Buschmann [1996], *Pattern-Oriented Software Architecture*, deals with larger-scale, system-structure patterns. We need more descriptions of whole systems, explaining system concepts. By and large we have that for a few operating systems only.

Studying Design Rationales of Exemplars

How should designers study exemplars in their fields? To study an architecture, one can read the manual. To study an implementation, one can read maintenance documentation. But for overview, one has to study the technical papers and books about the products to get the rationales.

Most technical papers, however, emphasize the *whats* and give skimpy coverage to the *whys*. And many designs never get explicated by their original designers at all; the creators are too busy on their next designs.

The exceptions cluster around the early days of any technology and around later revolutions, when approaches vary widely and debates are hot. These papers, like reports of military victories, are always after the fact, and they are usually rationalized; that is, they are far more rational in retrospect than was the actual design process. For most of us, that process was rich with potholes, blind alleys, mistaken turns, and alterations of goals. We learn a lot from the few exceptions to this *post hoc* smoothing.

Computer processor architecture provides a fruitful example for a study of exemplars. The technology is recent enough that there were many venues and outlets for descriptions. The field began with a wide diversity of design approaches and has converged to a "standard architecture." Blaauw and I elaborate on this evolution in Chapter 9 of our *Computer Architecture* [1997]. Revolutions—virtual memory, minicomputers, microcomputers, and RISC architectures—punctuated the historical development. Each occasioned fresh debates and hence stimulated fuller rationales.

First-Generation Computers

The most important computer paper ever written is

Burks, Goldstine, and von Neumann [1946], "Preliminary discussion of the logical design of an electronic computing instrument."

It is an incredible piece of work—must reading for every computer scientist. It cogently sets forth the stored-program concept, the three-register arithmetic unit, and many other ideas besides. The coverage is complete; the reasoning, compelling.

Maurice Wilkes says of an earlier draft,

> *I sat up late into the night reading the report. … I recognized this at once as the real thing, and from that time on never had any doubt as to the way computer development would go.*[4]

Wilkes further says there that this paper sets forth the ideas generated at the University of Pennsylvania in discussions among Presper Eckert, John Mauchly, and John von Neumann. He regrets that the extremely fruitful ideas are usually credited to von Neumann alone and has been at some pains to correct this misunderstanding.

After "Preliminary discussion" appeared, many groups in many places started building stored-program computers, using vacuum-tube logic. The first successes were at Manchester, with a running but unusably small Baby, and at Cambridge, with the first useful stored-program machine, the EDSAC. These rationales are very well documented: Williams [1948], "Electronic digital computers"; Wilkes [1949], "The EDSAC."

The most important early supercomputers are the IBM Stretch and the Control Data CDC 6600. Buchholz [1962], *Planning a Computer System: Project Stretch*, gives mostly rationale papers. However, the most noteworthy paper is Chapter 17, which describes a radically different sort of computer—a data-streaming coprocessor designed for cryptanalytic use—with hardly any description of the application or rationale for machine features.

The CDC 6600 quickly succeeded the Stretch as the world's fastest computer and came to dominate scientific supercomputing. It is the ancestor of the Cray family of supercomputers. Thornton [1970], *The Design of a Computer—The CDC 6600*, gives lots of rationale.

Third-Generation Computers

Second-generation computer architectures ran out of gas; that is, they lacked enough address bits to handle the large memories that had become economical and indispensable. An incompatible break in many product lines' architectures became inevitable, although painful. Fortunately, integrated circuits provided a large improvement in realization cost, and high-level languages enabled recompilation, so that the switch to new architectures could be afforded. New architectures occasioned new rationales.

Blaauw and Brooks [1997], *Computer Architecture*, while not a rationale book, nevertheless includes rationales for many of the System/360 architectural decisions. Those are the examples we could explicate from personal knowledge. Amdahl [1964] and Blaauw [1964] give abbreviated synopses of the System/360 rationale.

Virtual Memory

The Manchester Atlas introduced the automatic paging of blocks of instructions and data from a slower backing store into a smaller high-speed memory. Developers of time-sharing operating systems at Michigan and MIT soon proposed generalizing this concept into a full-fledged virtual memory, with vast namespace. GE and IBM built such computers. Again a revolution; again new rationales: Sumner [1962] (Atlas), Dennis [1965], Arden [1966].

The Minicomputer Revolution

Transistor-diode logic offered a radically cheaper way of realizing computers. Such a machine, the DEC PDP-8, changed the world by making a computer that individual departments, not whole institutions, could afford and control. This sociological advance was at least as important as the technological performance/cost advance. Minicomputers were made by the thousands, coexisting with, rather than replacing, the so-called mainframes.

The mainframe makers were content with their business models, and—fat, dumb, and happy—they universally missed the minicomputer revolution. Many new computer makers started up. The most successful was Digital Equipment Corporation. Bell [1978] treats the rationales and evolution of DEC's minicomputers.

The Microcomputer and RISC Revolutions

A similar sociological and technological revolution took place with integrated circuits. Radically lower costs meant that individuals, rather than departments, could have and control their own personal machines. Microcomputers are made by the millions.

This time it was the minicomputer makers, quite successful at what they were doing, who were fat, dumb, and happy. They missed the microcomputer revolution. Hewlett-Packard survived; DEC did not. Some of the mainframe makers, notably IBM, got back into the game and became major suppliers of personal microcomputers.

Again, the revolution spawned a cascade of rationales: Hoff [1972] (one-chip CPU), Patterson [1981] (RISC I), Radin [1982] (IBM 801).[5]

Experts in other disciplines can readily develop similar lists, giving the flow of history, the revolutions, and the milestone documented exemplars.

What Should a Discipline Do to Improve Exemplar-Based Design?

If indeed designers need to thrust beyond their own personal and corporate experience to master the ideas and techniques of their whole craft, how can the craft help?

Collections of Exemplars

The foregoing section shows that for computer architecture, there are plenty of documented exemplars. The obvious next step is the assembling and publishing of systematic collections. Gordon Bell and Allen Newell were the first to provide enough detail to help designers in their great 1971 book, *Computer Structures*. Hennessy and Patterson in 1990 contributed their valuable *Computer Architecture*, whose Appendix E is very helpful. Blaauw and I added to the collection with Chapters 9–16 of *Computer Architecture*.

Beyond Collection

The next step after collection is careful, evenhanded criticism of particular exemplars. In computer design, we see this both in the books of collections and in journal reviews of particular machine descriptions.

Next beyond criticism comes analysis, comparing one exemplar against another, assessing the differences in light of the objectives of each. Analysts are tempted to criticize the selection of product goals, rather than the effectiveness of the designing meeting those goals. Such analysis doesn't much help future designers.

A further step needs to follow comparative analysis. Some features of a design seem strong, others weak. Some approaches to design problems work; others do not. Hence careful analysts will derive from each example Rules of Good Practice to guide new syntheses. In most engineering disciplines, these rules are collected into handbooks, and ultimately into standards.

What about Software Design?

Computer design has progressed far through the sequence of collection, criticism, comparative analysis, and rules for synthesis. Software design is way behind.

Perhaps this is merely a question of youth. Software engineering as a discipline dates from 1968;[6] computer engineering, from 1937.[7] So far we have descriptions of individual exemplars of operating systems,[8] collections for programming language descriptions and rationales,[9] and little else.

Describing an operating system architecture is much more difficult than describing that of a computer. The functions are individually more complicated, and there are more of them. Moreover, the semantics of the operation Link are more difficult to describe than those of Divide. I believe we are dealing with two orders of magnitude more complexity. That will surely retard the collection, criticism, analysis, and synthesis of major software exemplars. I rejoice that Grady Booch has undertaken to assemble a *Handbook of Software Architectures*, currently as a Web site, ultimately for print.[10]

Who? Systematizing exemplars for study is a task of scholarship, not of design. Scholars and designers are different in taste and temperament. Designers often drive on from the conclusion of one project to the initiation of another, without pausing for much reflection, much less works of scholarship. Only as a discipline matures does it attract scholars (or matured designers, ready to reflect).

How Encouraged? Does modern engineering academia value and praise the work of the systematizer? Can one get tenure for doing such? In many institutions this work would be valued in a History of Science and Technology Department, but not in an Engineering Department.

Exemplars—Laziness, Originality, and Pride

Whoa! The above discussion on exemplars in design skips lightly by some issues very real for each designer:

- Isn't copying an early design, a precedent, just an exercise in laziness? Can an honest professional do that with integrity?
- People become designers because they like to make things. What fun is there in confining one's self-expression within the iron cage of another's style?
- The world highly values originality and innovation and rewards them with respect, reputation, and sometimes fame and fortune.
- One's special contribution to the human race depends upon one's own unique vision. Isn't it a disservice to neglect or suppress this originality?[11]

Some Perspective

Lest there be misunderstanding, I most emphatically do not assert that most design problems can be solved by adapting exemplars, nor do I advocate their slavish copying.

I do assert that

- The designer should know well the exemplars of his craft, their strengths, their weaknesses. Originality is no excuse for ignorance.
- In engineering, if not in the arts, gratuitous innovation (that is, not anticipated to be "better" in some useful sense) is a foolish idea and a selfish indulgence of pride—because of the unavoidable risk of unintended downside consequences.
- Designers who master the styles of their predecessors have more treasures upon which their originality can draw.

Laziness

Certainly the lazy or slack designer can minimize his work by picking an exemplar and just modifying it to fit. By and large, those who just copy do not draw on ancient or remote exemplars but only on those that are most current and fashionable. The world is full of lazy Bauhaus architecture and mediocre ranch-type homes done in Frank Lloyd Wright's "prairie" style.

Not laziness, but a high level of enthusiasm and diligence is required for the mastery of the corpus of exemplars available in any design domain.

Originality and Pride

It seems to me that the current premium on design originality misleads. To paraphrase Vitruvius, whatever the medium, one wants a design that meets the functional need, is robust and durable under stress, and gives the user pleasure. So with Shaker furniture, with Revere's tableware, with Peck and Stowe's needle-nosed pliers.[12]

What then of originality? Well, it can certainly delight. We have all seen new designs so sparkling fresh that we rejoice at the elegance of the solution—a Leatherman folding pocket tool, a Slinky toy, a cable-stayed bridge.

But the delight lies in the superior elegance of the new solution to an old problem, not in its novelty per se. This is shown by the new delight each time we use the tool or toy. It does not fade. On the other hand, mere novelty is a cheat for satisfaction. The seven-day wonder grows old. As its novelty fades, so does the delight. The novelty seeker is perpetually driven. There is no resting delight.[13]

Originality as Goal or By-product.   He who seeks originality is apt to find novelty, but not permanence of delight. On the other hand, he who seeks to make designs that really work is most apt to come up with new designs of enduring value, almost as a by-product.

Pride.   Closely tied to the striving after originality is pride, a desire to make a name for oneself. This ancient cause and consequent of humanity's fall infects all design, and ruins much.

Early on it manifested itself in the Tower of Babel. "Come, let us build a tower to heaven, and *make a name for ourselves.*"[14]

Shelley in one of his poems captures the ancient and modern desire: "My name is Ozymandias, King of Kings; Look on my works, ye Mighty, and despair."

The desire to be original has degraded many a work.[15]

Notes and References

1. Howard [2006], *Dr. Kimball and Mr. Jefferson.*

2. Tovey [1950], "Johann Sebastian Bach" says, "Indeed, there is no branch of music, from Palestrina onwards, conceivably accessible in Bach's time, of which we do not find specimens carefully copied in his own handwriting."

3. Lehman [1976], "A model of large program development"; Parnas [1979], "Designing software for ease of extension and contraction."

4. Wilkes [1985], *Memoirs of a Computer Pioneer*, 108–109.

5. Hoff [1972], "The one-chip CPU—computer or component?"; Patterson [1981], "RISC I"; Radin [1982], "The 801 minicomputer."

6. Naur [1968], "Software engineering."

7. Aiken [1937], "Proposed automatic calculating machine."

8. Multics, UNIX, OS/360, Linux.

9. Sammet [1969], *Programming Languages*; Wexelblat [1981], *History of Programming Languages*; Bergin [1996], *History of Programming Languages*, vol. 2.

10. Booch [2009], "Handbook of software architecture."

11. Wren's St. Paul's Cathedral shows that glory can be created within a tradition, as well as outside.

    I find delight in Disney World's exercises in working within styles and yet expressing wonderful originality. Consider Cinderella's Castle, Tom Sawyer's Island, the Haunted House, the Swiss Family Robinson's Treehouse, and the 19th-century Main Street. In that context, even the exaggeration and parodying of styles is workable and can be delightful.

12. Heath [1989], "Lessons from Vitruvius," is an excellent overview of Vitruvius. The assertion is that Vitruvius sets forth a design method, essentially a branching-tree approach, that leads one to choose among 45 house types. This is a major reference with respect to the use of exemplars and of simplified design methods.

13. I think this is a true test between godly pleasures and satanic counterfeits. For real pleasures give satisfaction (*satis* = "enough"). One gets enough food, enough sleep, enough work, enough play, enough

lovemaking. The perverted, however, always seeks a new delicacy, a different taste, a progressive weirdness.

14. Genesis 11.

15. I work in such a building. By its context, Sitterson Hall could easily have perfected a visual quadrangle with the facing Carolina Inn. This is the same height, an elegant colonial building, and made of the same brick. "Originality" led in Sitterson to a different and ugly steel roof and to third-floor dormer windows that are too high for seated occupants to enjoy the view. And the coherent visual quadrangle is not realized.

14

How Expert Designers Go Wrong

I beseech you, in the bowels of Christ, think it possible you may be mistaken.

OLIVER CROMWELL [1650]

But when I make a mistake, it is a beaut!

FIORELLO LA GUARDIA

The besetting mistake of expert designers is not designing the thing wrong, but designing the wrong thing.

Collapse of the aerodynamically misdesigned Tacoma Narrows Bridge
AP Wide World Photos

Mistakes

In any field, the amateur makes lots of little mistakes that a professional would never make. Training, internship, and practice have drilled the professional on good technique.

Professionals, when they goof, do it in a big way—making bridges that collapse during construction, houses with no stairs between stories, computers that radically waste memory bandwidth, programming languages that are too rich to be learned.

Henry Petroski has suggested that after each revolution in materials or technique, designers do in fact

- Tread cautiously at first
- Master the new approach
- Begin to extend it boldly, often forgetting the underlying assumptions
- Overreach in their boldness and self-confidence, pressed perhaps by hubris and competitiveness

He cited a study documenting a consistent 30-year period between major bridge collapses and suggested we were due for another.[1] The I-35W bridge collapse in Minneapolis proved him right.

Probably a major cause of professionals' gross failures is the appearance of a new generation of designers, trained from the start in the new technique. Not having suffered through the birth pangs, which often consist of controversy that probes assumptions, the new professionals are much less conscious of the assumptions and caveats.

They are also usually quite unconscious of how the new technique fits into the whole armory of possible techniques. The professional, I would suggest, is apt to be familiar with the trees, doesn't see the woods, and is slow to ask, "Does what I am doing make sense in the large?" To paraphrase Thomas Jefferson, the professional is often so preoccupied with *doing the thing right* that he fails to stop and ask, *"Am I doing the right thing?"*

In the development of the System/360 computer family, our superb group of seasoned computer architects rejected automatic memory management, an omission that had to be remedied almost before the paint was dry.

Success is dangerous for the professional designer. Failure stimulates analysis, scrutiny, rethinking. Success stimulates confidence both in design technique and in oneself. Both trusts may be misplaced.

The Worst Computer Language Ever

A vivid example of expert failure is IBM's Operating System/360 Job Control Language (JCL), now known as MVS Job Control Language for z/OS. It is, I am convinced, the worst computer programming language ever devised by anybody, anywhere. It was developed under my supervision; there is blame enough to go around among all the supervisory levels.

It is instructive first to examine JCL's deficiencies as a programming language. Then one must inquire how a software team of real experts, having on call, for example, designers of the original Fortran and leading language theoreticians, could go so radically wrong.

Although the mistakes were made 45 years ago, JCL is still in use, in essentially the same form. The mistakes continue to curse us. And the lessons are timeless.

What's JCL?

OS/360 was originally designed as a batch operating system, although from the first, terminal users could interact in sending jobs into the work queue, setting them up, inquiring about status, and retrieving results. The Job Control Language is a scripting language that specifies the options and priorities to be used for computing a batch job, the input files to be mounted, the disposition of each output file, and a host of other lesser functions concerned with the management of program and data files. A JCL script might specify, for example, compilation of a source program, linking with library programs, execution against particular datasets, and the printing, recording on disk, and archiving on tape of the several outputs.

JCL is really hard to learn and use. A set of JCL commands that successfully controlled a computing process would therefore be copied blindly by other users. Only the boldest would go inside the JCL script to change anything except obvious parameters. Even today, archived programs in Fortran and COBOL are stored away with the attendant JCL, in "dusty-deck" files.

So What's Wrong with JCL?

The biggest flaw of all was that JCL is indeed a programming language, but it was not perceived as such by its designers.

One Scheduling Language for All Programming Languages. JCL is deeply flawed in its very concept.

OS/360 provided compilers for a rich variety of programming languages, at least six besides Fortran and COBOL. Each user had to know at least two languages: JCL and his programming language of choice. Most did not, hence the borrowed JCL and the dusty decks.

What one wants, instead of a single schedule-time language like JCL, is a schedule-time capability, just like the compile-time capabilities provided for PL/I and for the S/360 Macro Assembler. Then each programmer could work within a single language, specifying some actions for compile time, some for schedule time, and most for run time.

Like S/360 Assembler in Syntax, Rather than a High-Level Language. Having mistakenly decided to have one schedule-time language, the designers chose the wrong one. As early as 1966, one year after the full OS/360 was up and running, assembler-language jobs accounted for only about 1 percent of all jobs. A major paradigm shift had happened, and it wasn't recognized.

But Not Exactly Like S/360 Assembler Syntax. Enough deviations crept into JCL that knowing S/360 Assembler syntax did not mean knowing JCL syntax.

Card-Column-Dependent. Fortran, for reasons having to do with the 36-bit word of the IBM 704 (1956), allowed statements of 72 characters, plus continuation lines. Characters beyond the

72nd in a line were ignored. (Card columns 73–80 were originally used to serially number program cards, so that if dropped they could be readily reordered!)

JCL followed this punched-card-based format, exactly when the rest of OS/360 was being predicated on terminal access. (Terminals then, and later, didn't even indicate a numeric character position, so users didn't know when they had reached position 73.) A major paradigm shift was happening, even being pushed by this very system product, and it wasn't recognized.

Too Few Verbs. The designers' proud boast was that JCL has only six verbs: JOB, EXEC, DD, and so on. And so it does. But the number of functions the language has to perform far exceeds six.[2] With an imposed "elegant" simplicity not up to the actual complexity inherent in the task at hand, the complexity inevitably breaks out in jury-rigged solutions.

Declaration Parameters Do Verbish Things. The verb functions have to be provided somehow. So in JCL a Data Declaration (DD) statement is provided with a (too-)rich set of keyword parameters. Many of these are imperative verbs in disguise, such as DISP, which commands what to do with the dataset after a job step ends.

Almost No Branching. Central to most programming languages is the concept of a conditional branch. JCL has no such central concept—branching is an afterthought, restricted in action, achieved through a parameter.

No Iteration. There is no direct primitive in JCL to accomplish iteration; it must be fashioned out of the awkward branching. The designers did not imagine an iterative action in a schedule-time script.

No Clean Subroutine Call. Similarly, the designers did not perceive any need for a subroutine call in a schedule-time script. This is harder to understand, for many JCL programs make extensive use of open subroutines, that is, repeated sequences of commands identical except for a few parameters.

How Did JCL Get That Way?

The professionals who designed JCL brought too much experience to the task. Their familiarity with what they thought to be the problem blocked their thinking about it afresh, in its wider setting. In this case, following an exemplar brought disaster.

The key thinkers on the OS/360 JCL had come to the OS/360 project fresh from the highly successful IBM 1410/7010 Operating System (1963). In terms of function, the 1410/7010 OS was perhaps two orders of magnitude simpler than OS/360. It was strictly a batch operating system designed for classical file-maintenance applications, without teleprocessing. Scheduling functions such as file names and I/O device assignments were specified by a few simple control cards placed before each job's deck as it was put into the punched-card reader, a technique dating from tape-based operating systems.

The designers of OS/360 JCL saw their task as being a replay of their 1410/7010 experience—designing, as they explained it, "a few control cards for the scheduler." This was the fatal mistake. Each part of this goal description turned out to be wrong in concept, and stating it wrongly led to wrong thinking throughout the design.

Few types of control cards did indeed characterize the 1410/7010 operating system, and fewness equated to simplicity as a goal for OS/360 JCL. This led to having too few verb types. Not only was fewness of card types wrong; so was the implicit assumption that each job would be controlled by a few cards of each type. In the event, JCL scripts usually contained dozens of statements.

Cards was the second conceptual misleader. The whole JCL programming language was conceptually built around the punched card just as it galloped into obsolescence.

Control cards implied that each was separately interpreted and almost independent in action—and indeed, that was the case in early operating systems. This accounts for the limited branching, iteration, and subroutine facilities of this poor stunted programming language.

Thinking of the cards as separate complete commands explains, I think, why none of us ever recognized that JCL was going to be a programming language—one interpreted and executed at schedule time. Our basic problem was a *pedestrian vision*.

A consequent problem was that JCL was never really designed—it just grew. Had it been recognized as a system language, it might perhaps have been designed as a language, using the expertise and experience of our language designers.

But, it wasn't. Initially, as the "layout of a few control cards," it was a by-task incidental to the main job of designing the job scheduler itself. As the tasks of file system management, teleprocessing network management, and so forth, grew during OS/360 design, every new schedule-time function or specification got loaded onto JCL. Since the language had little flexibility, generality, or comprehensive structure, the new specification ended up as a new keyword parameter, most often in the DD statements. So what should have been adjectives in declarations became imperative verbs with all sorts of action consequences.

Lessons Learned

1. Study failure examples even more carefully than you study successes.
2. Watch yourself after success. Success stimulates confidence in the design technique, in the design itself, and in oneself. All may lead to overconfidence.
3. Think at the top level about the object you are designing and its assumptions about the environment in which it will be used. Is a paradigm shift under way? Will your assumptions still be valid a decade hence? Are you designing the right thing?

Notes and References

1. Petroski [2008], *Success through Failure*. He cites the original study, Sibly [1977], "Structural accidents and their causes."

2. A few more verbs have been added during JCL's evolution. A current JCL standard (November 2008) is given at http://www.isc.ucsb.edu/tsg/jcl.html. The original one is in IBM Corp. [1965], *IBM Operating System/360, Job Control Language*.

15
The Divorce of Design

*Around the sixteenth century, there emerged in
most of the European languages the term "design"
or its equivalent. . . . Above all, the term indicated
that designing was to be separated from doing.*

MICHAEL COOLEY [1988]

Wright Brothers' first flight, Nags Head, North Carolina
Library of Congress

The Divorce of Design from Use and from Implementation

One of the most striking 20th-century developments in the design disciplines has been the progressive divorce of the designer from both the implementer and the user.

Consider the 19th- to turn-of-the-20th-century inventors. Edison fabricated working versions of all his inventions in his laboratory. Henry Ford made his own car. Wilbur and Orville Wright built their airplane with their own hands.

A century later, what computer engineer can *make* his own chips, much less start with sand and copper? What airplane designer is a master of the complex manufacturing processes that will build the plane, much less the complex software that will dynamically stabilize it? What architect does his own structural engineering and earthquake strengthening?

Similarly, in many disciplines the designer is divorced from the user as well. In architecture, the designer of a hospital, a crematorium, a nuclear-fuel-processing plant, a biophysics laboratory, brings little personal experience as a user and must elicit expected user behavior from representative users or, worse, user surrogates who are themselves removed a step or two from real users. Few naval architects have commanded a ship, much less wielded one in battle.

This is in sharp contrast with the situation only a generation ago. Today's cars were designed by senior engineers who had spent their teenage years taking old cars apart under the proverbial shade tree. Today's senior communications experts mostly had ham licenses and probably crafted one-tube radios in school. Some of today's British senior mechanical engineers were the product of 1-3-1 "sandwich" programs: a year of hands-on training with the company, three years in university at company expense, another year of hands-on training before starting to design. Many of America's engineers are the product of co-op programs that interspersed college with hands-on industrial experience.

Fortunately, there are exceptions to the divorces. Software engineering, for example, is still so young that system architects were once programmers. The designers of personal products such as the iPod, the iPhone, and cars are, first of all, users, and their own use-vision illuminates their designs.

The designers of UNIX and especially the Open Source designers of Linux start with their own needs, build tools for their own use, and share with their own peers. I reckon this accounts for both the use success and the user passion.

Why the Divorces?

The first reason is obvious. The stunning 20th-century advances in all implementation technologies demand specialization and protract learning times. Keeping up with just earthquake engineering or just manufacturing with composite materials is now a full-time job.

A second reason is less obvious but perhaps as strong. The things we design are so much more complex that just their *design* demands specialization, protracted learning times, and all the designer's energies. There are now few unsophisticated technologies. Consider the complex manufacturing process of the simple Twinkie, where good taste has to be combined with good shelf life and with continued separation of the filling from the cake.[1]

Fallout from the Divorces

So what? What consequences can we see? *Miscommunication abounds.* Architects build elegant buildings that are hard to work in. Engineers design control panels that nuclear reactor operators find confusing. Over-specified implementations cost way more than they should, with little added function or performance. Both the user-designer link and the designer-implementer link narrow radically in bandwidth. Communication *between* people is always much poorer than communication *within* a person. Instances of disastrous, costly, or embarrassing miscommunication abound.

Remedies

The first implication is that designers must recognize that the 20th-century divorces have occurred, and that much extra deliberate and focused effort must be marshaled to mitigate their painful effects.

Remedy 1: Use-Scenario Experience

Even a small amount of use-scenario experience is better than none. Even a good simulation of a use experience is better than none. Full-scale mock-ups enable dry runs of kitchen or cockpit scenarios. So do virtual environments.

When assigned to design an operator's console for the IBM Stretch computer, I had only hearsay evidence as to what operators actually did, much less the relative frequencies and importances of their several tasks.

The Stretch team stopped for two weeks in the summer while most took vacations. So I went to the computation center that operated 709 computers for the Poughkeepsie laboratories, and I applied to be an apprentice operator for two weeks.

It was immensely informative. Mostly, I mounted tapes, but I soaked in the rhythms of a scientific computer center and sharply watched what the chief operators did.[2]

This "user" experience led to the design of the first operator's console to be program-controlled (essentially a close-connected terminal) rather than directly reflecting and affecting the hardware, a capability that enables multiple consoles for multiple operators, and a flexible allocation of tasks among operators, as well as online interactive debugging of programs.

I must admit that the overly fancy console I designed seems to have been rarely used in any Stretch installation in the ways I envisioned. Online interactive debugging did not become a reality until considerably later, partly because Ted Codd's multiprogramming operating system for Stretch was an option, not the standard Stretch software.[3]

The experience became more fruitful when I was engaged in the Operating System/360 design. All the factors were in place for online interactive debugging, and the previous exploration led to a leaner terminal and full software support.

A similar experience was a semester's sabbatical in Dave and Jane Richardson's biochemistry laboratory at Duke. Daily exposure helped me understand their needs for molecular graphics tools for studying protein structure and function.

Philippe Kruchten systematized this sort of exposure when he was the lead architect for Canada's air-traffic control system:

> *All the software people were sent for hands-on training on air-traffic control, going to ATC classes, then spending days sitting next to controllers in a live Area Control Center, trying to understand what was the essence of their activity. Similarly, the ATC specialists were sent to courses such as Object-Oriented Design, Programming in Ada, to reach the point where there was enough common vocabulary for them to efficiently work together and leverage each other's skills.[4]*

Remedy 2: Close Interaction with Users via Incremental Development and Iterative Delivery

Harlan Mills's system of incremental development and iterative delivery is the best way to stay quite close to users right from the very start of the project.[5] One builds a minimal-function version that works; then one gives it to users to use, or at least to test-drive. Even products being built for a mass market can be tested on a sample of users.

In my own practice, building interactive graphics systems as tools for scientists, I have usually been surprised by early user reactions to our prototype systems. Almost invariably I have made wrong assumptions about how they would use the new tool.

My team spent some ten years realizing our dream of a "room-filling protein" virtual image. My idea was that the chemists could more readily find their way around in the complex molecule by knowing where the C-end and the N-end were positioned in the physical room. After many disappointments, we finally had a suitable high-resolution image in a head-mounted display. The chemist could readily walk around in the protein structure to study areas of interest.

Our first user came for her biweekly appointment; all went well and she moved about quite a bit. Next session, same thing.

Third session: "May I have a chair?" A decade's work shot down by one sentence! The navigation assistance wasn't worth the physical labor.

We had a similar experience with a radiation-treatment planning system. The radiologist's task is to find directions of multiple beams that will impinge on the tumor while avoiding sensitive organs such as eyes. We hung the patient's semitransparent virtual body in space, so the physicians could walk around and sight through from all viewpoints. No, they much preferred to sit and rotate the virtual patient through all angles.

Remedy 3: Concurrent Engineering

Designers need to dig more energetically and personally into the actual experiences and processes of implementation. Even an isolated and unrepresentative implementation experience can wonderfully inform a designer's often idealized or inchoate vision of how implementation is done. I recommend it highly.

There is a danger that a modest sample experience of implementation will unduly influence a design, if the designer's personal experience is all that is available—it is by nature unrepresentative. Probably the best balance is achieved with concurrent engineering as the main design practice. Here, the true implementers are intimately involved in the design process; their broad experience provides the balance for a designer's limited implementation examples. (In the software field, this same practice sometimes is called just an agile method.)

Pulling implementers forward into the design process makes its own demands. Shipyard workers who are skilled at following standard engineering drawings may be less skilled at envisioning the finished construct from the standard plans and sections, hence unable to catch mistakes or to foresee implementation "gotchas." Augmenting the standard plans and sections with richer visuals, even virtual-environment explorations, may provide the tools that lubricate the concurrent design process.

Remedy 4: Education of Designers

Design curricula simply must include both techniques for and practice at *understanding* users' needs and desires.[6]

In a classic and durable 1985 paper, Gould and Lewis enunciated three design principles, giving first place to *understanding* users and their tasks by *"direct contact from the outset."* They found many designers who thought they were doing this when in fact they were hearing or reading about them, examining user profiles, "presenting," "reviewing," or "verifying" designs with users late in the process.[7]

Implementation experience in the machine shop, at the job site, actually building the software, is just as crucial for the designer's education.

The students' needs for direct user contact and actual implementation experience argue strongly for more project courses and experiences, even at the expense of book learning. Analytical techniques and formal synthesis methods are necessary tools, but advanced methods can be self-taught when needed. Gut instincts are harder to acquire. Today's design curricula must reckon with the divorce of design and make strenuous efforts to introduce the young designer to the real worlds of implementation and use.

Notes and References

1. Ettlinger [2007], *Twinkie, Deconstructed*.

2. And listened to the sounds. I share Grady Booch's nostalgia: "I miss the sounds that old computers made. I could tell what my program was doing by the sound the computer made."

3. Codd [1959], "Multiprogramming STRETCH."

4. Kruchten [1999], "The software architect and the software architecture team." He further reports, "Some balked, sensing a waste of time, but were later amazed at how much it helped them do their jobs."

5. Mills [1971], "Top-down programming in large systems."

6. In some 22 offerings of a software engineering laboratory course, I have found it necessary and possible to solicit outside users, with whom student teams must work, and whom they must satisfy. The users have to commit time for weekly meetings with the team, in

return for which they *may* get usable prototype software. I ask for projects that would be useful if successful but not necessary. The student team must be allowed to fail.

7. Gould [1985], "Designing for usability": "These principles are: early and continual focus on users; empirical measurement of usage; and iterative design."

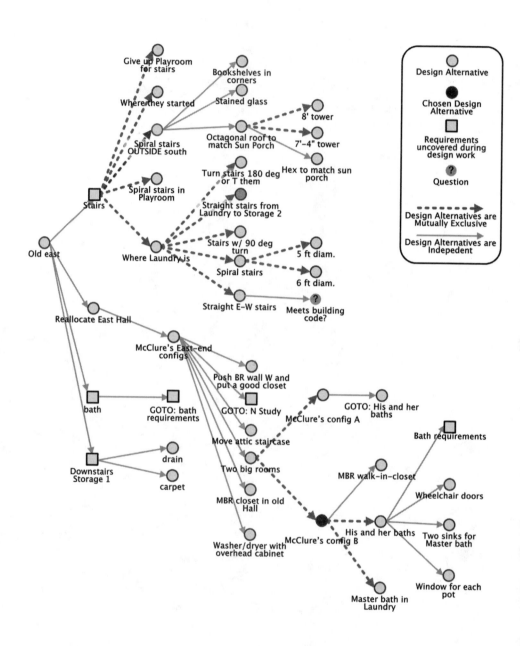

Legend:

- Design Alternative
- Chosen Design Alternative
- Requirements uncovered during design work
- Question
- Design Alternatives are Mutually Exclusive
- Design Alternatives are Independent

Stairs

- Give up Playroom for stairs
- Where they started
- Spiral stairs OUTSIDE south
  - Bookshelves in corners
  - Stained glass
  - Octagonal roof to match Sun Porch
    - 8' tower
    - 7'-4" tower
    - Hex to match sun porch
- Spiral stairs in Playroom
- Where Laundry is
  - Turn stairs 180 deg or T them
  - Straight stairs from Laundry to Storage 2
  - Stairs w/ 90 deg turn
  - Spiral stairs
    - 5 ft diam.
    - 6 ft diam.
  - Straight E-W stairs
    - Meets building code?

Old east

- Reallocate East Hall
  - McClure's East-end configs
    - Push BR wall W and put a good closet
    - GOTO: N Study
    - Move attic staircase
    - Two big rooms
    - MBR closet in old Hall
    - Washer/dryer with overhead cabinet
    - McClure's config A
      - GOTO: His and her baths
    - McClure's config B
      - His and her baths
        - MBR walk-in-closet
        - Bath requirements
        - Wheelchair doors
        - Two sinks for Master bath
        - Window for each pot
      - Master bath in Laundry
  - bath
    - GOTO: bath requirements
  - Downstairs Storage 1
    - drain
    - carpet

16

Representing Designs' Trajectories and Rationales

In collaboration with Sharif Razzaque

There are many ways of making a fool of
yourself with a digital computer, and to have
one more can hardly make any difference.

SIR MAURICE WILKES [1959], "THE EDSAC"

Be careful how you fix what you don't understand.

Portion of a Compendium chart for Brooks House Wing design
Sharif Razzaque

Introduction

For designers to get the most learning from each design experience, they need to document how it evolves: not only the *what*s of the design, but also the *why*s by which it was reached. Moreover, such a rationale document is a priceless aid to system maintainers; it prevents many ignorant mistakes. Documenting trajectories and rationales is much harder than it at first appears.[1]

Several research groups have tackled the problem of making computer tools to assist in this process.[2] So Dr. Sharif Razzaque and I decided to develop a computer representation of a specific design project's trajectory. We took as our raw material the 235-page prose log that my wife, Nancy, and I contemporaneously kept while designing a 1,700-square-foot addition to our house. (That design project is briefly sketched in Chapter 22. A larger portion of the design tree for this project is posted on this book's Web site.)

This chapter shares our observations both about the nature of a real design trajectory and about documenting design trajectories. Herein our usage is as follows:

- *We* for work we did together
- *I* for work Razzaque did solo
- *I* for Razzaque's comments and hypotheses, but
- *We* when Brooks agrees with them

Linearizing the Web of Knowledge

As Vannevar Bush acknowledged in the design for his proposed Memex system, the representation of all the interrelations among items of knowledge requires a general graph, in general a non-planar graph.[3]

But such a graph is difficult to represent and nigh impossible to comprehend. So in all disciplines people linearize the knowledge representation and supplement the linear representation with one or more auxiliary representations.

The process is:

1. Cut edges in the graph until it is a tree. This process imposes a hierarchical order where there was none before, whether that order is wanted or not.

2. Map the tree onto a line in any of the several well-known ways, but usually depth-first.

Consider a book, for example. The subjects it treats are intricately interrelated. But the book itself is perforce linear: page follows page; line follows line; word follows word. So the author organizes the subject matter into a tree and shows the tree in the table of contents: chapters of sections, sections of subsections. The page numbers show the mapping from the tree to the linear form.

The table of contents is, however, not the whole story by any means. In the back of the book is an index, which organizes the book contents alphabetically by term. The page numbers for any given term essentially define a linked chain through the book. The index restores many of the links that were cut in mapping the web of material to the table of contents tree.

The same process yields the organization of a library. The Library of Congress numbering system (or the Dewey Decimal System) maps all the interconnected books to a tree. The tree is mapped via a depth-first traversal to a line, yielding a shelf order. But this mapping is supplemented by multiple indices, each restoring cut links to form chains: an author index, a title index, a subject index.

The subject index is especially interesting because the shelf-order mapping was already based on principal subject. The subject index recognizes that any work treats many subjects besides its principal one.

A Wikipedia article solves this web-structure representation by rich cross-linking, instantaneously accessible. This capability is a significant new addition to our intellectual toolbox.

Any design space has the same sort of web structure, so the representation of designs is challenging. And if designs are difficult to represent efficiently, design processes are inherently more so.

Simon's Rational Model of design, Chapter 2, seems to assume the existence of a design decision tree that shows at each alternative node the subordinate design decisions occasioned by that choice. Ideally, one would associate with each choice the rationale for that decision. But decisions are interrelated in many complex ways, each with both simple reasons applying to it alone and reasoning that is shared with siblings and cousins.

Our Capture of a Design Trajectory

Our goals were to capture the implicit design tree of the Brooks House Wing design, both to supplement the abbreviated prose case study of that design process in Chapter 22, and to represent the design trajectory through time. More important, we wanted to get insights into the Brookses' design process:

- How consistent is the log with Fred's recollections?
- What and where were the struggles?
- When and how did the breakthroughs occur?
- Did Fred and Nancy explore the design tree systematically?
- Do findings from this analysis support the arguments in the rest of this book?

As it turned out, what we learned in *trying* to reconstruct the design tree is more revealing than the tree itself. In fact, the tree itself yielded disappointingly few insights. This exercise was an experiment that failed.

Our Process for Studying the House Design Process

We started with a search for off-the-shelf software for drawing design trees. We eventually settled on Compendium,[4] a tool now primarily intended for recording and focusing the design process as it unfolds.

I seeded the design tree from the notes on the very first page of the log and proceeded page by page, transcribing the notes into nodes and links in the design tree according to a written *transcription scheme* that I first prepared. We quickly ran into difficulties that forced us to wonder if we were transcribing properly. This led me to tweak the transcription scheme, veering from Compendium's implied guidelines.

Our process settled into a pattern: Each time we adjusted our transcription scheme, I would go back to page one and rework our Compendium tree to match the new scheme. We would then advance further into the log and inevitably run yet again into a log entry that didn't fit into our transcription scheme. This would cause us to reexamine

- Our (evolving) transcription scheme
- Our use of Compendium to reconstruct the decision tree
- The design process itself

This process—encountering problems with the transcription scheme, adjusting it, and starting over—happened over and over, every day at first and then less and less frequently. We gradually converged to a better scheme and surrendered to living with the remaining flaws, just so we could make progress transcribing the log into a design tree.

What Is a Design Tree?

It wasn't until much later that I realized that our problems in finding a transcription scheme for the design tree flowed from our lack of a precise *definition of* a design tree. My mental definition had been informal, implicit, and vague. The search for a usable tree transcription scheme was also a search for a definition of *design tree* that would be *rigorous, comprehensive, and precise enough to be operationally useful.*

Because my definition was informal and implicit, it did not even occur to me to construct a sample pen-and-paper design tree and for it a transcription scheme independent of the software tool.

Our vague starting notion of a design tree matched that in Figure 2-1. This notion is like the tree of options one meets when configuring a built-to-order laptop. Each design question (that is, decision to be made) is a node. Sibling design questions such as "Visibility" and "Alarm" are orthogonal to each other, and the designer must answer each of them. In Blaauw [1997], these are called *attribute branches*.

Each design-question node has a child node for each of its alternative design options. In the laptop example, one must choose the display size from several options. These options are mutually exclusive *alternative branches*. The designer chooses one for each independent design question.

Most choices raise more design questions (for example, having decided to use a luminous dial, one must choose its light mechanism). These design-question nodes are children of the previous solution node. Thus such a *decision tree* includes both independent and mutually exclusive design choices, and the finished product is represented not by the selection of a single node, but rather by the set of many design-alternative nodes, one at the leaf chosen for each independent design question.

To represent rationale within the tree, each option should associate with nodes for its pros and cons. Each design-question node would also have an associated node designating the choice made and why.

This first notion of a decision tree with rationale seemed to fit naturally with Compendium's predefined node types. I chose this mapping: Each design question was represented as a question icon. Each design alternative was an idea icon. Each idea icon had pro-icon and con-icon children. The alternative chosen became an agreement icon with a *why* note.

Finally, we thought design questions, even independent ones, should be sorted hierarchically, by house spaces. For example, we expected to group all the Living Room issues under one "Living Room" node to match the structure and labeling of the log entries.

Brooks early on had divided the design task into three separable problems (Figure 16-1).

Insights into the Design Process

Design Isn't Just to Satisfy Requirements, but Also to Uncover Requirements

Page-by-page analysis of the log quickly showed that even though an architectural program had been defined, the requirements

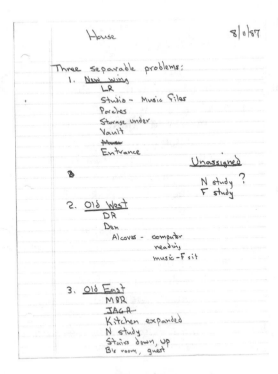

House   8/0/87

Three separable problems:
  1. New wing
       LR
       Studio - Music files
       Porches
       Storage under
       Vault
       ~~House~~
       Entrance
                              Unassigned

  ℬ
                              N study ?
                              F study

  2. Old West
       DR
       Den
       Alcoves - computer
                  reading
                  music - F sit

  3. Old East
       MBR
       ~~JAGR~~
       Kitchen expanded
       N study
       Stairs down, up
       Bk room, guest

Figure 16-1   Division of the house wing design task into separable problems

were still changing. For example, architect Wes McClure had proposed adding pavilions, one to the north and one to the south.[5] The Brookses ultimately rejected this idea because (a) the resulting house did not have any central place where the family would naturally congregate, and (b) the South Pavilion would require removing a precious large black oak tree. But neither the central place nor preserving the oak tree were recognized requirements when McClure devised the pavilions. Analyzing a proposed design solution, the pavilion idea, caused the Brookses to see these requirements.

We see this pattern again and again in the log. Design work doesn't just satisfy requirements, it elicits them. Our experience resonates with Schön's theory in Chapter 3. A good design process will encourage this phenomenon, rather than suppress it.

Design Isn't Simply Selecting from Alternatives, but Also Realizing Their Existence

Once the designer has posed a design question, it's not usually possible to simply enumerate all the possible alternatives. Some are obvious or preexisting options (perhaps borrowed from exemplars). But others are novel and require breakthroughs. In the log, we see the Brookses struggle between two possible Music Room configurations, and after much analysis and several attempts at tweaking each, neither is deemed acceptable. They discover a third configuration that they instantly like. The log notes: "Config C—A real way forward!"

This pattern also repeats again and again in the log. As Chapter 3 tells, Brooks's purchase of land from his neighbor was not an obvious solution to the problem of siting the Music Room. A major part of design is realizing that design options exist. Once again our experience resonates with Schön's theory.

The Tree Changes as the Design Changes—How to Represent That Evolution?

The three separable problems look very much like a laptop configuration tree, except that the lowest nodes are not leaf options, but rather sub-design questions. But the tree indicates that *some amount of design has already been done.* Why is the Entrance in the New Wing? Assignment to the New Wing, and not the Old West section, is itself a design decision. The tree of the design questions has implicit in it some design decisions.

But as we worked through the log, it became unclear why certain rooms were assigned to one wing versus another during the design process. Brooks then had the insight that he thinks of the house both as the original house (before this construction project) and also as it was finally built. For example, today he thinks of Fred's Study as a child of the New Wing node, because that's as built. When he wrote that first log page, Fred's Study was downstairs, and it was undecided where it would go. But there are many different designs between those stages.

Each of those high-level designs carries with it a different organizational tree structure. As the design changes, the same rooms and parts are grouped under different high-level nodes. For example, the original house and the 1987 design have the Master Bedroom in the East Wing, whereas the final design has it in the New Wing. Which tree structure should we adopt? How do we show the trajectory through time?

Our approach was to hang all nodes off the organizational structure of the *as-built* house, in order to have a stable structure for the design tree. The final house design is divided into Phase I (in turn subdivided into the New Wing and Old West) and Phase II (Kitchen and Playroom).

Certain design alternatives are necessarily nodes high in the design tree. For example, "Flip house end for end" must be at a level above Phase I and Phase II (or New Wing, Old East, and Old West). But this particular node confuses the reader, because it survived only briefly in the design process. But such a high-level node is always thereafter visible and intrusive.

We considered grouping several such short-lived explorations into a top-level node called "Early Wanderings," noting that many projects explore several radical designs early on. But abandoned design alternatives occur at each stage of the design. Those abandoned early are really similar to ones abandoned later, except they affect larger portions of the tree; far-reaching changes become fewer and fewer as the design evolves and stabilizes.

The very structure of a decision tree changes over time. Documenting such changes requires a new dynamic tool that doesn't yet exist. It must track not only how the tree grows leafward over time, but also how nodes and their sub-trees get cut from one branch and grafted into another.

Tree of Decisions versus Tree of Designs

As Figure 2-1 shows, the final complete design (that is, a product) is represented not by a single node in a decision tree, but rather by the set of leaves. From such a tree, it is difficult to visualize what is the best complete design so far on any given day of the design project.

The space of all possible designs is a different tree altogether, where each node specifies a sub-tree of products, alike in all the decisions down to that node, further differentiated below it. We call this *the tree of designs*. Each leaf is a different complete design.

The tree of designs is combinatorially larger than the corresponding tree of decisions. For example, a decision tree with n independent binary design questions yields a tree of designs with 2^n nodes. But for any substantial design this tree will be so large that it seems implausible that a human could construct it, or that doing so would result in any insight. The tree of designs is much too cumbersome for actual use in designing.

But the very concept of a tree of designs is instructive and clarifying. For example, there is an analogy to agile software development: each nightly build corresponds to a node in the tree of designs, and each represents the best complete design thus far.

Modular versus Tightly Integrated Designs

In transcribing the Brooks house decision tree, we found that the selection among a decision's alternative options is rarely independent of the choices for others. For example, the Music Room could have been in the north or west portion of the New Wing—a high-level decision—but its placement affected the possible placements of the Studies, Living Room, and Kitchen!

This resulted in an awkward decision tree, because some alternative solutions had to be combinations of several attributes. For example, instead of a "Music Room location" decision with a set of simple alternatives, we had these compound alternatives:

Music Room west; Living Room north

Music Room north; Kitchen south

Music Room north; Kitchen north

And even these were not independent of other design alternatives.

In *Notes on the Synthesis of Form*, Alexander [1964] explains how this tight dependency (that is, lack of modularity) is a disadvantage, because it makes it hard to revise the design. Thus a designer may not just choose among the merits of alternative designs per se, but may intentionally and rightly trade off design quality against the ease of a future modification. This is precisely what Parnas [1979] urges in his extremely fundamental paper, "Designing software for ease of extension and contraction."[6] Moreover, one may need to trade off quality of the design for speed and ease of the *design process* itself.

Modular designs are more readily represented as decision trees. Indeed, this may be what we mean by a *modular* design.

On the other hand, complete modularity also has drawbacks. Optimized designs have components that achieve multiple goals. Consider the unibody car: the body is not just for esthetics and holding passengers, it is also the structure. The unibody design is lighter and stronger than a ladder-frame body. But a ladder-framed pickup truck can be converted to an SUV more easily than can a unibodied one.

Compendium and Alternative Tools

We investigated several software packages in hope of finding one suited for reconstructing and analyzing our specific example of a design decision tree. Here's what we found.

Task Architect

Task Architect[7] could indeed be helpful for design, but not in the way we were hoping. Task Architect is a tool to facilitate *task analysis*—the structured study of how a job is carried out. Examples include both manual tasks, such as installing headlights on a car assembly line, and mental tasks, such as deciding whether to abort a landing.

Thus, for the Brooks house project, Task Architect might have been used to get a better understanding of the Brookses' use cases (cooking, hosting a meeting, teaching music, and so on). Task Architect is neither designed nor readily adapted for reconstructing the decision tree (but we surely did try!).

Project Management Tools

Like Task Architect, project management tools, such as Microsoft Project, OmniPlan, or SmartDraw, might be useful for the process of designing a system but don't appear appropriate for representing decision trees.

Critical-path methods such as the Program Evaluation and Review Technique (PERT) are the underlying models of project management tools. PERT seems to support only the Waterfall Model. Because there are no conditional tasks/nodes, the PERT technique implicitly assumes the major design decisions have already been made.[8]

IBIS and Its Descendants

IBIS (Issue-Based Information System) was designed in the 1980s for collaboratively making decisions and documenting the rationale behind them.[9] Like Compendium, it is intended to be used during the decision-making process, to keep design meetings productive and to help identify weak logic.

For each tool we evaluated, I sketched a transcribing scheme to fit our needs to that tool. We first took a quick look at Compendium, and then Task Architect. When we came to IBIS, we found that it very naturally supported many of the fields and node types that we had decided we needed.

IBIS was a command-line program. gIBIS, by Conklin, was a graphical version of IBIS.[10] gIBIS would have been more appropriate for our needs than Compendium, but we could not find a version that worked on our computers. Compendium is in fact a descendant of gIBIS. So, back to Compendium.

Compendium

Compendium has many advantages. It is remarkably flexible; it is becoming even more so. An active team of developers are extremely responsive to requests and cries for help. Compendium's request- and bug-tracking database is online and public. A large community of users share a very active online discussion forum. Hence Compendium is always growing to handle new uses.

Nevertheless, in retrospect we can't recommend this tool either for design itself or for documenting a trajectory and design rationales.

As to design itself, we are concerned that if designers use a structured annotation or software tool *during* design, it will restrict the ease of having vague ideas, impeding conceptual design. In much in the same way, a CAD tool is too precise for the quick exploration of creative ideas, whereas sketches allow the designer to be vague. Conklin himself noted that gIBIS was too structured and cumbersome for certain creative aspects of the design process.[11]

For our task of reconstructing the decision tree, I don't think Compendium is the most appropriate software tool. Our final transcription scheme ended up being very different from Compendium's target usage. Rather than using Compendium's affordances to help me reconstruct the design tree, I had to find creative ways of repurposing Compendium's features (such as using Compendium's Reference node to describe requirements).

Beyond that, our trees (even with great efforts to reduce their size) appear much bigger than Compendium's user interface readily accommodates, and this design task was small compared to most substantial software projects. It is difficult to find nodes in such large trees, and even harder to print or graphically export them.

Our final transcription scheme uses

- Work-arounds for Compendium's structures
- Our own self-enforced structures to ensure a consistent design tree, rather than Compendium's

Hence I believe that a generic diagramming tool, with features such as automatic layout of trees, automatic rerouting of relationship arrows, and searchable associated notes, is better suited to tree capture. Microsoft Visio or SmartDraw might be such a choice.

DRed[12]—A Tantalizing Tool

The biggest success story we've heard about in computer-aided design rationale documentation is the widespread use of DRed at Rolls-Royce (RR). DRed was developed by Rob Bracewell at Cambridge University's Engineering Design Centre, under the sponsorship of Rolls-Royce, BAE Systems, and the UK Engineering and Physical Sciences Research Council.[13]

DRed is designed for capturing design rationales as decisions are made. Its conceptual structure is quite like that of gIBIS. In use, it looks very similar to Compendium. But because it has been used primarily for rationale capture, DRed's evolution has focused on that function, as distinguished from facilitation of design meetings.[14]

Adoption of DRed in RR was radically facilitated because there was *already a strong rationale-capture culture in RR*. (The project's other sponsor, BAE Systems, has not had such a culture, and DRed has not been widely adopted there.) RR engineers were already required to write a design-rationale prose report. The big step was a management rule that allowed project teams to do a DRed document *instead of* the previously required prose report. DRed documentation is much easier to do.

As Marco Aurisicchio relates, the adoption at RR has been extensive. Aurisicchio is Cambridge's point person for the relationship with RR and is most familiar with how RR uses DRed. He teaches many of the use courses at RR. Michael Moss, of the RR corporate staff, is RR's point person for DRed, to whom RR engineers go for direct support. He also filters and prioritizes feedback to Bracewell's team at Cambridge. In Brooks's view, this dedicated two-person link between users and builder has played a major role in DRed's success.

Use modes vary by group, but it is common for DRed content to be created on a whiteboard during a design meeting. Then one person is tasked to turn the captured whiteboard sketches into formal DRed documentation. DRed is also created during solo design sessions. It is used for both conceptual and detailed design. Designers, reviewers, and downstream manufacturing engineers use DRed themselves, always without a facilitator.

About 30 percent of all RR engineers, some 600 in several divisions and in RR labs across the world, have had at least short-course training in DRed use. New engineers learn RR engineering practice in a six-week project course, in teams of four. A typical project is a real problem that some group wants solved and doesn't have the manpower to do; but not an essential project, so trainees are allowed to fail.[15]

The largest DRed tree the Cambridge team has seen comprised 190 charts, with an average of 15 nodes per chart. There is also for such projects an *overview chart*, with a node for each of the detailed charts.

Of course, RR's designs evolve. Their DRed charts and other documents evolve with the design. The DRed charts are very useful to both presenters and reviewers in the multiple reviews. The DRed document is not itself under formal revision control. Formal RR revision control is seen as so cumbersome that "if DRed were under it, DRed wouldn't be used."

A widespread use the developers never imagined for DRed is as a tool for steering and documenting the diagnosis of faults by product engineering groups responding to field reports from all over the world. "Here's the data as to when, where, and how the engine quit, and all the readings captured then. Now, what caused it?"

Unfortunately, DRed is not generally available. RR and BAE Systems own the intellectual property, and they currently choose to keep it proprietary.

Notes and References

1. MacLean [1989], "Designing rationale," and Tyree [2005], "Architecture decisions," argue for rationale capture. Moran [1996], *Design Rationale*, is a rather complete compendium of the published papers on design rationale. Madison [1787], *Notes on the Debates in the Federal Convention of 1787*, is a stunning example of complete rationale capture. Madison's text is also available on the Web at http://www.constitution.org/dfc/dfc_0000.htm.

2. Noble [1988], "Issue-based information systems for design"; Conklin [1988], "gIBIS"; Lee [1993], "The 1992 workshop on design rationale capture and use"; Lee [1997], "Design rationale systems"; Bracewell [2003], "A tool for capturing design rationale"; Burge [2008], "Software engineering using RATionale."

3. Bush [1945], "That we may think," the great paper proposing a Memex system with generalized linking and personalized link trails through a knowledge graph much like today's World Wide Web. The technology proposed was primitive, but the concepts are visionary and prescient.

4. Shum [2006], "Hypermedia support for argumentation-based rationale"; http://compendium.open.ac.uk/institute/, accessed July 25, 2009.

5. See the plans in Chapter 22.

6. Parnas [1979], "Designing software for ease of extension and contraction," uses a tree of designs as its basic framework.

7. http://www.taskarchitect.com/index.htm, accessed July 25, 2009.

8. This isn't exactly right—PERT can help a manager choose among design alternatives, based on the schedule implications for each.

9. Noble [1988], "Issue-based information systems for design."

10. Conklin [1988], "gIBIS."

11. Conklin [1988], "gIBIS," 324–325.

12. This section is based on a joint interview of Bracewell and Aurisicchio by Brooks on June 19, 2008. Brooks saw a full demonstration that showed the system capabilities.

13. Bracewell [2003], "A tool for capturing design rationale."

14. Aurisicchio et al. [2007], "Evaluation of how DRed design rationale is interpreted."

15. UNC–Chapel Hill's software engineering project course applies exactly the same criteria for project selection from real users.

IV

A Computer Scientist's Dream System for Designing Houses

17

A Computer Scientist's Dream System for Designing Houses—Mind to Machine

Pyramids, cathedrals, and rockets exist not because of geometry, theory of structures, or thermodynamics, but because they were first pictures—literally visions—in the minds of those who conceived them.

EUGENE FERGUSON [1992], *ENGINEERING AND THE MIND'S EYE*

UNC GRIP Molecular Graphics System user console

James Lipscomb

The Challenge

Suppose one could imagine into existence an ideal computer system for the architectural design of houses and other buildings. What would it be like?

A Vision

A professional architect is obviously better equipped than I to envision an entire "building design" system. Yet because I've done a little amateur house design, because building architecture is more concrete and accessible to a general audience than is software architecture, and because I have for more than 50 years worked on human-computer interfaces, I presume to postulate my version of the designer-computer interface for a Dream System for Designing Houses.

The interface proposed will heavily reflect the experience of my students and me in evolving the UNC–Chapel Hill GRIP Molecular Graphics System. Evolution of this real-time interactive graphics system took place over years, as we worked with brilliant protein chemists on tools for challenging tasks.[1]

This essay will treat only the process of functional design of houses, not the processes for structural or systems engineering, although I think the same system would be useful for the structural engineering, the mechanical and electrical systems, and even the furnishings.

There have been other dream systems for design. Ullman [1962] devotes an essay to such a system for mechanical design.[2] Yet our scopes are quite different. Ullman seeks a program to handle as much of the knowledge management as possible, a valuable objective. I am here principally concerned with the communication between the designer's mind and the automatic system, for I consider the designer's mind to be paramount.

Progressive Truthfulness

Good design is top-down. One starts a prose document with an outline that identifies the key ideas and then the subordinate ones. One begins a program by thinking about a data structure and an algorithm. One starts thinking about a house plan by identifying the functional spaces based on the use cases, and then their connectivity. One early on addresses a building's esthetics in terms of massing.

Great designers, even the most iconoclastic, rarely start from scratch—they build on the rich inheritance from their predecessors.[3] They take an idea from here, an idea from there, add some of their own, and wrestle the mix into a design that has conceptual integrity and a coherent style of its own.

The usual technique is to begin a design with precedential ideas but blank paper. One sketches in the big units and then proceeds by *progressive refinement*, adjusting dimensions and adding more and more detail.

Turner Whitted in 1986 proposed that another, perhaps better, way to build models of physical objects (originally in the context of computer graphics) is to start with a model that is fully detailed but only resembles what is wanted. Then, one adjusts one attribute after another, bringing the result ever closer to the mental vision of the new creation, or to the real properties of a real-world object.

Whitted called his technique *progressive truthfulness*.[4] In a very real sense, progressive truthfulness is precisely the program of the natural sciences over the past few centuries, as their models approach the existing natural creation.[5]

With human design of artifacts, the very process of designing occasions changes in the mental ideal that the design approaches. Progressive truthfulness radically helps. One has at every step a prototype to study. The prototype is initially valid; that is, there are no inconsistencies in structure. The prototype is always fully detailed, so that visual and aural perceptions of it do not mislead.

So one can imagine a house design sequence such as this:

- "Give me the Three-Bedroom Georgian House."
- "Face it north."
- "Mirror-flip it left to right."

- "Make the living room 14 feet wide."
- "Shrink the kitchen depth by a foot."
- "Make the exterior white stucco instead of brick."
- "Make the roof pantiles instead of shingles."

I find Whitted's vision convincing, and I will postulate that approach for this Dream System. It could bring about a change in how one does design. New tools can lead us to better ways of thinking.

The Model Library

Hence the Dream System starts with a rich library of fine specimens of fully detailed designs. Starting with exemplars that themselves have consistency of style ensures that such consistency is the designer's to lose. The model library itself grows as the system is used. For remodeling, computer-vision methods of capturing a 3-D object and reducing it to a structured model will be necessary.

In our first imagined house-uttering sequence, the designer acted as if intimately familiar with the exemplar library: he called out an exemplar by name.

No matter how experienced the designer, as the library grows, this easy familiarity will be lost. As with any large terrain, one will be quite at home in parts, passably competent in others, and an explorer elsewhere. The novice will explore everywhere. Hence the ability to scan the library hierarchically and otherwise is crucial.

Structuring the library most helpfully is a prime taxonomic task, but much terminology and conceptual structure already exist.[6]

Hazards of the Progressive Truthfulness Mode

Although I postulate that progressive truthfulness is how the most productive and easy-to-use design systems must be built, it has its inherent hazards.

Some will argue that broad exposure to exemplars will implicitly limit the designer's creativity. Could the designs of a Brunelleschi, a Le Corbusier, a Gehry, a Gaudí, emerge from the minds of designers so indoctrinated?

I submit that they did. None were amateurs. All trained by studying precedents. Like Bach, they innovated from mastery, not ignorance. The Grandma Moseses of the world are few.

Perhaps more relevant, these "but what about?" examples represent a minute fraction of designs, and a great tool doesn't have to provide for discontinuities.

The true hazards of progressive truthfulness lurk in the library. Bad models, too few models, too narrow a variety of models—these shortcomings will most limit the emerging designs. This hazard will be worst at the beginning.

A Vision for Input from Mind to Machine

Whether designing from an exemplar or *de novo*, how does one transform thought-stuff into a computer model?

One wants to utter one's castle in the air into existence, using the voice, both hands, the head, and conceivably the feet. Buxton, his colleagues at Alias Systems, and his students at the University of Toronto have pioneered two-handed interfaces.[7] The dominant hand makes the precise manipulations; the non-dominant hand provides framing context (hereafter *right* and *left*, for simplicity). Both hands together provide approximate dimension—"So big."

The Noun-Verb Rhythm

In design languages, as in imperative languages in general, each utterance has a verb and a noun, the object. The noun may have a selecting "which" adjectives, phrases, or clauses. The verb may have an adverbial phrase (Figure 17-1). A linguistic curiosity is that many verbs assign adjectives to the object noun: "Make this door 32 inches wide." "Color the west wall green."

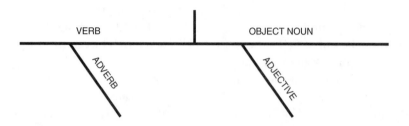

Figure 17-1   Structure of an imperative sentence

In spatial design languages, one usually wants to specify the noun by pointing—a task for the hand(s). The voice is the natural instrument for verbs; the Windows-Icons-Menus-Pointing (WIMP) interface uses an unnatural input, the menu. To be sure, the menu has the tremendous advantage of showing the options. For the user traversing familiar tasks, however, this is not necessary.

Users at work at a WIMP interface proceed with a regular rhythm: point to or key in a noun specification; then point to a menu command (verb). Thus, in editing a document, one selects a block of text, points to "Cut"; perhaps selects another, points to "Copy"; selects an inter-character location, points to "Paste."

Specifying Verbs

The one-handed rhythm is in fact irritating and counterproductive. By moving the pointer away from the noun field to the verb menu, one loses one's place. The next noun is usually close to the previous one—back goes the pointer to about where it was. To avoid this disorientation, special ways have been developed for high-frequency verb specification. Double-clicking becomes an "Open" verb; keying specifies an "Insert."

The most common verbs have keyboard equivalents, executed with the left hand. This technique is a brilliant invention.

The novice always has available the standard technique—verb selection from a menu. The expert has techniques that are faster, exploit both hands, and leave the pointer positioned in the noun field. Best of all, the novice can acquire expertise one verb at a time, according to his own use frequencies.

Voice Commands. But voice is the natural mode for giving commands. So our Dream System will have a limited-vocabulary voice recognizer with wide tolerance for voice differences, a rich synonym vocabulary, and a user-modifiable dictionary. The menu option is kept active, as is the keyboard one. The hoarse user has lost no options.

General Verbs. Today's architectural CAD systems embody a richly developed set of general verbs, based on years of customer experience. There are perhaps too many, but if any user can choose a personal palette and thereafter select most readily from it, usability is not hampered.

Examples include

- Rotate
- Replicate
- Group
- Snap
- Align
- Space Apart
- Scale
- Select Object from Library
- Name

Select Object from Library is perhaps the most useful of these, whether or not one takes the progressive truthfulness approach. We do, and that approach elevates library selection in frequency and importance.

The library will have all objects in one scale; the frequent verb will be Select and Scale, where the scaling is automatically set by the current working scale.

Specifying Nouns

What a variety of ways we use for specifying objects and regions of the space and time continuum!

By Name. In most conversation we specify objects by an explicit name or a name implicit via a pronoun. We want to do the same in the Dream System. Even with 100 percent effective voice recognition, this is still harder than it looks. To what does "the left one" refer? "The front one"? "The red one"? "The biggest one"? "It"? Even when the pointing is unambiguous, the scope of selection is often not. Making a system as smart and natural as a three-year-old requires syntactic analysis, semantic analysis, and the saving and use of context.

Moreover, the same object is called by different names, and different objects by the same name. Deriving standard definitions for a joint Army–Navy–Air Force database proved a huge job. Just "What time is it?" was challenging. The Air Force used Greenwich time; the Army used local time; each Navy ship used the local time where its battle-group aircraft carrier was.

So our Dream System must enable individual users and user groups to create individualized synonym dictionaries that supplement and override the system dictionary. Rationalizing model library nomenclature is much too deep a morass for our system builders; the users must have and wield the tools.

By Pointing in 2-D. The stunning success of the WIMP interface demonstrates the power of pointing for selecting defined and visible objects. This mode will indeed have very high use frequency.

But it is not sufficient. When we built the GRIP system, I assumed our first client chemist would select one of several hundred amino-acid residues in a protein by pointing to it. No, he wanted a keypad so he could specify a residue by a three-digit residue number. He had worked with that particular protein for years; he knew the numeric names of those residues as well as he knew the names of his children! Pointing required adjusting the viewpoint until the target residue was clearly visible in the 3-D tangle. Moreover, extending the arm holding the light pen was fatiguing.

By Sketching in 2-D.   Architects design 3-D entities. But their principal mode is 2-D drawing, both rigorous and sketchy. This is true even though their fanciest 2-D projections are such limited portrayals of 3-D objects. Sketching appears essential to the thought process.[8]

I do not believe this primacy of 2-D drawing will ever change, no matter how rich and handy the 3-D modeling tools become. The retina is 2-D. The flat surfaces that so easily guide the hand are 2-D. Therefore, our Dream System must feature 2-D pointing and sketching, as with a pen pad that detects not only position but also pressure.

For defined 2-D spaces, such as maps or blueprints, one often needs to specify both *where* and *how much region*. Hierarchical subdivisions such as states, countries, or rooms make this *how much* specification much easier.

Precise specification of both *where* and *how much* calls for a two-handed operation. Consider drawing a line of a precisely specified length. The right hand holds the pen telling *where*; the left works the numeric keypad telling *how long*.

Pointing and Sketching in 3-D.   All of the above considerations for 2-D apply in 3-D. Pointing is inherently more fatiguing—one must hold the hand up. Finger-wrist-elbow movements have about the same relative precision as hand-elbow-shoulder movements, so one wants a primary working volume where both elbows rest most of the time.[9]

Specifying arbitrary spatial regions and their rotations is more difficult than specifying objects and their positioning. In conversation we usually specify arbitrary regions with two hands in motion: "The cloud was shaped like this." That's how our Dream System should work. Much work has been done on widgets and affordances for 3-D specification.[10] Much of the work aims to yield freehand specification; much of it just provides more awkward substitutes for it.

Specifying Text

Most text blocks will be short strings, mostly names and dimensions, on the design drawings. Voice recognition is the tool of choice for these, as with verbs.

Specifications will consist of blocks of text, standard paragraphs chosen from a database and parameterized. For creating new substantial text, dictation has largely died out because one can type and edit paragraphs much faster than one can dictate and edit. For both of these kinds of text tasks, one needs an alphanumeric keyboard.

In our UNC GRIP system, we found it advantageous to slide the keyboard away under the work surface. In practice, it stayed there most of the time; I would expect the same to be true in the Dream System.

Specifying Adverbs

"Move."
  "Which way? How far? To Where?"
"Rotate."
  "Which way? How far?"
"Duplicate."
  "How many? Which direction? Spaced how?"
"Select door and scale."
  "How wide?"

The command dialog consists of not only verbs and nouns; most verbs have adverbial modifiers, usually prepositional phrases.[11]

Most Such Adverbs Will Be Quantitative. Moreover, those must be precise; pointing on a tablet rarely suffices. Much of this precision is specified indirectly by auxiliary verbs: Snap To, Align With, and so on.

Much is specified by selection from limited menus: color palettes, materials lists, finish schedules. Menu selection is cognitively and economically cheap. House designs, like computer memory accesses, exhibit very strong locality—for any given design decision, there may be many independent choice alternatives, but most choices are made from a small subset. Customizable menus are essential.

The remaining quantitative precision is best specified by a numeric keyboard. In our experience, this gets much use. One doesn't want to put it away as one does the alphanumeric keyboard.

Specifying Viewpoint and View

Most creative architectural work is done on plans and sections, but one checks the work by looking at the 3-D design whole, and from many vantages including walking through it. Specifying the current view of a 3-D house design is an important special case of noun + adjective specification.

One changes some viewing parameters continually and some infrequently. This distinction is not the same as dynamic versus static. One wants even infrequently changed parameters to change dynamically and smoothly.

Interior Views

In simulating a walk through a house, x, y location and head *yaw* change continually. One slides a viewpoint about on a 2-D drawing representing one building floor and turns the gaze in the same plane.

Eye height above the floor changes rarely. Most often, one moves to the same height on a different floor. Infrequently, one adjusts *eye height* proper, to fit a different designer or to envision the perspectives of different users.

Roll is rarely changed. We just don't roll our heads much. *Pitch* movements are much more common—look down, look up—but they are far less frequent than x, y and *yaw* movements.

The EyeBall. We found a special I/O device to be ideal for specifying interior views in architecture. The EyeBall consists of a six-degrees-of-freedom tracker housed in a billiard ball whose bottom half inch has been sliced off. It is equipped with two buttons readily pushed by the forefinger and the middle finger (Figure 17-2). One glides it over a work surface to move a V-shaped cursor on the plan.

Figure 17-2   UNC–Chapel Hill EyeBall viewpointer device
Kelli Gaskill, University of North Carolina

This device enables natural continual specification of all six view parameters—viewpoint (3 parameters), view direction (2 parameters), and view roll (1 parameter)—while heavily favoring x, y, yaw. The forefinger's button is that of a one-button mouse; the other button is a clutch. One moves the viewpoint to an upper floor by raising the EyeBall, clutching, lowering it to the table, and unclutching. Eye height above the floor stays unchanged. A nice property is that the viewpoint continually moves in z, as if one is in a glass elevator; there is no visual discontinuity, so one doesn't get lost in the model so often.

The EyeBall has another mode of use besides gliding over plans to specify interior views. Assume one always has, as a context index, a 3-D model on one side of one's workstation, with a "You are here" light showing viewpoint. Then, one can easily point within this index and say, "Put me there, looking that way."[12]

In either mode, eye height is set by a slider, usually very rarely. Two buttons default it to that of the 5th-percentile woman or the 95th-percentile man.

Exterior Views

The "Toothpick" Viewpointer.   As I elaborate in the next chapter, any design workstation needs multiple views of the object being designed: the workpiece on which one is manipulating plus context views.

For a house, one context view may be a view from the outside, or a view of a whole room or interior wall. For specifying an arbitrary exterior view of an object, we have found the most useful device to be a two-degrees-of-freedom positional joystick, as shown in Figure 17-3.

Figure 17-3   Toothpick viewpoint device; copy of a UNC device made by Professor Charles Molnar's group at Washington University, St. Louis

This is readily manipulated, usually by the left hand, to specify the direction from which one is looking at the object. The rest position has the Toothpick pointing to the user. To give a full 4π-steradian selection of views, we doubled the angle of displacement of the Toothpick from its rest position. Thus, when it is moved completely to the left or right, one's view moves around the object to look at it from the very back. Our users found this doubling easy and natural, rather to my surprise. This is supplemented with frequently used default buttons specifying the four elevations and some three-quarter views (from the corner of an aligned encompassing cube), and a rarely used slider that specifies the viewing distance.

Depth Perception.   Massing, the relative placement of filled and empty volumes, is an important consideration in architectural esthetics. Perceiving it requires 3-D perception. The most powerful depth cue is the kinetic depth effect, the relative motion of eye and scene. This cue is stronger even than stereopsis, and the two together are very powerful.

So how does one specify the motion wanted? Clearly the EyeBall can be used to move the viewpoint arbitrarily, but that requires work. One would like to study massing while thinking. On the UNC–Chapel Hill GRIP Molecular Graphics System, we found that rocking the entire scene about the vertical axis greatly helped perception while thinking, so we provided a rocking mode in which the scene behaved like a torsion pendulum whenever no action was being taken. The controls enabled the user to specify both the amplitude and the period of the rocking, although usually default values were used.

Notes and References

1. Brooks [1977], "The computer 'scientist' as toolsmith"; Britton [1981], *The GRIP-75 Man-Machine Interface*; and Brooks [1985], "Computer graphics for molecular studies," describe the system. The user interface was remarkable in that it had 21 degrees of freedom for

modifying the model and controlling the display, plus keyboards. All were in fact used. No device had more than three degrees of freedom; there was no device overloading. Users instinctively reached to known locations to change values.

2. Ullman [1962], "The foundations of the modern design environment," in Cross [1962b], *Research in Design Thinking*.

3. Alexander, *Notes on the Synthesis of Form* [1964], *A Pattern Language* [1977], and *The Timeless Way of Building* [1979], are all highly relevant here.

4. Turner Whitted, personal communication [1986].

5. Computer graphics also used progressive refinement in scene illumination, back when computers were slow. In the first 1/30 second, one renders an image with simple ambient lighting. In subsequent frame times, one iteratively calculates the more sophisticated radiositized illumination. The visual effect is dramatic—in a building interior image, for example, the shadows flee away to the corners of a room as the lighting sweetens from ambient to radiositized.

6. See, for example, the 40 styles of houses at http://www.houseplans. net/house-plans-with-photos/ (accessed July 30, 2009).

7. Buxton [1986], "A study in two-handed input."

8. Goel [1991], "Sketches of thought."

9. Arthur [1998], "Designing and building the PIT."

10. For example, Conner [1992], "Three-dimensional widgets."

11. One can imagine building the system so that it asks such follow-up questions after a noun or verb is incompletely specified. If so, one must be able to turn it off; expert designers will know implicitly what must come next, and the distraction would be intrusive.

12. Stoakley [1995], "Virtual reality on a WIM."

Andrei State 2009

18

A Computer Scientist's Dream System for Designing Houses— Machine to Mind

When we mean to build,
We first survey the plot, then draw the model;
And when we see the figure of the house,
Then we must rate the cost of the erection;
Which if we find outweighs ability,
What do we then but draw anew the model
In fewer offices, or at least desist
To build at all?

WILLIAM SHAKESPEARE [1598],
HENRY IV, PART 2

Vision for a house design workstation
Drawing by Andrei State

Two-Way Channel

Mind-machine collaboration demands a two-way channel. The broadband path into the mind is via the eyes. It is not, however, the only path. The ears are especially good for situation awareness, monitoring alerts, sensing environment changes, and speech. The haptic (feeling) and the olfactory systems seem to access deeper levels of consciousness. Our language is rich in metaphors suggesting this depth. We have "feelings" about complex cognitive situations on which we need to "get a handle" because we "smell a rat."

Visual Displays—Multiple Concurrent Windows

Computer-using designers have customarily worked with one active window. Yet computer scientists have long understood that designers need at least two, and that screen sizes have been far too small.[1] What visual displays would one in fact want in a Dream System for Designing Houses?

The Drafting Table and Drawing View

Since I believe 2-D drawings will always be primary for actual design, the first display is an electronic drafting table.

- **Angle.** In standard manual drafting, a vertical display and tiltable work surface are perforce combined, but electronics liberates. Separating the two means the hand and arm no longer obscure the view. Studies show that users have no difficulty moving a mouse or pen on one surface correlated with a display on another.
- **Work surface size.** Drafting tables vary, but 30 x 48 inches is common. These dimensions are set by the arms' reach.
- **Display resolution.** It should be that of the human eye, about one minute of arc—a 1,920-pixel computer screen at a distance twice its width. Such flat-screen displays now grace many offices.
- **Display viewing distance.** Projection on a screen 6 to 8 feet away relieves eyestrain for the individual designer.

The object on the table is almost always a 2-D drawing. The object on the screen may be the drawing, other renderings, and so on. Layering of the displayed drawings with controllable transparency, as is routinely done today, is an indispensable technique for focusing attention on some one aspect while maintaining conceptual context.

The 2-D Context View

In all our UNC systems where we've watched users doing real design work, whether architectural, molecular, or 2-D diagrams for publication, we see a universal sequence:

1. Study a big spatial chunk for context.
2. Zoom in.
3. Create or manipulate some local portion.
4. Zoom out.
5. Repeat.

Obviously, the historical limitation of one time-shared window enforced this unnatural and wasteful behavior. One wants a context view and a detailed view simultaneously, switching by movement of eyes rather than hand. We must provide that. Moreover, it won't do to provide the context window as a thumbnail in some corner of the detailed view—one needs to see the details in it, too. With current prices, no serious design shop can have any excuse for being display-constrained. Have two big screens showing these two views all the time!

Usually, the context view will be spatial, normally the entire plan. But for operations such as object selection from a library, one view might well be the library (a hierarchical tree representation or the contents of a particular node), the other still the drawing where the object is to be placed.

The 3-D View

People live and move in 3-D houses, not 2-D abstractions. In the Dream System, the designer continually sees the 3-D house as currently specified—always in full detail.

Projection virtual-environment technology seems quite suited for this. One doesn't want a completely immersive environment, such as a CAVE; a small vertical dome would be superb. Even a single standard 3-D view window would serve nicely. The designer is surely seated at the drafting surface, not walking about. He surely has a set of controls handy. This 3-D display is an auxiliary creation tool, whereas the CAVE was designed for viewing, not creation.

Several technical issues arise. First, one does not want to wear stereo glasses all the time while designing. The eyes work hard enough without that burden. So one wants a mode switch—perhaps a foot switch. Or, the 3-D display can be autostereoscopic.

Next, houses generally have flat walls, and so can projection screens. Of course, one wants the viewpointer, ideally an EyeBall, to control standard modes where yaw rotations spin the scene around the viewer and vice versa. But the Dream System also wants a snapping mode that aligns the view to a flat house surface.

Exterior Views

Especially useful viewings are the house from outside, with a wide field of view. As with interior views, one wants viewer controls of the hourly and seasonal positions of the sun.

Viewpoint control for exterior viewing is ideally different from that for interior viewing. One usually wants to specify x, y on the context display and to have view direction continually default toward the center of the house. Thus one easily walks around a house.

A dramatic exterior view is the house at night with the interior lights ablaze. The effect, if overly exploited by the painter Thomas Kinkade, is charming, attractive, homey.

I have found a third exterior view to be unexpectedly useful—the night view with the near wall dynamically eliminated. Circumnavigating a building in this mode gives a comprehensive grasp (Figure 18-1).

Figure 18-1   **Cutaway view of an apartment**
DeltaSphere, Inc.

The Workbook View

Yet another window concurrently displays the designer's work-book. Designers come to design stations with

- In-progress designs
- Action plans

They take away

- Updated in-progress designs and future action plans
- Logs capturing all actions; these, or the version-control sys-tem, enable automatic backtracking
- Notes, ideally dictated so as to leave the hands free to design, as to what was tried, and *why*, what was rejected, and *why*, and what was kept, and *why*

The *why*s, which cannot be captured from the action log, are cru-cially important for any complex design. They wonderfully aid refreshment after interruption. They remind one of the branching thought trails skipped as one explored a particular design alternative. The *whys* are priceless for new team members and for a designer's project heirs.

Ideally, the action plan and the resulting notes are interleaved in one document, distinguished by color or font.

In the Dream System, two page-corner inserts in the action log show the current value of the cost estimate and of some other budgeted commodity, such as square feet.

The Specification View

Construction requires not only drawings, but also prose specifications. Ideally, these grow to finality contemporaneously with the drawings, not afterward.

This is not nearly so hard as it first seems, given the progressive truthfulness mode of design. Specifications are highly stylized. If each of the starting models in the library has its specs, the designer can work by changing them as he goes. This task is made radically simpler by the vast collection long called Sweets File, now Sweets Network.[2] Many million products are listed, pictured, described, and specified there. McGraw-Hill Construction maintains the file and its taxonomy; product vendors provide the contents; architects and contractors subscribe to the service. Everybody wins.

So the Dream System needs a fourth 2-D window, the continually refined prose specifications. Ideally, a change made in this display can be automatically reflected in the drawing display. Since many Sweets Network product descriptions already include CAD models in standardized form, this link is not conceptually difficult. Propagating changes from the drawing back to specification is much more difficult—a research problem.[3]

Audio Display

I was stunned, many years ago, to watch a videotape in which a group of Helsinki architects showed a computer graphics simulation of a proposed redevelopment project. The visuals were good but not exceptional. But the video included recorded playground sounds. Even though no people were visible, the offstage noises made the whole scene leap to life.

Delivering audio displays is easy; building the sound models to be displayed is challenging. One wants to plant, at locations both indoors and outdoors, sound sources: a TV, traffic, a washing machine, young children playing/squabbling. Then, as one walks through the virtual house, one wants to hear the result, to look for both pleasure and nuisance.

The necessary acoustic simulation technology is well in hand.[4] What cannot currently be done in real time can be approximated and the display progressively refined. The march of processor speed will solve such difficulties.

The challenge is doors and windows. Which ones are open? How far? The combinations explode. Both designer specification and designer exploration seem easy in principle and tedious in practice. An obvious exploration aid would be a sound-intensity plot, as of ear height, gridded over the entire house drawing, and responding to interactive opening and closings of orifices. This visual display could suggest where to listen. The EyeBall is again a handy device for specifying the location and orientation in the model for the listening head.

Haptic Display

Haptic displays seem to get to our guts (and hearts) like no other modalities.[5] Nevertheless, try as I might, I have not conceived of any plausible use of existing haptics technology in the Dream System.

Generalization

From the specifics of the Dream System for Designing Houses one can readily generalize to many other domains. A dream system for building software, for example, would not benefit from all the 3-D capabilities. But it should incorporate the rich starting library, the Design Display, the Context Display, the Workbook Display, and a Test Cases Display, all suitably cross-linked.

Feasibility

Can the Dream System now be built? Unquestionably, yes. All the technologies are well within reach. Can it now be an affordable tool even for relatively modest projects like the design of individual houses? I believe it can, at least in larger firms that can invest the capital and can time-share the system among multiple designers.

How would one build it? Incrementally! Any all-at-once project to build such a superficially pondered system would almost surely fail. But growing it, incrementally, with continual trials by real designers, would work. The hardest part would be assembling a good initial library of starting models.

One can imagine an academic research project that develops a framework, and the necessary standard input format and description format, and then solicits Open Source contribution of models. This is a place where the prestige incentive of the Open Source model could work well.[6] I should think that architects might view having their house, room, or other project in the library as yielding not only prestige, but also advertising, like having it featured in a magazine. It would not be too hard to automatically winnow a massive central library based on usage. If it isn't viewed, out it goes.

Notes and References

1. Brooks [1995], *The Mythical Man-Month*, 194.

2. http://products.construction.com/.

3. The heavy machinery in the system basement required to do *two-way* linking, even in the much simpler case of text editing, may be grasped from Ken Brooks's Lilac system, described in "A two-view document editor with user-definable document structure" [1988] and "A two-view document editor" [1991]. The difficulty is that one view contains much more information than the other, so making modifications in the simpler view requires deducing and injecting information into the complex view.

4. Svensson and Kristiansen [2002], "Computational modelling and simulation of acoustic spaces."

5. Meehan [2002], "Physiological measures of presence in stressful virtual environments."

6. Raymond [2001], *The Cathedral and the Bazaar*, Chapter 4, "The magic cauldron."

V
Great Designers

19

Great Designs Come from Great Designers

Not from Great Design Processes

The basic premise underlying the SEI's [Software Engineering Institute] work on software process maturity is that the quality of a software product is largely determined by the quality of the software development and maintenance processes used to build it.

MARK PAULK [1995], "THE EVOLUTION
OF THE SEI'S CAPABILITY MATURITY
MODEL FOR SOFTWARE"

...[W]hile some may see them as the crazy ones, we see genius, because the ones who are crazy enough to think that they can change the world, are the ones who do.

STEVE JOBS, APPLE COMMERCIAL (1997)

Thomas Jefferson
iStockphoto

231

Great Designs and Product Processes

The authors of the opening quotes could hardly disagree more. Who's right?

I have earlier listed a little personal classification of well-known computer products, divided according to whether or not a product has passionate fans. It is expanded as Figure 19-1, with some more recent additions. I believe this division reflects some greatness in the designs. (It does not at all correspond to commercial success, which depends complexly on many factors besides design quality.)

A striking thing about this chart is that, so far as I can determine, every one of the right-hand products was produced by a formal product process, one involving many inputs and many approvals. Each of the left-hand products was produced *outside* a normal product process.

Examples abound in other fields: the atomic bomb, the nuclear submarine, the ballistic missile, the stealth airplane, the Spitfire, penicillin, the intermittent windshield wiper. Each of these innovations was produced by a small team, either naturally or intentionally set apart from normal product processes.

Yes	No
iPhone	Cell phone
Apple II	PC
Macintosh Interface	Windows
UNIX	z/OS (MVS)
Pascal	Algol
Fortran	Cobol
Python	Appletalk

Figure 19-1   Computer product fan clubs
(After Brooks [1995], *The Mythical Man-Month*, Figure 16-1)

Product Processes—Cons and Pros

This observation, even if true frequently but not always,[1] raises important questions:

- Why do so many great products issue outside product processes?
- What are product processes for? Why have them?
- Can one do a great design within a product process? How?
- How can we make product processes that encourage and facilitate great designs, rather than inhibiting them?

Do Product Processes Stifle Great Designs?

I believe that standard corporate product design processes do indeed work against truly great and innovative design. Considering how and why corporate processes evolve, this is not hard to understand. Product processes exist to bring order out of the natural chaos that develops new products.

By its very nature, process is *conservative*, aiming to bring similar but somewhat different things within one orderly framework. Hence the really dissimilar, the highly innovative, doesn't fit the framework. Consider the personal computer, not really the same thing at all as the institutional glass house of the 1960s or the central departmental minicomputer of the 1970s.

By its very nature, a product process *aims at predictability:* a product roughly defined by business needs before any great designer has spent substantial time on the problem, to be delivered at a stated time at a stated price. Predictability and great design are not friends.

By its very nature, a product process *"fights the last war,"* encouraging tactics that have worked in the past and discouraging those that have failed. Hence for the product addressing a new war—a totally new need or mode of operating—both kinds of tactics may be irrelevant. Consider the iPhone, not really the same thing at all as a simple mobile phone, much less the landline instrument Alexander Graham Bell invented and his AT&T monopolized.

By its very nature, a product process is *veto-oriented*, aimed at blocking bad ideas and catching oversights. The process aims to inhibit products that won't sell as hoped, products that cost more than expected to deliver, promises about function and schedule that can't be kept. More subtly, a corporate product process also aims to inhibit a confused product line, where one's own products are one's most deadly competitors, and customers don't know what to buy. Since failure can arise from many causes, product processes typically demand *consensus* by many people, each expert in a separate cause of potential failure.

Such consensus stifles great design in several ways. First, each expert watchdog is paid to avoid mistakes, not to make great things happen. So each is separately biased toward finding reasons not to proceed. Even when a really new product is not vetoed, consensus mechanisms often take off the sharp edges by forcing compromises. But the sharp edges are the cutting edges!

Next, product processes require not only consensus among the living and present, but consensus with the past, as codified into rules. Product processes grow, and as with all bodies of rules, each mistake-experience begets new rules or new approvals to prevent repeats. There are few barriers to the birth of such extra rules, and, once they are born, there are no forces for their elimination until a crisis comes. By the very nature of things, bureaucracies become more Byzantine, processes heavier, and organizations less nimble as they succeed and grow.[2]

When I was managing the development of IBM's System/360 computer family hardware in the early 1960s, our S/360 Model 20 mainframe was being developed in IBM's laboratory in Böblingen, Germany. This team had great talent and strong leadership. Yet, although they had been in operation for many years and had produced successful products for specialized markets, they had never quite succeeded in getting a product into IBM's main product line, its worldwide market. For the "bet your company" System/360 project, this was scary, so I went to investigate.

The reason became clear. The engineers had always conscientiously and scrupulously followed IBM's official Corporate Product Procedure, as documented in a manual of more than 100 pages. Successful project managers in other labs made bold "exceptions" to the procedure rules at the right times; the secret to success was choosing wisely![3] I sent such an experienced procedure manipulator to manage the project. He enabled the strong talent there to realize its potential. The S/360 Model 20 became phenomenally successful.

Finally, consensus processes starve innovative design by eating the resource. Consensus building takes meetings, lots of meetings. Meetings take time, lots of time. Great designers are few and far between; their time is exceedingly precious.

So Why Have a Product Process at All?

Am I quixotically advocating a revolutionary overthrow of all corporate design processes, in favor of creative chaos? I am not. Many of the reasons for process noted above are inescapable. At some point, corporate approval to go ahead must be obtained; at some point, experience should be tapped to catch obvious oversights; at some point, a product schedule and budget must be agreed. The trick is to hold "process" off long enough to permit great design to occur, so that the lesser issues can be debated once the great design is on the table—rather than smothering it in the cradle.

Follow-on Products. Further, a product design process will always have an important role because most designs are not intended to be highly innovative. This is for good reasons. Once users get their hands on a successful and truly innovative product, at least four separate effects follow:

- Use reveals shortcomings that need to be corrected in follow-on products.
- Users will put the innovation to unexpected uses, enlarging the product concept, usually in an incremental way.
- The innovation's demonstrated usefulness creates a demand for a more capable product, and a readiness to pay more for it.
- Yet simultaneously with all these drivers for change, popularity breeds lock-in; users don't want the next product to be "revolutionary"—they want what they know and like.

Thus, follow-on products are much more highly constrained and have less room for true innovation. At the same time, success breeds multiple opportunities and possible directions for enhancements in follow-on products. Yet no organization can do everything. So these follow-on products must be carefully selected from the range of possibilities. Their development must be monitored to ensure that the product stays on track to accomplish its chosen objectives and reach its forecasted customers.

Product processes, with their repeated cycles of

- Product definition
- Market forecast
- Cost estimate
- Price estimate

efficiently accomplish this selection and this monitoring.

But accurate market forecasting depends on having some sales experience with similar products. Accurate cost estimating depends on having some development and manufacturing experience with similar products.

Thus, product processes are, properly, designed for follow-on products. For innovation, one must step outside of process.

Raising the Level of Design Practice. Product design and release processes cannot turn good designers into great ones. They rarely produce great designs without a great designer. But the disciplines imposed *can* bring up the low end of the design curve and improve the average performance of the art. That's nothing to sneeze at.

The software engineering community has given much attention to its development processes. It has needed to, for I know of few design communities where average practice is so far behind best practice, and where worst practice is so far behind average practice.

The work of Watts Humphrey and the Software Engineering Institute in developing the Capability Maturity Model and energetically prosecuting its adoption has been valuable.[4] The CMM is a disciplined measure of components of a good design process that have generally been found to be useful. When a design shop does a CMM audit and scores poorly, it is time to look not only at its own practices but at those of more successful shops. Process improvement is most valuable in raising the floor of a community's practice. The CMM has done a good job of that.

There is no magic there. No amount of process improvement can raise the ceiling of the community's practice. Great designs do not come from great processes; they come from talented people doing hard work. Apple is quoted as saying, "We're at Level I [on the Capability Maturity Model] and will always be."[5] Yet Apple's results speak for themselves.

Isn't Process Necessary Even for Innovative Designs? I've been asked, "Surely the S/360 project, coordinating international labs and the business needs of multiple markets, made use of a great deal of process. How did you harness it without being stifled by it?"

Our core design team was well insulated from normal IBM oversight processes, with strong support from several levels of bold managers. We had exceptional capabilities to recruit talent from other company groups. We had enough money.

Getting the designs out as products required going through the standard processes. From the top came the word that this gamble was known to be revolutionary, and that it would require some bending of normal processes. The weekly struggle was our team's pushing for more innovation in forecasting, estimating, pricing, and so forth, and the process teams' proper pushing back. The talents of the process people were, however, of high order, and their skills were essential to our success.

The Clash: Process Stifles, Process Is Unavoidable; What to Do?

Great Designs Come from Great Designers; Find Them!

As a tone-deaf nonathletic man, I think it evident that not only are talents, whether for music, pitching, dancing, or design, unevenly distributed, but the range for any particular talent is enormous.

Even within a team of people of similar education and experience, gifts vary widely. I have had some team members and some students who were superbly gifted designers—they glitter in my memory. The history of the arts is bejeweled with examples.

Moreover, no two people have the same bundle of talents. (I think God did this so that each one of us will have something unique to give to other people, some unique way to serve.) Hence a wise leader organizes by drawing responsibility boxes around the people he has and can get, rather than putting people into the boxes he dreams up as abstractly ideal.

Our right and fundamental democratic concern is that all people be equal before the law and, a much more difficult goal, have equal opportunity. But pursuit of these goals must not blind us to the wildly unequal distribution of native talents, and the unequal drives to grow, hone, and express native talent.

Hence our structures and processes must cold-bloodedly recognize that people who have done great designs are more likely to make yet others if entrusted with freedom and authority to do so.[6]

Great Designers Require Bold Leaders Who Demand Innovation

First and foremost, the top leader of the organization must passionately want innovative products with great designs. This was clearly true of Apple under Steve Jobs's first reign, less true under his successors, and true again when he resumed the throne. It was true of IBM under both Thomas J. Watson (CEO 1914–1956) and Thomas J. Watson, Jr. (CEO 1956–1971). Other examples abound.

How to Make a Process That Encourages Great Designs?

I have suffered under burdensome processes, and I have some experience in bypassing or violating such, but I have no experience in pruning or restructuring them. Every organization needs to do that from time to time. I should want to delegate that job to a first-class talent with a sweeping authority for a limited task and time.

If one is designing a new product procedure or restructuring an existing one, how does one build in the counterforces necessary to overcome the natural inhibitory tendencies? How can one make a process that allows, enables, and even encourages great designs?

First, the product procedure must explicitly identify the matters of fundamental importance and constrain those, *and those only*. It is inherently a protective mechanism. It must securely protect the crown jewels, but, equally important, it must eschew building high fences around the garbage cans. This requires discretion and restraint—the instinct of protectors is to overprotect. Chapter 27, "Case Study: A Joint Computer Center Organization," illustrates how the separate identification of matters of fundamental importance worked in a specific case.

Second, the product procedure must provide easy and swift exception mechanisms, exercisable at the appeal of any project manager and the approval of only one sufficiently high-level boss. In other words, judgment and common sense must be explicitly provided for and readily available: "All rules can be broken."

Go for Conceptual Integrity: Entrust Your Design to a Chief Designer

Since conceptual integrity is the most important attribute of a great design, and since that comes from one or a few minds working *uno animo*, the wise manager boldly entrusts each design task to a gifted chief designer.[7]

Entrusting has many implications. First, the manager himself must not second-guess the design. This is a real temptation, because the manager is quite apt to be a designer, but one whose design gifts may not be as great as the best who report to him (design and management are very different jobs), and one whose attention is surely fragmented among other tasks.

Next, it must be crystal clear to all that the chief designer, although perhaps managing only a few assistants, has complete authority over the design, and that he ranks equal with the project manager sociologically.

Third, the chief designer must be shielded from watchbirds from outside the project and protected from time diversions.

Fourth, he must be provided with tools and help as he sees the need. What he is doing is of prime importance.

Notes and References

1. Air Force Studies Board [2008], *Pre-Milestone A and Early-Phase Systems Engineering*, states that it is true for many of the most successful and innovative weapons development projects.

2. This universal phenomenon hits software as well, as convincingly documented by Lehman and Belady's classic study of the growth of entropy over time in IBM's Operating System/360: Lehman and Belady [1971], "Programming system dynamics." A more thorough treatment is in an important paper: Lehman and Belady [1976], "A model of large program development."

3. See the essay "Template zombies," Chapter 86 in DeMarco [2008], *Adrenaline Junkies and Template Zombies*. I do not believe this IBM lab was afflicted with the form-versus-substance disease of the template zombie but was just conscientiously following the written rules sent from afar.

4. This has been recognized by the award of a National Medal of Technology in 2005.

5. James Robertson of the Atlantic Systems Guild gave me the Apple quote in 2008 (personal communication).

6. Cross [1996b], "Winning by design," is a delightful case study of the methods of Gordon Murray, a winning racing car designer. The account reports a chief-designer team, avoiding most kinds of process, and benefiting from constraints.

7. The British Deputy Prime Minister sought from the Royal Academy of Engineering a report on how to make rail travel safer. The RAE delegated the task to a committee of only one person: its President, Sir David Davies. The report was done in record time and is crisp and forthright, rich with concrete recommendations (Davies [2000], *Automatic Train Protection for the Railway Network in Britain*).

20
Where Do Great Designers Come From?

Genius will live and thrive without training, but it does
not the less reward the watering pot and pruning knife.

MARGARET FULLER [1820–1850], DIARY ENTRY

Every man who rises above the common level has
received two educations: the first, from his teachers; the
second, more personal and important, from himself.

EDWARD GIBBON [1789], *MEMOIRS
OF MY LIFE AND WRITINGS*

John Cocke (1925–2002), computer genius
IBM Watson Research Laboratory

I have just argued that great designs come from great designers, not from great design processes. Although technical designs are now always the work of teams, we still identify the great designers around whom the teams formed: John Roebling (the steel-cable Brooklyn Bridge), George Goethals (the Panama Canal), R. J. Mitchell (the Spitfire), Seymour Cray (the CDC 6600, the Cray 1 supercomputers), Ken Thompson and Dennis Ritchie (UNIX).

A peculiar concern facing producers of high-technology designs is the inherent conflict between the solo design paradigm that has yielded great works in the arts, literature, and engineering, and the team design paradigm now demanded by the complexity of our artifacts and the tempo of our economies.

- How can we grow great designers?
- How can we develop design processes that support and enhance great designers instead of shackling them and homogenizing their work?
- How can we best support great designers with teams?

We Have to Teach Them to *Design*

Our formal education of designers is often dead wrong. Schön,[1] paraphrased, says: "Technical Rationality holds that all professions should be taught as engineers still are taught: first the relevant basic and applied science, then the skills of application."

Schön strongly disagrees with Technical Rationality on this point. He argues that all professional skills are mastered by *critiqued practice*. He argues that this is true of medicine, law, the ministry, architecture, art, music, social work, and indeed engineering. Medical education recognizes this, and from third year on, students spend more and more of their time in clinics, in grand rounds, and taking responsibility for patients. Architectural education has never lost sight of this truth, so studio dominates in all years.

On the other hand, in America most engineering designers spend most of their formal education in the classroom, or in the lab doing prescribed experiments, not doing designs to be critiqued. The same is even more true of software engineers.

Schön's argument rings true to me. In such education we are misusing the most precious commodity in the education process: student time. Increasingly, engineering schools are reinserting critiqued design practice into the curriculum, in spite of the high faculty investment required.

It has been argued that engineers, hardware or software, have to know the basic science underlying their practice, and they have to know it first. The best modern engineering education refutes this and starts critiqued design in the freshman year, concurrently with science education. Only rarely do computer science curricula do that.

Similarly, strong engineering curricula often include "co-op" or "sandwich" programs, in which students intersperse on-the-job practice (and company training) between initial and final academic education. This practice is still far too rare in computer science curricula.

The weakness of much academic formal education is its reliance on lectures and readings, as opposed to critiqued practice. Effective education in design styles will have the pupil doing a well-constrained computer architecture in the style of Cray, a fugue in the style of Bach, or a building in the style of Wren. A knowledgeable and discerning mentor will then point out stylistic inconsistencies and critique the overall excellence of the design for its constrained objectives.

Such critique requires a certain confidence, even boldness, on the part of the mentor in engineering and computer science. Our emphasis on science has made us perhaps reluctant to engage in free-form subjective criticism, and inexperienced in offering it. Yet such is essential for teaching design.

Students can also mentor each other in such critiqued practice. The most effective way for a designer to learn other design styles is to undertake to teach them to other designers.

We Have to Recruit for Design Brilliance

All too often a manager recruiting new designers assesses them subconsciously on the criteria for the manager's own job—"Could he do well the job I'm doing?" This favors the articulate, the leader, the person who will be effective in meetings. It tends to overlook the introvert, the slow-spoken, and especially the unconventional. But brilliant designers come in these packages, too! (I do not assert that brilliant designers are more likely to come in such packages. I don't know.) We managers overlook these gifted ones to our great loss, theirs, and society's.

How can we select better? First, by reminding ourselves what we seek. Second, by looking at portfolios of the design work itself, not just oral presentations about the work. Microsoft, for example, has candidates craft programs; this is not yet a universal practice among software engineering firms.

We Have to Grow Them *Deliberately*

Most substantial industrial and military organizations have elaborate and well-developed processes for growing people from worker to manager to executive to top executive. At each career stage, there is another education program for the new lieutenant, new major, new general. Promising talents are identified early and tracked. Mentors are assigned. Rotation of assignments gives a carefully planned variety of experience. The most promising are assigned to hitches as aides to the top professionals. The most promising young lawyers clerk for Supreme Court justices.

God trains many leaders this way. Moses, by a "fluke," was trained to lead a nation by growing up as a prince in the court of a pharaoh. David, as King Saul's harpist, observed how a kingdom was run and fair judgments were made. The apostle Paul was prepared to articulate and expound a totally new understanding of God's ways by a superb education in the Old Testament at the feet of Gamaliel, the greatest rabbi of his day.[2] He was then radically transformed by an encounter with the risen Jesus Christ and sent for a period to the desert, to think it all through afresh.[3]

I do not see most technical organizations giving thought to crafting a similar in-the-trenches approach to the development of nonmanagerial technical leaders, much less the great designers on whom the company will critically depend.

Make the Dual Ladder Real and Honorable

The first task for growing designers, as opposed to managers, is to craft a proper career path for them, one whose compensation and sociological status reflect their true value to the creative enterprise. This is commonly called the *dual ladder*. I have treated this elsewhere; here I only repeat that it is easy to give corresponding salaries to corresponding rungs (and market forces tend to make that happen), but it requires strong proactive measures to give them equal prestige: equal offices, equal staff support, reverse-biased raises when duties change.[4]

Why does the dual ladder need special attention? Perhaps because managers, being human, are inherently inclined to consider their own tasks more difficult and important than design and need to deliberately assess what makes creativity and innovation happen.

Plan Formal Educational Experiences

Budding designers, like budding managers, need a combination of continuing formal education interspersed with actual hands-on practice that is guided and critiqued by a master designer.

Why formal education? Today's world continually changes. In the high-technology disciplines, the rapid obsolescing of a technical education is self-evident, and almost frightening. Since I got into the computer field in 1952, my professional intellectual life has been a big sea bath in a heavy surf. As soon as one stumbles up after one breaker, here comes the next! Thoroughly invigorating, thoroughly enjoyable, and ever varying. So the first reason for formal education is continual retooling.

I have personally found formal short courses an effective and economical method for retooling—I have averaged one per year. Why? Can't one keep up by journal-reading and conference-going? Indeed one can! But I am a believer in formal education—a good teacher who carefully prepares a balanced overview of a subject can improve my learning efficiency by a factor of two or more and can quickly give a balance and perspective that would require studying literally dozens of journals. As a teacher who undertakes to deliver that kind of learning efficiency to my customers, I try also to buy it for myself.

A second reason is *deepening* and *broadening*. This is most effectively done by studying both good and bad designs of predecessors and contemporaries. For this purpose the principal advantage offered by formal education is *detachment*—the professional teacher is more apt to study competing design concepts and styles. As the culture inside any design shop emphasizes its own traditions and viewpoints, so does company-sponsored formal education. This is the best reason for budding designers and their mentors to seek formal education outside.

My most productive single act as an IBM manager had nothing to do with product development. It was sending a promising engineer to go as a full-time IBM employee in mid-career to the University of Michigan to get a PhD. This action, which at the time seemed to a busy computer architecture manager to be just a quite incidental personnel activity, had a payoff for IBM beyond my wildest dreams. Ted Codd's PhD prepared him for a research career; his research led him to invent the relational database concept and to receive a Turing Award.[5] Relational databases have been the principal application of IBM's most profitable computer line for over 25 years.

Plan a Varied Set of Work Experiences

As the best organizations now do for budding managers, so we need to do for budding designers. The critical word is *plan*; the course of the young career should itself be designed—for variety, for depth of involvement, for spiraling challenge and responsibility.

Often the most fruitful of early assignments have young designers serving in the organizations of the users of the objects they design. My own short-term jobs in a commercial data-processing shop building a 40-state payroll program, in a scientific computing shop calculating rocket trajectories, in a cryptanalytic shop, in a telephone switching laboratory identifying dialers on four-party lines, and in an engineering-physics lab measuring ground vibrations in milli-inches have been priceless in helping me understand computer users' requirements viscerally. As described in an earlier chapter, my two-week stint as an apprentice computer operator, hanging tapes in a glass house, also gave me a blast of reality when I designed an operator console. Dewey was right that we learn by doing; the effective growth curriculum of the designer must include a variety of experiences.

Plan Sabbaticals Outside the Organization

The mid-career designer can be refreshed and broadened by a sabbatical outside the organization—perhaps on loan to a customer; perhaps teaching at a university; perhaps on assignment with a federal agency. Preventing stagnation of creative people is a great investment.

We Have to Manage Them Imaginatively

The John Cocke–Ralph Gomory story.   John Cocke was probably the most brilliant and surely the most creative person I have ever known. We both joined IBM in its Stretch supercomputer project in July 1956, with fresh PhDs, and we shared a bullpen then and later a two-person office. That arrangement was fine because John, single, worked at night, and I worked in the daytime. John was passionate about computers, all aspects. I suspect he spent more hours every day thinking about computers than he did thinking about everything else combined. He understood in depth not only computers, but all the supporting science and technology.[6] And he was a rare combination—both deeply thoughtful and outgoing; like the Ancient Mariner, "he stoppeth one in three" to explain his latest ideas. It was impossible not to love John—genial, generous to an extreme degree, and always excited. Harwood Kolsky's memoir vividly captures many aspects of John's personality, style, and presence.[7]

Cocke attracted great collaborators, who helped capture and helped implement his incredibly numerous ideas. Three of these ideas, each worthy of the Turing Award, were instruction pipelining with Kolsky,[8] global compiler optimization with Fran Allen and Jack Schwartz,[9] and the reduced-instruction-set computer architecture with George Radin.[10]

Now how could an idiosyncratic genius like John Cocke, who couldn't manage a group, rarely published anything, and mostly just thought and talked to bright people, make so many major contributions? There are two geniuses in this story, and the other is Ralph Gomory, IBM's Director of Research and Senior Vice President for Science and Technology. Like Cocke, Gomory received the National Medal of Science for his own contributions.

Gomory created an organization, atmosphere, and organizational management style that aimed to *enable* each person in IBM Research to contribute in the way that best suited his particular bundle of talents. Ralph says, "I didn't treat John any differently from anyone else." But his statement misses the point: he treated *each* of his great minds differently—according to their nature and needs. He also says, quietly proud, that "John was the highest-paid person in IBM Research, because he was the highest contributor."[11]

We Have to Protect Them Fiercely

Protect Them from Distraction

Once we have great designers, we want them to design. Design productivity requires *flow*, an uninterrupted mental state of high creativity and concentration. We designers have all experienced and covet its delights. DeMarco and Lister have an excellent discussion of flow, its importance, and how to achieve it in Peopleware.[12]

The modern organization has many hindrances and diversions to prevent flow:

- Meetings
- Phone calls
- Emails
- Rules and constraints
- Staff bureaucracies and "service" groups, who make rules to simplify their own jobs
- Customers
- Professional visitors and journalists

Many creative organizations have adopted procedures such as "quiet mornings" to enhance flow. When IBM was trying to catch up with Apple after the introduction of the first personal computers, CEO John Opel established a closed laboratory in Boca Raton to develop IBM's entry. Other IBM employees, including even corporate staffers with defined relevant responsibilities, simply were not permitted to go in.

Similarly, I closed the System/360 project to non-project visitors, both IBMers and customers, from January to April 1964. We had too much work that needed flow.[13]

I interviewed Jeffrey Jupp, Technical Director of Airbus UK, on the design and manufacture of wings in Britain for Airbus planes whose fuselages were designed and manufactured in France. Late in our fascinating conversation I asked if I could speak with his chief designer. "No" was the simple answer. I understood and respected it.

Protect Them from Managers

A mediocre or insecure manager can smother any designer's creativity. Often a mediocre manager fails to recognize the jewels on his team. Sometimes he doesn't realize the crucial nature of design to his team's success. Sometimes he doesn't understand his own role of enabling design magic.

Sometimes the manager resents, or cannot admit, that the "subordinate" designer is in fact the better designer. Sometimes the manager is offended if the exceptional designer is paid more than he. The result is lack of encouragement, lack of facilitation, petty put-downs.

The task of higher management is then quite clear: they must actively change the first-line manager, ideally by raising his vision of his own talents and special role, and by training him in team encouragement and leadership.

Protect Them from Managing

I have seen potentially great designers sidetracked from design into management. They never reached their potential. The culture of our organizations, alas, encourages or even forces this. Intention, nay, determination, is required to swim against that culture.

Seymour Cray, the greatest supercomputer designer ever, furnished an inspiring example. Cray was a designer of first-generation vacuum-tube computers in the hotbed at St. Paul, Minnesota, first at Engineering Research Associates, and then at Control Data Corporation. To design the CDC 6600, he moved his team of "thirty-five people including the janitor" away into seclusion and disentangled himself from all other CDC responsibilities.[14]

When the dramatic success of the 6600 involved him again in CDC management, he arranged a departure, with CDC's blessing, to found Cray Computer Corporation, working on a secluded prairie site. He personally oversaw all aspects of the Cray 1, from circuits to refrigeration to the Fortran compiler.

Then, as Cray Computer blossomed with success and involved him again in management, he pulled a team away to Colorado to form Cray Research Corporation. Only a drunk driver ended the determined pattern.[15]

Growing Yourself as a Designer

Suppose you are a technical designer and want to improve. Is there any counsel from outside your own discipline that can help? I think so. You must start by planning your own growth program.[16] You alone are responsible for it.

Constantly Sketch Designs

Designers learn to design by designing. Some of the sketches need to be fully detailed, for the devil is indeed in the details, and many a grand scheme has foundered on a little submerged rock. Leonardo's *Notebooks* are a rich example of how this is best practiced. The aspiring young software designer might well keep a notebook of patterns he encounters and invents in his own constructions.

Seek Knowledgeable Criticism of Your Designs

Donald Schön, in his superb book *Educating the Reflective Practitioner*, argues extensively that critiqued practice is in fact the only successful method of teaching practice. He cites discipline after discipline—law, medicine, architecture, masonry, the medieval craft guilds—as having evolved (probably independently) to this method of teaching.[17] The modern PhD dissertation is exactly such a method of teaching the practice of research.

Study Exemplars and Precedents

In this practice, you emulate many great designers. Robert Adam studied Christopher Wren. Wren studied Palladio. Palladio begged support from his father to go to Rome and measure and draw the remnants of great Roman buildings. The Romans studied and fused the architectural styles of the Etruscans and the Greeks. Each great designer mastered the rich legacy of his predecessors and then added his own new concepts.

The proper study of exemplars demands humility of approach. Those precedents whose reputations have survived centuries of criticism have some deep excellence. In newer fields, the available span may be only decades. But however deep the pool of precedents, the task of the student is to find and master the excellence that has gone before, even if his muse or his new circumstance then drives him in a totally different direction.

The computer architect needs to study the whole variety of commercially produced machines. Someone thought they were good enough to merit the investment of real money. (The much more numerous published-only architectures have passed no such stringent test and hence merit far less study.)

In approaching a precedent design, it is crucial to assume competence—the right question is

"What led such a smart designer to do that?"

rather than

"Why did he do such a fool thing as that?"

Usually, the answer lurks in the designer's objectives and constraints; discovering it usually brings new insights. Whereas in marital disagreements, the wise and usually truthful answer to the "Why did you . . . ?" or "Why didn't you . . . ?" question is "Lack of sense," that is rarely true when one probes a design decision.

When possible, listen to contemporary designers discussing their work. When possible, read what designers have written about their works.

Gerry Blaauw and I have found it very instructive to cast our own studies of others' computer architectures into a common format—common structure, standard sketch scale, common prose description elements, common formal description language—with a short prose critique of the highlights and peculiarities of each.[18]

A Self-Education Project—Floor Plan for a 1,000-Square-Foot House

From a beginning design course at the North Carolina State University School of Design comes a useful self-education exercise for designers, no matter what their design disciplines.

The Program.   Design the plan of a 1,000-square-foot home for a family with two parents and two children, a son aged three and a daughter aged six. The site is in northern Virginia, suburban, 50 feet on the street, 70 feet deep, somewhat wooded, and facing south.

Journal.   Keep a dated journal of your design questions, decisions, and reasons. Here are some questions to address:

- Fabricate a more detailed architectural program, using your imagination. Put it in your journal.
- What constraints did you deduce from the given program?
- What was the budgeted commodity? How did you manage it?
- What desiderata did you follow, explicitly or implicitly?
- How did you decide which of two design alternatives was better?
- Did you use a CAD tool? If so, assess it versus sketching, for the different phases of your task.
- How did you proceed? Analyze your journal and sketch your design trajectory.
- Assessment: What are the good points in your design? The weaknesses?

Notes and References

1. Schön [1986], *Educating the Reflective Practitioner*.

2. Acts 22:3; Wikipedia on "Gamaliel" (http://en.wikipedia.org/wiki/Gamaliel), accessed on April 25, 2008.

3. Galatians 1:17–18; Acts 22:3. However, in contrast with all of these, Jesus was blocked from getting training by the Old Testament experts and had to rely on memorizing the Scriptures and coming to a totally new understanding of them by meditating on them in the carpenter shop for many years (Luke 2:41–52).

4. Brooks [1997], *The Mythical Man-Month*, 118–120, 242.

5. Edgar Frank Codd, if you want to seek his work.

6. Even in his last illness, though chair-bound, Cocke regaled me with some new science and his latest ideas for how it could be applied to computers.

7. http://www.cs.clemson.edu/~mark/kolsky_cocke.html, accessed on November 26, 2008.

8. Cocke and Kolsky [1959], "The Virtual Memory in the STRETCH Computer." This is really about instruction pipelining, not virtual memory as we know it today.

9. Cocke and Schwartz [1970], *Programming Languages and Their Compilers*; Allen and Cocke [1971], "A catalog of optimizing transformations."

10. The Reduced Instruction Set Computer (RISC) concept is often misunderstood. The basic idea is not a *reduced set* of instructions, but a set of *reduced instructions*, that is, more primitive. In extreme form, there are no subsequenced instructions, not even a Shift N Bits or a Multiply. This enables the accumulator-adder-accumulator loop to be minimized, and with instruction cache and an optimizing compiler, everything goes faster. I know of no one besides John whose mastery of both computer design and compiler optimization could have so wedded those concepts. George Radin was an important collaborator, but the original papers, Radin [1982], "The 801 minicomputer," and Radin [1983], "The IBM 801 minicomputer," should

have borne Cocke's name as lead author, although I suspect he didn't write a word.

11. Ralph Gomory personal communication [November 2008].

12. DeMarco [1987], *Peopleware*.

13. Samples of the letters of February 4, 1964, to the head of the Marketing Division, and to my boss and the laboratory manager are on the book's Web site.

14. Murray [1971], *The Supermen*.

15. http://americanhistory.si.edu/collections/comphist/cray.htm, accessed on August 12, 2009.

16. The best advice I've seen for planning an academic career is given in Gilbert Highet's *Art of Teaching* [1950], 21:

> *When a young German scholar was beginning his career, he used to choose three or four large fields in which he felt a real interest, on which there was a good deal of work to be done, and which—an important point—were all linked with one another, and which—most important of all—he felt to converge on the very center of his subject. He would contrive as far as possible to make these the subjects of his first classes and seminars. He would write groups of lectures on them, and nurse and nourish each group until it grew into a book. If he were energetic enough and percipient enough, he would thus become the author of three or four books, each of which would recommend and illuminate the others. He would then continue . . . enlarging [each field] strategically from year to year until he had built up a really authoritative knowledge of the whole subject. ... Scholars who planned their learning and their teaching in that way usually found ... that they had enough interests and nearly enough knowledge to fill three careers.*

17. Schön [1986], *Educating the Reflective Practitioner*.

18. Blaauw and Brooks [1997], *Computer Architecture*, Chapters 9–16, "A computer zoo." The standard format is described in Chapter 9.

VI

Trips through Design Spaces: Case Studies

In retrospect, most of the case studies have a striking common attribute: the boldest design decisions, whoever made them, have accounted for much of the goodness of the outcome. These bold decisions were due sometimes to vision, sometimes to desperation. They were always gambles, requiring extra investment in hopes of getting a much better result.

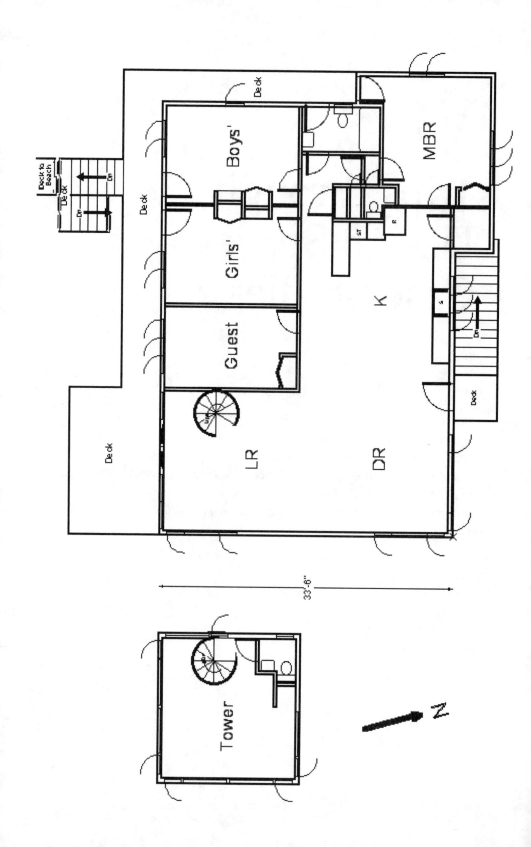

Deck

Boys'

Girls'

Guest

Deck

LR

DR

K

MBR

ST

R

S

Deck to Beach

Deck

Dn

Dn

Dn

Up

Deck

Deck

33'-6"

Tower'

N

21

Case Study:
Beach House "View/360"

The Most Beautiful House in the World
(is the one you build yourself).

WITOLD RYBCZYNSKI [1989]

Main-floor and Tower plan of "View/360" beach house

Highlights and Peculiarities

Why This Case? It documents for a simple, understandable structure how very many decisions must be specified and the numerous considerations affecting them.

Bold Decision. Place the house as close to the ocean as possible, while still on the warranty-deeded lot. It is about 40' forward of all the neighbors' houses, at somewhat greater risk of wash-away.

Budgeted Resource. For this house design, the budgeted resource turned out to be inches of oceanfront, hence of view and breeze.

Serendipity of the Spiral Staircase. This wooden staircase, included because of floor-space cramping, turned out to be a piece of spatial art and a visual delight.

In-Construction Changes. Changes in the design made during the construction process substantially improved the visual delight, the feel of the house, and its commodity. Not all of the opportunities created by in-construction changes were exploited, which was a mistake.

Placement of Pilings. Both the amateur and the professional architect failed to give careful thought to the placement of the pilings under the centers of weight, and their distribution so that the load on each was about the same. The pilings settled unevenly into the sand, and the house sagged where pilings should have been and weren't.

Introduction and Context

Location:

321 Caswell Beach Road, Caswell Beach, NC; Latitude 33°53.6' N, Longitude 78°2.1' W. The site is on an east-west island with one central road. One row of lots lies between the

Atlantic Ocean and the road, a second row between the ocean and the Cape Fear River and its marshlands. The house is on the oceanfront and faces 15° *west* of south!

Owners:

Frederick and Nancy Brooks family

Designers:

Frederick and Nancy Brooks, architecture; Arthur Cogswell, FAIA, structural engineering and roofline for Tower

Dates:

1972, shell closed in and occupied
1997, construction completed

Local Family as of August 1972:

Parents: Frederick and Nancy
Children: Kenneth, 14; Roger, 10; Barbara, 7
Grandmother: Octavia, 71
Close child friend: Chandler, 10

Objectives

Primary Goal. Our primary goal was to build a comfortable, informal vacation home for family and friends that would capitalize on the natural riches of an oceanfront setting. The house was not intended as a rental.

Other Objectives.

- Capitalize on the view.
- Create a casual, unpretentious, restful interior.
- Capitalize on the sea breeze for day and night.
- Sleep 14 on beds and feed 22 at one seating.
- Provide a Grandmother/Guest Room, a Master Bedroom, a Boys' Dorm, and a Girls' Dorm—4 bedrooms.
- Provide plenty of showers and toilets.

- Build the house to withstand hurricanes with winds of at least 100 mph. Hurricanes threaten about two times a year and hit about once a decade.
- Design the Kitchen to be workable for one but also for 4 to 6 workers.
- Isolate the noise from our boys and their friends.
- Keep maintenance requirements low.
- Make the house a do-it-together project for family training and bonding.

Opportunities

Building Site.   The lot has 75' of ocean frontage. To the southeast there is a fine view of Bald Head Island (Cape Fear) and ship traffic in and out of the Cape Fear River. *Front* is defined as the ocean side, not the road side, of the house. The soil is coarse beach sand; the vegetation is low scrub, sea oats, and smilax vines.

Dunes.   The house can readily be as close as 65' to the high-water mark because it is protected by a row of dunes.

Views.   Due to the narrowness of the island, there is not only a 180° view of the beach from the front of the house, there is a 135° view of the Cape Fear River and its marshes from the back.

Breeze.   The house site naturally faces 15° *west* of south. The prevailing sea breeze is south to southwest and blows most of the time in warm weather.

Constraints

Budget.   There was not enough money to build a finished four-bedroom house at one time.

Time.   The family's available time for construction during any one summer was limited.

Code and Deed Requirements.

- The house must be on 16' pilings, 8' of which must be in the ground.
- The setback requirement from each lot side was 10'.
- The house must be a single-family residence.
- Electric and septic tank codes must be met.

Foredune.   The foredune could be disturbed only minimally, for example, by a boardwalk over it.

Services.   The site was serviced with only electricity and water, not gas or sewer.

Deed.   Some 65' of the ocean-side part of the lot had accreted since the lot was platted in 1938. We have a quitclaim deed, not a warranty deed, to this land.

Appearance.   External appearances were not constrained, nor did we consider them important.

Design Decisions

Build the house over a relaxed period of time.

- Have a dried-in campable shell put up at once, with one bathroom plumbed, the septic tank installed, and temporary electricity provided to the house.
- Invest all initially available cash in maximizing square footage and windows.
- The family would do all interior work, including walls, doors, cabinets, wiring, and most of the plumbing.

Exploit the 75' lot width.   Most beach lots are 50'. Most ocean-front houses are long and narrow. In order to use most of the 55' allowable width, we turned the house sideways, so that it is wider than it is deep. Therefore, a custom floor plan was needed, not a book exemplar.

Exploit the views.

- Set the house as far forward on the lot as feasible, but stay on the warranty-deed land.
- Build a view-maximizing Tower room on the front of the second floor, with glass on four sides.
  Corollary: The roof pitch is limited. The ridge can be no higher than the windowsill level of the Tower.
- Put numerous and large windows in all the elevations.
  Corollary: The structure had to be strengthened against skew.

Exploit the breeze.

- Give every bedroom some ocean frontage.
- Plan to keep the house open to the breeze—install no central air conditioning.
  Corollary: Expect to have moisture and salt spray everywhere.
- Put a 6' sliding-door pair in the front of the Living Room.
- Provide an ample front deck, with protection from the sun.
- Use casement windows, which maximize the opening area and can be directed to scoop in the breeze.
  Corollary: Install the windows to open facing southwest or northeast.

Build to resist moisture.   The house needed to resist both normal breeze-borne moisture and hurricane leaks. Use wooden paneling to minimize drywall. Use no carpets, just separate rugs, many of them small.

Optimize for spring, summer, and fall use.   Provide heat for occasional winter use. Use electric baseboard heat instead of central heating; it has a higher operating cost per day used, but a substantially lower capital cost.

Localize/minimize noise.

- Provide each of the Girls' Dorm, Boys' Dorm, and Master Bedroom with a private external door so early risers can slip out to the beach without disturbing sleepers.

- Divide the house into a bedroom zone and a public-room zone; partition off the bedrooms, baths, and Hall serving them from the public areas.

Isolate the boys' noise.   Put the Boys' Dorm at the far end of the bedroom zone.

Design a casual, unpretentious, restful interior.   Use paneling, not paint or wallpaper, for all walls. Use dark paneling and floor-boards for the Living Room and Tower where glare is the greatest; for the Kitchen and Dining Room public rooms; and for the Boys' Dorm. In all cases, provide a dark, quiet, cool feeling. Use light paneling for the other bedrooms for cheer. Use arctic white paneling for the Halls, which get no daylight.

Sleep 14.   Four can sleep in the Boys' Dorm, 4 in the Girls' Dorm, 2 in the Master Bedroom , 2 in the Guest Bedroom, 2 in the Living Room, and 2 in the Tower. Provide two sofas, suitable for sleeping, in the Living Room. Provide convertible/storable beds for two in the Tower. Provide two fold-up bunks and two perma-nent single beds each in the Girls' Dorm and Boys' Dorm.

Feed 22.   Fill the middle of the house with three tables—two for 8 each, one for 6.

Don't install ceilings.   For economy and visual effect, use no ceilings except in the bathrooms and the Living Room. The rafters are doubled 2 x 12s on 4' centers, designed for a load of up to 1' of snow. The roof consists of tongue-in-groove 2 x 6s with an insulat-ing pad on top, then built-up tar-cloth roofing, then white stones to reflect heat. The visible part of the interior is just varnished. **Corollary:** The open ceiling complicates hiding the wiring.

Optimize the footprint of the Tower stairs.   To put the Tower forward, the stairs have to be in the front of the house, where space is precious. The Living Room is to be the only front public room, so the stairs go there.

If the Living Room is to maximize its view on the south and be open to the other public spaces on the north, the stairs must be along the east or west wall. The east wall has windows for view, light, and breeze, so the stairs go on the west wall.

It seemed a better use of precious space to give the stairs a square footprint rather than a rectangular one, which would narrow the whole Living Room. So we used spiral stairs. Salt spray argues strongly against steel, so the stairs are wooden. Given the stairs as a necessity, feature them as a bit of sculpture.

Design the eaves for light control. The eaves must be 4' to admit midday sun into the front rooms from September to March, but not from March to September.

Rationing the Frontage

The opportunities and constraints give a maximum house width of 55', or 660". Since ocean breeze and ocean view are to be maximized, frontage becomes a critical design budget.

Living Room. The Living Room has the highest claim on ocean view and breeze. Clearly it gets a substantial chunk. An arbitrary decision was to make it 16' wide. The Living Room can have side windows as well as front window and doors, so we put the Living Room in the southeast corner of the house to exploit the southeast view, the mouth of the Cape Fear River and shipping.

West Deck. Run a narrow deck along the west end of the house, to provide direct beach access and major breeze to the Master Bedroom and to provide a direct path from the beach to the interior showers without having wet people track through the house.

Bedrooms versus Dining Room–Kitchen. Given the decision not to air-condition, breeze for sleeping becomes very important. Direct bedroom access to the beach is secondary, but more than just a nicety, given the personalities of our children. So the bedrooms go forward and divide the remaining frontage.

Girls' Dorm, Boys' Dorm. These are the highest priority among the bedrooms, since they will be used on every beach trip (as opposed to the Guest Room) and may need to serve as reading retreats for the children.

Guest Room. The Master Bedroom is needed primarily for sleeping. The Guest Room may well be used as a reading retreat, so it wins out for a position on the front.

Configuring the Boys' Dorm. Site the Boys' Dorm on the house's southwest corner for isolation. One bed goes under the front windows, and one bunk on the west wall overlapping it. Another bunk can go high (for adventure) if it goes on the north wall near the ridgepole. The closet therefore goes on the east wall. The minimum room width equals door width plus bed length.

Configuring the Girls' Dorm. The lower beds feel much less confining if not completely under an upper bunk. Put a bed under the window, a bunk on the east wall. Another bunk can also go on the east wall and share a ladder. Put another bed on the north wall and a closet on the west wall. The minimum room width equals door width plus bed length.

Configuring the Guest Room. This room needs only a double bed. It needs no door to the beach. The minimum width equals bed width plus passage around the bed. There is plenty of room depth, so put the closet on the north wall.

Sizing the House

Square Feet. The available money led to an upper bound of 2,000 ft^2, given the abundance of windows.

Roof Structure and Room Depth. The deflection of a uniformly loaded beam supported at both ends is very sensitive to length:

$$d = k \, l^4 / w^2 \, t$$

where w is the width of the timber, t the thickness, and l the effective length. The effective length is shortened by any cantilever beyond the point of support. I chose 4' eaves, based on summer and winter sun angles. The whole calculation yielded a maximum horizontal span length of 16' for twinned 2 x 12s on 4' centers. This determined the depth of the front bedrooms, the Living Room, and the Tower.

Sizing the Dining Room–Kitchen.   It appeared that the Master Bedroom would benefit from a door directly into the Kitchen, as well as the one into the Hall. The critical dimension then became the Kitchen west wall, whose length had to be at least one work surface width plus a stove width plus a refrigerator width and a bedroom door width, plus a work surface between stove and refrigerator.

I chose to make the Kitchen depth also the depth of most of the back of the house, for simplicity. This gave a good working size to the Kitchen. It also required the addition of flitch plates to the roof beams to support the 17' span.

False Starts

Breaking-Wave Roof.   Initially I planned to make the roofline suggest breaking waves, as shown in Figure 21-1.

Cogswell strongly advised against it: "My architecture prof told us, 'If you can design a house to keep the rain out, boys, you will have done well.' Maybe you can find a contractor in Brunswick County who will make that trough so it won't leak, but I doubt it." I followed his back-to-fundamentals advice.

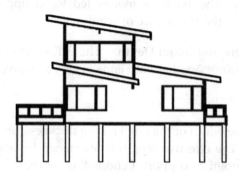

Figure 21-1   Brooks's proposed roofline

Figure 21-2   East elevations by Brooks and by Cogswell

Dull Symmetric Tower Roofline by Brooks. I did a perfectly dull roofline for the Tower. Cogswell substantially improved it as shown in Figure 21-2.

Design Changes after Design, before Construction

Designed two exterior showers on the ground floor. To keep sand, salt, and wet bathing suits out of the house, we designed two ground-floor exterior showers; changing to and from bathing suits would occur there. We provided each with ample dressing space for multiple occupancy, so parents can help children.

Replaced the planned shower off the Hall with closets. That space became a big linen closet and a full-height miscellany closet, 12' wide, with a shelf to store a rollaway bed below, window screens above.

Moved the eating area from the Dining Room to the Kitchen. Mock-up studies showed this to make serving much more convenient. This made a sitting, working, game, puzzle area in the Dining Room.

Doubled the size of the ground-floor enclosed Storage Room from 8' x 16' to 16' x 16'.

Swung the Master Bedroom screen door the other way. When the bathroom window was open, the screen door wouldn't open—a design goof discovered during construction.

Design Changes after Shell Construction and Initial Occupancy

Decided against constructing a partition between the bedroom zone and the public rooms.

Installed let-in diagonal braces. Braces on the east and west walls of the Living Room, the north wall of the Guest Room, and the west wall of the Boys' Dorm improved parallelogram skew resistance to wind. The work was done after the shell was up, before any paneling.

Installed hurricane clips. The shell contractor did not install the specified vertical tie rods, so we substituted these to hold the roof down in high winds.

Added water faucets on the deck for rinsing.

Provided an awning for the big front deck. An awning provided shade for all or part of the deck. We used a trailer awning, designed for 70 mph wind speeds on the highway. Much later, we replaced the awning with a fixed roof, extending halfway out to enable sitters to choose sun or shade.

Replaced and enlarged the Tower windows. Hurricane Diana (1984) blew out all the original Tower windows, glass and frames. We replaced the front multiple small panes with two single large panes. These afford a much better view in both size and presence—and stronger wind resistance.

Added a door in the West Hall. This allows the north half-bath to be either grouped with the Master Bedroom into a suite, or made part of public toilet facilities.

Made removable plywood shutters. We use these for boarding up the two windward sides of the house for winter and for hurricanes.

Ripped out the extra sound insulation (and wall thickness) between the Living Room and the Guest Room, after framing, before paneling. Grandmother Brooks died in 1973, so the room became the Guest Room instead of Grandmother's Room and no longer needed the special sound isolation.

Replaced the east railing of the front deck with a bench, especially for facing breeze and sunsets.

Installed a foundation sill (1997) to stabilize settling pilings.

Installed supports under the west wall of the Boys' Dorm (2000). The original plan had the pilings under the edge of the west deck rather than under the west load-bearing wall, an error in the structural design.

Assessment (after 37 Years)

Delight

Tower. The Tower has turned out to be a wonderful study, with horizon views to rest the eyes, the ability to watch action on the beach, a fine southeast view for watching shipping in the ocean channel, a fine northeast view for watching shipping traverse the river, and plenty of light. Much of *The Mythical Man-Month* was written there.

Open Plan. Omitting the partition originally planned between the Kitchen and the Hall substantially adds delight. It increases the visual space, enhancing one's perception of roominess upon entering the house. It brings daylight and sea breeze to the main passageway. The cook can see the ocean through the Girls' Dorm and its open exterior door—a big morale booster. The colored bedroom doors became major decorative elements, and the white Hall wall is ideal for hanging maps.

Spiral Staircase. The oak spiral staircase is a visual delight as a sculpture. In daylight, it is silhouetted against the glass front wall.

Design Rationale. My consulting architect, Arthur Cogswell, once derisively called "View/360" "the damned-logical beach house" because of the detailed rationale described here and shared with him. I've never been sure with what he was contrasting it. The rationality is a private delight for me when I'm there.

Exterior. The house is interesting but not beautiful from the exterior—form follows function (Figure 21-3). Cogswell's asymmetrical roofline for the Tower is just right; it seems to leap forward.

Usefulness

Objectives Met. The house is very livable.

Design Changes. The changes made after the original design proved to be big improvements.

Wall Omission. The omission of the wall originally planned between the Hall and the Kitchen makes the biggest Kitchen work surface available from the Hall. Meals are served buffet-style from that work surface, a convenience not contemplated in the design. Multiple cooks can more readily work.

Toilet in Tower. Putting a toilet in the Tower makes it a separate bedroom suite, an unexpected benefit.

Figure 21-3   "View/360" house from the southeast

Dining Room. Providing a separate sitting/conversation/ work/game area in the original Dining Room has added to livability. Essentially what was designed as an adjunct to the Kitchen has instead become a second living room. It sometimes serves as a second study, although it is not isolatable.

Master Bedroom. The Master Bedroom provides yet an unexpected third study, set apart, and with views over the marsh.

Accommodates Groups. Although not explicitly designed for groups, the house accommodates weekend groups of up to 25, but *not* beyond, based our on success and failure experiences. Sleeping (including rollaways and floor), feeding, bathroom, and meeting spaces are packed but workable at 25.

Family Size. The house now (barely) accommodates a simultaneous family gathering: our three children, two children-in-law, nine grandchildren, and us—quite a change from the family designed for.

Kitchen. The Kitchen readily accommodates a crew of cooks, but a single cook finds the sink somewhat far from the work surfaces-stove-refrigerator.

Deck. The deck along the west end of the house was a major mistake. It used 42" of the critical budget commodity, namely, the buildable ocean frontage. The deck is rarely used. The space would have been much better used elsewhere.

The late decision to put the major beach-serving showers on the ground floor obviated the need to provide an outside path from the beach to the master bath. Substituting the linen closet for the second interior shower further reduced the need. I should have rethought the deck decision when the shower decision was made.

Master Bedroom. The exterior door to the Master Bedroom is often opened for breeze but rarely for passage. The Master Bedroom occupants have quiet access to the beach through the Kitchen and back door. The Master Bedroom usually gets plenty of breeze via its west windows and its two interior doors. Its meager ocean view doesn't matter much because it was intended as a sleeping space, not a living space. So that door could be eliminated if the deck was.

Main Bathroom.   The outside door to the main bathroom stays open most of the time, ventilating the whole house. If the deck were not there, one would want a Dutch door with the bottom half nailed shut.

Privacy.   The openness of the Living Room, Dining Room, and Kitchen area is a disadvantage with respect to privacy of conversations and makes it hard to find a retreat from the hubbub of a full house. The Tower is visually and socially isolated but cannot be closed off acoustically.

Firmness

The house has resisted direct attack by three hurricanes and miscellaneous other storms.

- 1978 storm. We lost the built-up (tar-impregnated cloth monocoque) roof off the Tower. Wind and the Bernoulli effect lifted it off and deposited it in the backyard.
- 1984 Hurricane Diana. The eye came within 10 miles, and peak local winds were 135 mph, from the south. The wind lifted all the built-up roof except that of the Tower and deposited it as a unit in the backyard. Sixteen inches of rain leaked into the house. The storm blew out all the window glass and window frames in the Tower and blew mattresses, rugs, and lamps out into the marsh.
- 1996 Hurricanes Bertha and Fran. The eyes came within 10 miles. There was no damage except to one shutter and one windowpane.

Radically different loads on the pilings produce different settling rates in the sandy soil.   The design did not take variable settling into account. This is a strange oversight, since every house on pilings in sandy soil must be subject to this problem. The pilings under the two south corners of the Tower bore extra-heavy loads, hence settled more. The pilings under non-load-bearing walls settled less. This was particularly bad under the center of the big double Living Room door. The door track bowed upward in the middle, so that the sliding doors did not close properly. We installed in 1997 a 4" x 6" x 16' subterranean sill bolted to all three of the pilings under the Tower south wall, so future settling will be less, and uniform.

The westernmost row of pilings was put under the edge of the deck, rather than under the west wall holding the ridgepole and the roof weight. The floor joists bent under the unsupported weight. Pilings had to be added under that wall in the 28th year. Clearly this was just a general oversight. Neither Cogswell nor I carefully compared the main-floor plan and the piling plan.

Casement windows were a mistake. The breeze-scooping action worked well as planned. Although the windows were of wood, the crank-out mechanisms were of steel and had to be replaced every five years on the ocean-spray sides of the house, and every 15 years on the lee sides. So at the 35th year, as the old window frames were deteriorating, we replaced most of the casement windows with double-hung.

What factors led to the casement window mistake? Inadequate weighting of maintenance in a long-life project, combined with inadequate attention to all the materials of construction.

If I "Threw One Away"?

Suppose I were designing this house for this site and the 1972 family situation; what would I design differently, based on what I know now? The "Assessment" section above details various lesser miscalculations and mistakes; here are the big ones:

The first big lesson I would apply from the essays (Chapter 10) is to pay even closer attention to the budgeted resource, in this case, inches of ocean frontage. Now understanding that criticality, I would study the details of the side-line setback requirements (as to whether eaves count), and I would design to exploit every available inch, even breaking the square-foot budget.

The second big lesson (Chapter 11) would be to notice that the early addition of the under-house showers to the plan had removed the desideratum/constraint of outside access to the main bathroom. Hence I would remove the west deck and real-locate its 42" of frontage.

General Lessons Learned

The lessons learned here in the small apply generally to every substantial design project, whether hardware, software, or buildings:

1. Check your professional architect's work very carefully, and ask for rationale. Even honest, competent, and conscientious architects make mistakes.
2. Inspect often and thoroughly during construction. Even honest, competent, and conscientious builders make mistakes.
3. Think hard about all aspects of maintenance. One maintains any successful design a long time.

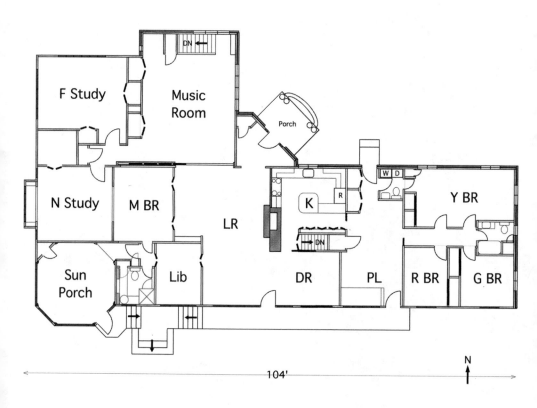

F Study

Music
Room

DN

Porch

N Study

M BR

LR

K

R

W D

Y BR

Sun
Porch

Lib

DN

DR

PL

R BR

G BR

N

104'

22

Case Study: House Wing Addition

In fact, architecture can almost be taken as a prototype for the process of design in a semantically rich task domain.

HERBERT SIMON [1981],
THE SCIENCES OF THE ARTIFICIAL

Plan of house after 1991–1992 wing addition

Highlights and Peculiarities

Why This Case?   For this design, we have some 235 pages of the contemporaneous log of design issues, pros and cons, and decisions made over 60 months. From this log we undertook a formal design-tree documentation, as detailed in Chapter 16. This case illustrates the interplay of design and the discovery of requirements treated in Chapter 3.

Bold Decision.   Defer budget constraints; design for function; then value-engineer. This decision was made halfway through the design process when nothing was working.

Bold Decision.   Move the Master Bedroom to the midst of the public and semipublic spaces. This decision was made late in the design process when a low-frequency use case revealed a hitherto unperceived requirement. This decision seemed at the time to mean essentially abandoning the east end of the house. As the family has subsequently grown, having that "hotel" end has been quite useful.

Key Decision.   Buy a 5' strip of land from the neighbor to solve an intractable design problem. The story is told in Chapter 3.

Phasing.   Undertake the total house remodeling in two phases, to simplify our design and supervision task, as detailed in this chapter and the next one.

Plenty of Design Time.   Design until we were satisfied, unconstrained by any construction schedule goal. In the event, the design happened over some 60 months (with substantial interruptions), whereas construction took only 9.

Introduction and Context

Location:

413 Granville Road, Chapel Hill, NC
The house faces precisely north, so descriptions will be given in N, S, E, W terms.

Owners:

Frederick and Nancy Brooks

Designers:

Frederick and Nancy Brooks
Advised at times by Wesley McClure, FAIA, and Alex Jones, ASID
Construction drawings by another draftsman

Builder:

Additions Plus (Stanley Stutts, contractor; Gary Mason, project master carpenter)

Dates:

Design, 1987–1992
Construction, 1991–1992

Supplementary Web Site:

During the design process, Fred and Nancy kept a detailed log of design issues, problems, thoughts, consultations with friends and professionals, and decisions, some 235 pages. Sharif Razzaque encoded the more significant parts of this as a Compendium graph, showing the decision tree, but not the detailed rationales for each decision. This tree may be consulted on the book's Web site, www.cs.unc.edu/brooks/DesignofDesign.

Context

1964–1965
The original house (Figure 22-1), built in 1960, was acquired in 1964, chosen largely because of the large wooded, creek-bordered lot and convenient location, and in spite of obvious house shortcomings. The most serious single design flaw was the traffic pattern, especially the bottleneck between the Dining Room and the Kitchen, through which all east-west traffic flowed. Moreover, each room in the house was experienced as somewhat too small for its function.

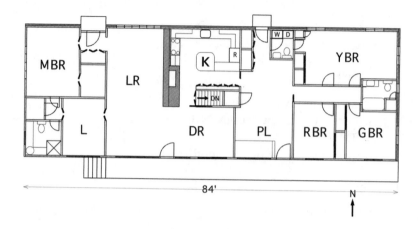

Figure 22-1   Main floor as of 1987

When in 1965 we moved in, we had two sons, aged 7 and 3, and a 6-month-old daughter. To be near the children, we used the Red Bedroom as the Master Bedroom, and the other three east-end bedrooms for the children. The original Master Bedroom, at the west end, was used as a guest suite from 1965 to 1986.

1972
We finished the basement as an apartment and relocated our older son there; the second son joined him later. This enabled us to remove the partition and closets between the two northeast bedrooms, creating one large bedroom, the Yellow Bedroom, for our daughter. The Green Bedroom became Nancy's Study.

1987
Our daughter graduated from college in 1986 and became an Army officer. Our sons were in graduate school or professional practice; one was married, with no children. With our children gone, we had more time for other activities, hence felt a need for more of certain spaces. Nancy Brooks had been teaching violin in the home since the mid-1960s; now she was able to teach more pupils.

Nancy's widowed father, Dr. Joseph Greenwood, had just come to live with us permanently, living in the Master Bedroom (Guest) suite at the west end. Nancy had inherited her parents' grand piano. This supplemented the one we owned, enabling two-piano music.

In various ways, the house was ready for a 30-year update. Fred's Study was in the (ground-level-access) basement apartment, in what had been the sons' quarters. Given our ages, it seemed wise to enable normal indoor living using only the main floor, should that become necessary.

Off and on over previous years we had tried to see how a 500 ft^2 addition might be used to make the house more spacious, ideally by shuffling functions so that each room's function got upgraded in space. These design efforts had been unsuccessful.

So now we began in dead earnest to design an addition.

Objectives

Original Objectives

- Improve the traffic pattern.
- Make more space in almost every room.
- Build a Music Room (MR) large enough to hold two grand pianos, a small organ, and a string octet with a 1' teaching margin around the outside of the octet. The room must also hold music files. This size would get the two grand pianos out of the Living Room, where they were filling the north end and made a narrows for entry from the front door. The Music Room should also accommodate small student recitals with an audience of parents. Ideally, it would have a separate entrance.
- Bring Nancy's Study (NS) from the southeast corner Green Bedroom to make it convenient to the Music Room and to Fred's Study. Enlarge it.
- Get Fred's Study (FS) upstairs to the main floor.
- Provide more function spaces: rooms and/or alcoves.
- Add a front porch (FP) large enough for a porch swing and other seating.
- Provide a screened back porch (this became the Sun Porch, SP).
- Modernize and enlarge the Kitchen (K).

- Enlarge the Dining Room (DR).
- Make the main entrance obvious as one approaches from the driveway (Figure 22-2).
- Improve the esthetics of design, especially outside, perhaps with a more interesting roofline.
- Enhance, or at least don't hurt, the yard and site.
- Preserve trees to the southwest and southeast, flowers to the north.
- Capitalize on the view of the yard and gardens from within the house, especially from the public rooms.

Discovered Objectives

- Better accommodate the biweekly meetings of a student group we advise, about 40 people.
- Accommodate some 40 coats for attendees at recitals and student meetings.
- Provide storage for family goods currently in rental storage.

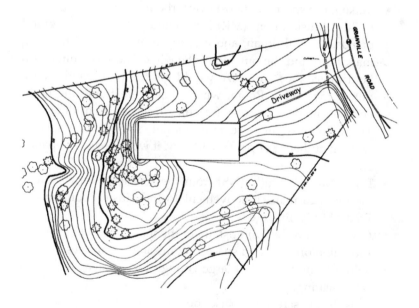

Figure 22-2   North part of house site

Constraints

Existing Structure. The plan, placement, and orientation of the existing structure determined the scope of the remodeling.

Site. The north property line and 15' setback, and the 17' shadow-casting requirements, constrained expansion.

Tree. A large black oak in the upper backyard was a main feature of the lot that we wished to keep.

Lot. The topography falls off fairly steeply to the west, starting at the end of the existing house.

Budget. Our target was $100K, and the expected cost of the addition was $100/ft².

Non-Constraints

Budget. Our target of $100K was not an absolute constraint, as the purchase mortgage had been fully paid.

Resale Value. There was no need to consider whether investment in the addition would increase the resale value. From life expectancies and our plans not to move, we could expect some 30 years to amortize the addition before selling the house, by which time it would be ready for another update anyway.

Acreage. There was plenty of land; the lot has more than 1½ acres.

Time and Effort. We had plenty of design time and willingness to invest lots of design effort.

Events

Several events changed the design as it proceeded:

- Dr. Greenwood died in late 1988.
- The architect's draftsman hired to make construction drawings misaligned the foundations drawing with respect to the

main-floor drawing. This discrepancy was discovered after the foundation was poured. The fix was to enlarge the main floor by 1' to the west and 1' to the north. The chapter frontispiece shows as-built, rather than as-designed.

Design Decisions and Iterations

Explorations

Flip the House End for End.   Redo the interior radically, making the existing bedroom wing into the public rooms—Music Room, Living Room, perhaps Nancy's Study—and fitting the master and guest bedrooms into the old Music Room. **Plusses:** There would be easy main and student entrances, and we could perhaps add studies as an extension to the southeast. **Minuses:** This would be a costly change; we would need more bathrooms at the west end; we would waste the fireplace; and we would separate the Living Room from the Dining Room with all traffic coming through the Kitchen. We abandoned this option quickly.

Southeast Wing.   Build a new Master Bedroom suite out from the southeast of the house, perhaps incorporating the Green Bedroom. We abandoned this idea to preserve the white oak and red oak trees at the southeast of the house, and the access from the driveway to the apartment and the backyard.

McClure's pavilions (Figure 22-3).   **Plusses:** The Music Room (North Pavilion) becomes almost entirely separate, with easy access from the driveway and good acoustic isolation from the house. The Living Room (South Pavilion) has superb views into the garden and yard. The freed-up Living Room converts to an inglenook around the fireplace for reading and conversation. **Minuses:** The South Pavilion would require sacrifice of the magnificent four-trunk black oak. We would not be able to use the living space to enhance the Music Room for recitals.

The South Pavilion was abandoned rather soon, so with it went the redesign of the Living Room to include the attractive inglenook.

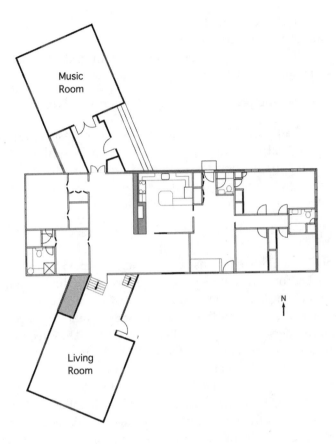

Figure 22-3 McClure's pavilion sketch

The North Pavilion stayed in the main line of design, under-going many shape and configuration explorations and ultimately becoming the north wing, incorporating the Music Room, Fred's Study, Foyer, and Front Porch.

Partitioning the Design Problem

As we proceeded, it became clear that we could partition the house redesign into three almost separate problems:

- Old East: the bedroom end, perhaps including the Playroom

- Center: the Kitchen, the North Hall and its closets, Playroom, Laundry/Toilet, basement stairs
- Old West: the Music Room, Dining Room, and West Bedroom suite, together with the new addition, New West

This partitioning proved liberating; all later design used it.

Phases. Fairly early, we decided to have two design and build phases, several years apart, chiefly to give manageability to the design and supervision tasks. Phase I would be the Old West–New West part; Phase II, the Kitchen and Playroom part. Phase II is treated as a separate case study in Chapter 23.

East End

Various East End redesigns were done, all aimed at giving the Master Bedroom its own shower-toilet and providing a comfortable suite for Dr. Greenwood. Some rather tentative explorations looked at moving the basement stairs to the Red Bedroom or sharing between it and the Playroom. After Dr. Greenwood's death, the requirement for a bedroom/bath suite in addition to the Master Bedroom vanished. As a result, after we moved the Master Bedroom to the West End late in the design process, we abandoned the East End redesign effort and left it as it was.

It serves as the Guest Suite, unheated and uncooled except when there are visitors. Roger's family now has five children; Barbara's has four. A visit from either fills this suite and the basement apartment.

Function Placement within West Half

The most extensive exploration concerned placement of functions in both Old West and New West, which were considered as one allocable space, although existing room walls were implicitly honored in most deliberations.

These explorations occurred before the decision to keep the Master Bedroom in the West End; the old Master Bedroom was assumed to be part of the allocable space. So all the early deliberations concerned only where to put the Music Room, the Living Room, the Dining Room, Library, Nancy's Study, and Fred's Study. The plan in the chapter frontispiece is misleading at this stage.

Having ruled out extension to the south, we considered additions to the north, to the west, and in both directions. Function allocations considered were

- Music Room west and Living Room north
- Music Room north and Living Room west

Change of Approach: Forget the Budget as a Design Constraint

As these explorations proceeded, it became evident that the budgetary constraint, translated into 1,000 ft², was inhibiting our thinking. So we decided to design to meet the objectives, then later cost-engineer and/or decide to spend more money if it then seemed worth it. This radically freed up our thinking.

I have for some years advocated this approach to the design of computer graphics systems. In that domain, I had discovered that the best way to make a cost-effective application system is to make an effective one, then cost-reduce it, rather than making a cheap one and augmenting it until it is useful. It took me too long to come to this same approach on the house.

Newly Discovered Requirement: Where to Put the Coats?

In November 1990, we were checking a tentative design by running various (extemporaneous and undocumented) use cases against it. We did this in more detail than we had earlier, because the design was more congealed. We ran the biweekly scenario of a dinner meeting of the 30- to 40-person student group for which we are faculty advisers and hosts.

As the guests enter in winter, they place their coats somewhere. Where? The Foyer coat closet clearly wouldn't hold them. On the music instruments? All over our Studies? Where do they put them now? On the bed in the Guest Room, adjacent to the Living Room. Oh—that room is gone in this design.

One solution would be to enlarge the coat closet, quite substantially. Another would be to keep the Guest Room in the West End, move into it as the Master Bedroom, and quit redesigning the East End. The gross cost: making the westward extension larger, by at least the present width of the Guest Room. The net cost: gross cost less the East End costs not undertaken.

Problem.   If there is a westward extension beyond the Master Bedroom, it must be integrated with it to meet code requirements for sleeping spaces; there can't be a closable door between the bedroom and windows.

Corollary 1.   If we put Nancy's Study as the westward extension, that integration is not problematic. No other room could go there. (Fred often studies while Nancy sleeps, but not vice versa, so his study can't go there.)

Corollary 2.   If the Music Room isn't to be in the west extension, it should be in the north one. This keeps it isolated from the main living quarters and makes it convenient for access from the driveway.

Convergence of Function Placement

Things then rather rapidly fell into place.

Living Room.   In order to meet the recital requirement, it would be desirable to integrate the Living Room and the Music Room sometimes, but not most of the time. This was solved by a 12' sliding door (four panels), moving into a new pocket on the outside of the north wall of the Master Bedroom.

The Living Room enlargement was accomplished by absorbing the original Foyer, the original Foyer coat closet, and the original Guest Room closet—all to be replaced in the new wing. Of course, moving the two grand pianos out to the Music Room made an immense difference in the Living Room's effective size.

Fred's Study.   The logical place for this now became a filling-in of the corner between the north wing and the west one. This was done with space for a new Master Bedroom closet off Nancy's Study and other closets. The North Hall also accommodates the copier, centrally adjacent to the Music Room, Nancy's Study, and Fred's Study.

Sun Porch.   The desired south porch nicely fits into the southwest corner of the New West wing. Originally we envisioned it as a ground-level porch. When we saw how the necessary steps down from the main floor would eat into its space, we kept it on the main-floor level. Likewise, use-case checking led us to glass it in, with many operable windows, rather than screening it. An outdoor porch would be underutilized—too cold in winter; too hot in summer.

Front Porch. The Front Porch went through several iterations; originally it covered the whole east face of the north wing. In the event, we kept the original diagonal orientation of McClure's North Pavilion, facing out directly toward the approach to the house from the driveway. It was made big enough to accommodate two facing porch swings, which has created an unexpectedly useful conversation site.

The porch gable created by the 45° orientation solved two problems. First, it provides an obvious entrance for the house. Second, it neatly smooths over the joint between the old house's 8' ceilings and the new wing's 9' ceilings and their corresponding eave lines (Figure 22-4).

Figure 22-4   View of the remodeled house from a northeast approach

Basement Storage. A late-discovered opportunity was the possibility of putting cheap storage space under the west wing, because the terrain falls off so rapidly. Modest excavation and low-cost finishing yielded a 530 ft² closed-in storage area under the Music Room, a small workshop, and space for the new wing's mechanicals. This enabled us to give up remote storage we had been renting, with more convenient access.

The Property-Line Setback Constraint. Chapter 3 tells the story of the most interesting single design problem and decision. The Music Room objectives were quite specific and constrained it to be rather squarish. This and any reasonable configuration of Fred's Study conflicted with the 17' shadow-casting setback requirement of the Town of Chapel Hill. Extensive design iterations couldn't solve the problem. We finally bought a 5' strip of land from our neighbor.

Dining Room. A simple extension of the Dining Room to the south was designed. This would put the long side of the room north-south instead of east-west. It required a roof gable, as well as some awkwardness in the deck along the south side of the house. After cost estimation, we gave it up, purely as part of our cost engineering.

Changes during Construction

Fred's Study Windows. As designed, the west windows in Fred's Study were 4' tall, starting 3' from the floor. During framing it became evident that the westward-falling terrain meant that the view from those windows would be just treetops. So the windows were changed to 6' tall, starting 1' from the floor. This did indeed improve the view and the feel of the room.

This is the sort of problem that plans and elevations would never reveal, but that a virtual-environment simulation would have shown during design.

Organ Niche Window. Son Ken Brooks suggested putting a narrow window behind the bench of the new organ. This provides light to the Music Room from a third side.[1]

Assessment—Successes and Unresolved Drawbacks

Some 17 years have elapsed since the completion of the Phase I project, 14 years since Phase II, the Kitchen-Playroom redesign.

We have no "Wish we had done that differently" list. The unusually long design effort, with close attention to detail, paid off in livability, function, and delight. Of course, not all ideals are achievable, given the constraints.

Kitchen–Living Room Door. Cutting the door from the Kitchen into the Living Room had the most dramatic effect. This radically eased the traffic pattern of the house and gave end-to-end visibility.

Master Bedroom. The plan is indeed somewhat weird in having the Master Bedroom surrounded by other functions. The design depends upon resale value not being a consideration. Few families would need the big Music Room, Fred's Study, and Nancy's Study.

Music Room. This space works well for lessons and individual practice, because it can be closed off. It accommodates a big organ very well. It works for recitals and an annual workshop because of the wide opening into the Living Room. But it has no separate access. Students put shoes and instruments in the Playroom, then trek through the Kitchen and Living Room.

Living Room. Getting the pianos out makes it a new room. The enlargement via closet incorporation is welcome. But the greater breadth would have worked better with a higher ceiling.

Photo and video projection is awkward. There is no good place to put the screen.

Dining Room. This room is still cramped. The table can be extended into the Living Room, and auxiliary tables set up there, so the house can feed a lot of seated people.

Front Porch. The two facing swings make a separate conversation nook that is often used. The main entrance is now evident; the appearance, much improved.

New Functions

The redesigned house turned out to meet needs that we didn't know we had. As noted in previous chapters, this is usually, not exceptionally, the case for products.

Sun Porch as Meeting Venue.   The Sun Porch has turned out to be a very suitable room for meetings of up to a dozen people. A new Christian school was founded there and held its board meetings there for some years.

Music Room as a Living Room Extension for Meetings.   An initial requirement was that the Living Room serve as a Music Room extension for musical recitals. It works well for that. Students and their parents, about 25 people, sit in rows of chairs that start in the Music Room and extend back into the Living Room.

The converse has unexpectedly turned out to be true. Meetings of the graduate InterVarsity Christian Fellowship normally run 30 to 40 people but have occasionally attracted over 50. These meetings focus on speakers by the Living Room fireplace, and the Music Room accommodates seating for the outer rows.

Deck, Steps, and Yard as Meeting, Eating Area.   The deck along the south exterior wall was brought down to the upper backyard with broad steps and equipped with a fold-down table. This has proved to be a good outdoor eating and meeting space for the IVCF chapter. The steps provide a lot of seating.

General Lessons Learned

1. Spend time on design. We spent much more time per square foot than might have been cost-effective if the designer time were part of product price. The same thing is doubtless true of much of Linux. On Operating System/360, we would have benefited greatly from more design time before implementation got under way. I do not think the product would have cost more in total.
2. Talk many times, lengthily, with the principal user(s), showing prototypes they can understand.

3. Run lots of use scenarios.
4. Double-check the work of professionals, such as architects, draftsmen, and decorators. Make sure you understand it, and that it's accurate.

Notes and References

1. Alexander [1977], *A Pattern Language*, advocates ensuring that each room is daylighted from at least two sides, preferably more. We followed this scrupulously, putting a skylight in Nancy's Study and Fred's Study (but carefully not in the Master Bedroom), and a window in the interior wall between Nancy's Study and the Sun Porch. Thus, each of the new rooms has some daylight from three sides.

23
Case Study: Kitchen Remodeling

If you can't stand the heat,
get out of the kitchen.

HARRY S. TRUMAN

Virtual-environment model of remodeled kitchen

Effective Virtual Environments Research Project,
University of North Carolina at Chapel Hill

Highlights and Peculiarities

Why This Case?   This simple case illustrates the power of design tools. Drawings, computer-assisted design (CAD) software, scale models, full-scale mock-ups, and a virtual-environment (VE) walk-through each benefited the design. The VE and the mock-up each added value that the other did not.

Bold Decision: Move the exterior wall. This change transformed the design.

Bold Decision: Cut a door between the Kitchen and the Living Room. Creating this door transformed all house traffic.

Skylights.   Two skylights transformed the dark, north-facing kitchen into a bright, pleasant space.

Introduction and Context

Location:

413 Granville Road, Chapel Hill, NC

Owners:

Frederick and Nancy Brooks

Designers:

Frederick and Nancy Brooks

Advised by Mary June Magó and Alex Jones, ASID

Dates:

1995–1996

Context

This design was Phase II of a 1990s remodeling of a 1960s house. Phase I consisted of the addition of a West Wing, a Foyer, and a Porch. It is described in Chapter 22. Phase II was scheduled a few years later than Phase I to enable ample design time for Phase II and plenty of oversight for Phase I construction.

Objectives

Primary Goals. Our principal objectives were to enlarge, re-arrange, and brighten a small, dark, north-facing kitchen–breakfast room.

Other Objectives.   In decreasing order of importance:

- Improve the traffic pattern for the house, in which all traffic between halves passed through the narrows by the basement stairs. We also needed to accommodate violin student traffic coming in the back door, emptying their cases, storing the cases in the Playroom, moving to the Music Room, and back.
- Move the kitchen table to the garden window for view.
- Arrange the spaces so the cook can talk with a seated non-working visitor.
- Make the kitchen convenient for each of
  - One cook preparing breakfast
  - One (short) cook doing general cooking, baking, and canning
  - Multiple (up to three) cooks preparing a big meal
- Conveniently serve, via buffet, groups of 30 to 40 students.
- Add substantially more counter space.
- Install a bigger sink.
- Design a walk-in pantry.
- Keep the exterior appearance pleasing.
- Brighten the "back" entrance to the house, which is the principal entrance for family, students, and often for informal guests.
- Subordinate the back door in the exterior façade.
- Add a decorative bird mural to the dull brick chimney wall.
- Conceal miscellany in cabinets.
- Display a small amount of glassware.

Opportunities

Smaller Family. The family had shrunk, due to the children growing up. So normal kitchen-eaten meals would be for two, occasionally three, exceptionally four, rather than routinely five.

Space Available in the Playroom. Due to the 1992 construction of a music-teaching studio in the new West Wing, a 5' x 5' space formerly occupied by an organ became available, as well as a 2' x 6' space formerly occupied by hi-fi equipment.

Three-Foot Eaves. Due to Frank Lloyd Wright's inspiration of 1960s ranch-style houses, this house had deep eaves.

Design Time and Effort Budget. These were essentially unlimited.

Constraints

User Height. The primary user of the kitchen is 5'1" tall.

Construction Budget. The budget was not cramped, but did not admit of major structural changes.

Exterior of House. The exterior of the house was finally made attractive by the 1991 addition (Chapter 22), which we didn't want to mess up.

Existing Kitchen. The size and shape of the existing kitchen (Figure 23-1) would determine the shape of the new one.

Brick Chimney Wall. This wall was 8" thick and constrained the traffic pattern.

Basement Steps. These could not be relocated.

Playroom Exterior Door. The function of this door was essential, but the placement was movable.

Back Door. Placement in the brick wall made moving it expensive.

Existing Laundry/Toilet. This room did not need to be changed.

Pantry. We needed to preserve the pantry's function and capacity, but not its placement.

Closets. The North Hall closets' functions and sizes had to be retained, but not their placement. This is an interesting example of the importance of probing existing use scenarios closely. The requirement could not readily have been inferred from a wealth of precedent kitchen designs. The strength of this requirement comes from the fact that we had followed particular use scenarios for 30 years and would suffer a high "chaos cost" if the closet contents were severally dispersed all over the house.

Structural Considerations. The structural vertical members in the basement staircase wall supported the roof.

Rest of House in Use. Other rooms would be in constant use during construction.

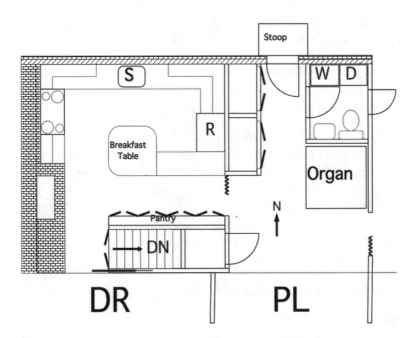

Figure 23-1   Kitchen plan before remodeling

Rationing the Critical Width Budget

Needed Width North to South

In all the early attempts to find a workable design, the width proved to be the stumbling block. Consider the objectives of

- An eating area by the window
- A sink where one could see out the window
- A sink where one could visit with people at the eating area
- Easy east-to-west traffic through the kitchen
- Enough counter/cabinet space
- A short stove-sink-refrigerator triangle

Tentative Design

This suggests an island with a sink, facing the window and eating area. Putting a counter with the stove against the south wall seems necessary.

Now the width at the tightest pinch point must be rationed among, from north to south:

- Eating table (not less than 30")
- Passage for traffic (not less than 24")
- Sink island (not less than 24")
- Walk/work space between sink and stove (originally estimated at not less than 36")
- Stove and counter (not less than 27")

This is a total of not less than 12'3". The original width was 12'.

The objective of seating up to four at the table occasionally can be satisfied by having the visitors sit in the passage, effectively blocking it. This is acceptable, since only occasional.

Mock-up studies, however, showed that the sink-stove space really needed 44", rather than 36", because of swing-out/pull-out cabinets, stove doors, and dishwasher pull-out. So the total width needed was not less than 12'11".

Alternative Width Solutions

Eliminate the Traffic Passage. A rejected design would have eliminated the passage and routed east-to-west traffic between the sink and stove, utterly interfering with cooking. Rejecting it meant the needed width was ≥12'11". This suggests

- Taking over the pantry and basement stairs' space, moving them elsewhere, or
- A bay window for the eating area, or
- Pushing the whole north wall of the kitchen out as the eaves allow

In either of the latter two cases, one would move the pantry elsewhere to pick up 9".

Move the Basement Stairs?   Extensive studies of moving the stairs elsewhere showed that the only workable alternative would be a spiral staircase tower outside the house, connecting to the Playroom's south exterior door. Other solutions either didn't work with existing or reasonable partitioning upstairs, or with reasonable partitioning in the basement.

The stair tower alternative was pursued for some months. It was finally rejected as expensive and unesthetic, although workable for traffic.

For the design process, concluding that all "move the stairs" alternatives were unworkable or unacceptable was a critical moment, radically narrowing the field of possible designs. This subdesign was a good example of Simon's "search the tree" process, as I explored multiple instances of the "spiral stair" design and, when none worked, went up a level on the design tree and ruled out moving the stairs at all.

Bay window or push the whole north wall outward?   Exterior mock-up studies showed that pushing the whole kitchen wall out northward would look much better than a bay window, and costs appeared roughly comparable. So that alternative was selected. The same mock-up studies showed that push-outs of 18" to 24" worked esthetically, given the 36" eaves.

Resulting Width Design

With an extra 24" from push-out and 9" from moving the pantry, the width constraint was greatly relaxed. The island was widened from 24" to 36" to provide serving, staging, and storage space. The north passage was widened to 39"; the south passage, to 44".

Rationing the Length Budget

The Length Pinch. The south wall became the length pinch. It had to accommodate the 48" stove, a work counter to its right, and a work counter to its left. The west work area was chosen as the breakfast-cooking corner, so it had to accommodate a microwave oven and a toaster, for a total of not less than 36".

The east work counter is the major general cooking and baking area, with access to dry ingredients, spices, mixers, and other cooking needs. Mock-up studies showed that a 48" counter length would be desirable.

Design. The south wall was lengthened eastward by 18", increasing the separation of Kitchen and Playroom into two rooms. Mock-up studies with the new Pantry in place showed that the 5' (diagonal) opening would suffice and yield a good visual effect.

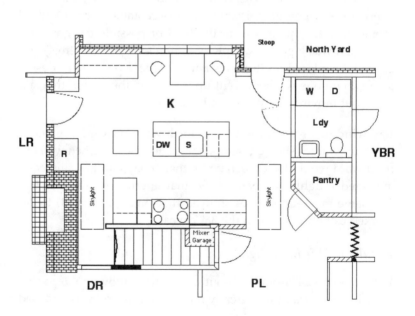

Figure 23-2   Kitchen plan after remodeling

Other Design Decisions

Doors. Should we cut a door from the Living Room to the Kitchen? Yes, even though it meant cutting through 8" of brick wall, hence was expensive. The house traffic pattern demanded it. From the Dining Room to the Playroom? No, the wall space in each room was more valuable.

Closets. Another decision was where to move the North Hall closets. We decided to move them to the Playroom east wall.

Pantry Shelves. We moved the pantry shelves (originally on the south wall) to a new Pantry built out from the Playroom north wall, into the space vacated by moving the organ elsewhere.

Configuration of the Kitchen-Playroom Opening. Positioning the Pantry door diagonally increased the visual opening.

Traffic. The south passage is for cooks only; the north passage is for visitors and all east-west house traffic.

Cabinets. Hanging cabinets over the sink island was an option, but a virtual-environment walk-through showed these to interfere with the visual space of the room.

Perimeter of the Sink-Stove-Refrigerator Triangle. The Small Homes Council recommends that the triangle joining these three workstations have a maximum perimeter of 26'. Our final design yields a 24' perimeter.

Storage for Plates, Glasses. Putting these items in drawers worked better than cabinet storage for the shorter user.

Rolling Auxiliary Island. The 26" x 26" island with a 12" flip-up extension provides storage for silver, glasses, and implements. It also provides staging for the refrigerator and an optional extension to the main island for buffet service.

Low East Work Counter. The east work counter was made low for the convenience of the shorter user. It also enables a tall-appliance garage.

Appliance Garage. This space is embedded in the adjacent closet through the south wall.

Lighting

Skylights. Two skylights, 2' x 4', were placed at the ends of the island and over the darker south part of the room. This design decision was suggested by Alexander's pattern of "Every room should have daylight on two, or preferably three, sides."[1]

Back Door. We replaced the solid back door with a glass one.

Windows. We installed new kitchen windows to fit the entire breakfast nook.

Artificial Lighting. Seven circuits yield different configurations for uses, moods, and traffic pattern emphasis.

Color Scheme. Off-white aids brightness and allows accent colors. We kept the old paneling in the Playroom and east Kitchen wall and covered the brick chimney with white drywall.

Assessment

Size. The 2'9" width enlargement by the push-out and the Pantry move changed working space and traffic space. Moving the closets lengthened the visual space by 2'3". The square footage in the Kitchen increased by almost 54 ft^2.

Traffic. The costly door to the Living Room radically transformed the whole house. Almost all east-west traffic goes through the new door. From the Kitchen one can see out the east windows in the Yellow Bedroom and the west windows in Nancy's Study.

Brightness. Skylights, glass, the off-white color scheme, and lighting transformed the room's feel.

Effect on Playroom.   The Playroom became noticeably narrower because of the closets, but it still proves quite adequate for

- Music student staging and instrument cases
- Music student siblings playing during lessons
- Grandchildren playing

South Door.   The path to the south exterior door is somewhat cramped.

Other Desiderata Satisfied.

- The eating area works well as a guest area. There is also an entrancing view of the bird feeder.
- The breakfast-cooking corner is convenient—standing in one place, one can reach the microwave, electric frying pan, toaster, drawer, stove, and dishes.
- Multiple cooks can work comfortably.
- The new Kitchen works well for group buffet feeding:
  - Traffic enters through the Dining Room and leaves through the Living Room.
  - People take serve-yourself silver from the southwest counter drawer.
  - Trays, plates, and supplies are stored in the southwest counter cabinet.
- The new Pantry is much more capacious and convenient.
- The exterior appearance was not hurt.

Use of Drawings, CAD, Models, Mock-ups, and Virtual Environment in the Design

Much effort was put into the design because

- Kitchen satisfaction accounts for much of the total satisfaction with a house.
- Kitchens are intensively used.

- This remodeling project was tightly constrained by the existing structure and its traffic pattern, creating difficult design problems.
- The designers had no limitation on the design effort budget.

The design turned out to use a full range of design tools.

Drawings and CAD. Most design was done with sketches, then rationalized into coherence and consistency with the existing structure, using the MiniCad architectural CAD system on a Macintosh. The MiniCad file served as the design document.

Most CAD work was done at 1/4" = 1' (1:48) scale, but the CAD system and a two-page monitor made it easy to do detailing at on-screen scales up to 1:6. Scales 1/2" = 1' and 1" = 1' were often used.

The CAD design was layered, with layers for original kitchen, removed construction, added construction, and appliances and furniture.

Design Log. The rationale behind substantial design decisions and the wanderings in arriving at them were contemporaneously captured in a design log. Edited sample pages are shown on the Web page for this book.

Isometric Drawing Kit. We also used a kitchen design kit that provided a set of isometric grids and a set of isometric drawings of appliances, cabinets, counters made to the proper scale and printed on electrostatically active plastic. It was easy to use, fast, and produced good results. The chief limitations were the set of furnishings provided and monochromaticity.

Models. Nancy made from 1/2" = 1' drawings a set of simple cardboard models to get a feeling for the 3-D geometry. These models proved to be substantially richer than the isometric drawings: they enabled one to view the interior of the kitchen from any angle, even though in miniature.

Mock-ups. Full-scale mock-ups were used to test the most critical design decisions. These proved invaluable.

The pushed-out exterior wall was mocked up with cardboard mattress boxes for prediction of external appearance. Interior counter arrangements were mocked up with tables, cardboard, and sawhorses, in a large interior space in another building. Then kitchen scenarios were carried out with various inter-unit spacings. This proved to be a very effective way to establish both the minimum tolerable spacings and the amount of ease effected by measured relaxations of those spaces.

This mirrored a previous experience I had on a church building committee. We ended up mocking up the church kitchen's spacings. It proved the only satisfactory way to determine them.

Virtual-Environment Visualization.   Because my UNC research team was developing a virtual-environment laboratory, Nancy and I tested the lab by testing our proposed kitchen design using it. The chapter frontispiece shows one of the views produced in the head-mounted display as the viewer walked about in the virtual kitchen. Our tracking technology allowed free walking movement over a 15' x 18' space, which encompassed almost the whole kitchen.

The illusion of presence during a 20- to 40-minute kitchen design session was very strong—one forgot the VE apparatus and concentrated on the kitchen.

VE Findings

- The most important finding of the VE sessions was that the hanging cabinets flanking the sink broke up the visual space and made the kitchen feel small and cramped. So we redesigned to remove those cabinets and still keep the required amount of shelf space.
- A hanging lamp at the breakfast-cooking corner was intrusive and needed to be replaced with a recessed ceiling fixture.
- The VE experience confirmed the desirability of the bird mural planned for the large chimney wall.
- The diagonal arrangement of the hardwood flooring was seen to be effective.
- Other findings showed improvements needed in the VE apparatus and techniques.

General Lessons Learned

1. The kitchen is indeed the most important room in the house. It rewards extensive design work.
2. Fourteen years later we can think of only minor details we would have done differently on this project. This happy outcome is partly due to the fact that as with Linux, the designers are the users, hence the use cases are realistic and representative.

   Another large factor is the time and effort invested in the design. As with the System/360 architecture (Chapter 24), we had plenty of time. Whereas with software, one wants to use extended design time to test prototypes with real users, we used much of it to test pseudo-prototypes—mock-ups and VE models—with extensive use cases.

   I am convinced that most projects need to devote a larger share of the total schedule to design.
3. Very wide consultation with friends yielded crucial good ideas, including the basic configuration.
4. Full-scale mock-ups, together with use scenarios, proved invaluable.
5. Virtual-environment technology provided important information beyond that which floor plans and even mock-ups provided, especially about visual space and the feel of the room.

   As a practical matter, VEs will become cheaper and easier. Mock-ups won't. So, the key question is not "Did VE add value beyond that provided by mock-ups?" but "Do mock-ups deliver key value that isn't subsumed in what VE delivers?"

   Both my experience in designing spaces and scientific results from our VE laboratory say "Yes." Insko found that adding Styrofoam mock-ups that could be felt (even though seen only as model images) to a VE experience significantly improved the sense of presence.[2] Those trained in a VE that included a touchable mock-up as well as a visual image traversed a real maze (blindfolded) significantly faster and with radically fewer errors than those trained in the same VE with only the visual images.

Consequently, I believe mock-ups, exercised by use scenarios, will continue to be worth their substantial effort and cost when one is designing an intensively used space, such as a kitchen, or one that will be widely replicated, such as an office in a multi-office building.

Notes and References

1. Alexander [1977], *A Pattern Language*.

2. Insko [2001], "Passive haptics significantly enhances virtual environments"; Whitton et al. [2005], "Integrating real and virtual objects in virtual environments."

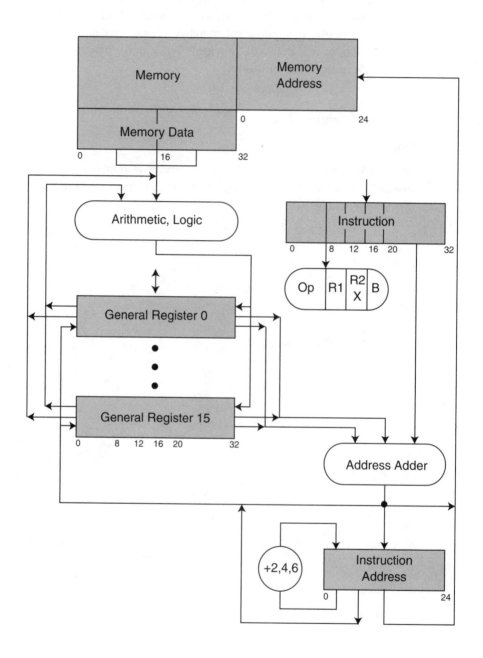

24

Case Study: System/360 Architecture

IBM's $5,000,000,000 gamble

TOM A. WISE [1966], *FORTUNE* MAGAZINE

[The IBM System/360 mainframe and its compatible successors]... was the workhorse of computers for such a long time and continues to be.

GORDON BELL [2008]

Basic programming model of the IBM System/360

Blaauw and Brooks [1997], *Computer Architecture*, Figure 12-78

Highlights and Peculiarities

Boldest Decision. Drop all further development of each of IBM's six existing product lines in favor of one new product line, exposing the existing customer base to competitors' computers compatible with the existing IBM product lines. Needless to say, this decision was made by the CEO, Thomas J. Watson, Jr.

Bold Decision. Make the new six-computer product line strictly upward- and downward-binary-compatible, with exactly one architecture. This initiative came from Donald Spaulding, and Bob O. Evans made it a decision.

Bold Decision. Base the architecture on an 8-bit byte, making obsolete all existing I/O and auxiliary devices, even card punches.

Introduction and Context

Owner:

IBM Corporation

Designers:

Gene Amdahl, Architecture Manager; Gerrit Blaauw, Second Architect and manual author; Richard Case, George Grover, William Harms, Derek Henderson, Paul Herwitz, Graham Jones, Andris Padegs, Anthony Peacock, David Reid, William Stevens, William Wright; Frederick Brooks, Project Manager

Dates:

1961–1964

Context

Few computer architectures have had their rationales so thoroughly discussed as the IBM System/360 product family. The "Notes and References" section gives some of the most important rationale discussions.[1] This case-study essay will therefore hit only the high spots.

In 1960 it was clear that IBM's second-generation (discrete-transistor technology) computer product lines were running out of architectural gas (memory-addressing capacity, principally). IBM's existing mutually incompatible product lines, each with its own software and market support, were

- IBM 650 (first-generation, vacuum tubes) and its incompatible transistorized successor, the 1620
- IBM 1401 and its incompatible successor, the 1410
- IBM 7070-7074
- IBM 702-705-7080
- IBM 701-704-709-7090
- IBM 7030 (Stretch, nine copies, no further marketing)

Of these, the first two, some two-thirds of the total fielded machines, were the responsibility of the General Products Division (GPD); the rest were the responsibility of the Data Systems Division (DSD). The 1410 and the 7070 competed directly with each other, as did the 7080 and the 7074. The several product lines represented quite distinct architectural philosophies and basic decisions.

DSD had started developing, in 1959, a new product line, the "8000 Series," based on second-generation discrete transistor technology, reflecting Stretch architectural philosophy and designed to serve as successor replacements to the 7074, 7080, 7090, and Stretch. The first of these engineering models was running, and four models of the 8000 series had been through "zero-level" cost estimating, market forecasting, and pricing by January 1961. A key component of the market forecast was a new set of applications based on telephonic computer communications.

During the first half of 1961, there was a raging product fight within DSD as to whether to proceed at once with the 8000 Series, as I mistakenly advocated, or to wait three years and design a new product line to be produced with the forthcoming new integrated-circuit technology. The latter plan, championed by Bob O. Evans, won out. The 8000 Series effort was stopped, and in June work started on a new integrated-circuit DSD product line. Evans put me in charge, a totally unexpected action by a very big-minded man.

Meanwhile, corporate technical staffer Donald Spaulding became convinced that IBM needed a unified, corporate-wide new product line, not just a new DSD line that addressed only the upper half of the market. He persuaded Vice President T. V. Learson, who convened a corporate-wide strategy committee, the SPREAD committee, to develop such a plan. The committee was shrewdly put under the leadership of John Haanstra, Engineering VP of GPD, who might have been expected to most vigorously oppose any constraint on GPD autonomy, and whose 1401 product line was proving immensely successful (the first computer to sell more than 10,000 copies). The SPREAD committee produced its report at the end of 1961, and the Corporate Management Committee adopted its recommended New Product Line as the successor for all existing product lines.[2] This stunningly bold move was later called, by *Fortune* magazine, "IBM's $5,000,000,000 gamble."[3] Evans called it "You bet your company." I was appointed Corporate Processor Manager to coordinate all the development activities. Fortunately, besides this staff-type corporate-wide authority, I had line responsibility for the market requirements and architecture efforts for the whole project, and line responsibility for the DSD computer engineering and all the programming efforts. Staff authority is paper signoff authority; line authority has money and people.

The SPREAD report called for six computers to be developed initially, with an ultra-low-cost machine and a super-supercomputer to come within a couple of years. The first six were christened.Models 30, 40, 50, 60, 64, and 70; the later two, Models 20 and 90. Models 20 and 30 would be GPD responsibilities; the others, DSD responsibilities.

Objectives

Primary Goals

- Create a strictly *upward- and downward-binary-compatible* computer architecture.
- The computers must be suitable and competitive for *business data processing*, *scientific engineering computing*, and *telecomputing*.

- Broaden the capabilities for new applications so that IBM would have a steadily growing sales dollar volume, even as cost per computer dropped in half. We could not expect IBM's market share of existing applications to increase substantially, or for those applications' volumes to double quickly.
- Make *each* of the models cost-effective (competitive) in its own market, from the *very low-cost to the fastest supercomputer*.

Other Important Objectives

- Develop a single new total software support, exploiting binary compatibility to enable a single rich system to replace the multitude of incomplete second-generation systems. This must include a new operating system incorporating the fast-developing concepts from second-generation computers' operating systems experience.
- Devise ways to help customers convert to System/360 from their second-generation systems, even as competitors offered compatible successor machines to IBM's discontinued product lines.
- Provide an architecture, sometimes to be implemented in hardened technology, meeting the needs of IBM's Federal Systems Division for both military and government civilian (such as NASA) products.
- Achieve new levels of reliability and maintainability, including ultra-reliable multiprocessor systems.

Opportunities as of June 1961

A New Architecture Necessary. Magnetic-core memories had proved to be quite reliable, and their costs had fallen radically. As a consequence, all customers wanted more memory. Since all the existing product lines had exhausted their addressing capacities, one or more major architectural revisions would be necessary. This gave us the opportunity to apply many lessons learned from first- and second-generation computer uses and users. These lessons were hard to exploit within the old architectures.

New, Cheaper Technology. IBM's technology division was in hot pursuit of integrated circuits and would have an important way-station, called Solid Logic Technology (SLT), ready for volume manufacture in 1964. This promised cost savings of about a factor of two for computers of any given complexity, along with smaller sizes, lower power, and higher reliability. This drastic performance/cost increase promised to be incentive enough for customers to go through the painful and costly process of conversion to a new incompatible system.

Plenty of Design Time. The timing of the new technology meant that for once the system architects would have plenty of time, almost two years, to do a thorough and careful job.

New Kind of I/O Device. Random-access disk technology had progressed rapidly, enabling entirely new data-processing approaches and a radically different approach to operating systems.

New Telecomputing Capability. Computer communications technology, originally developed for air defense, was beginning to be attractive for commercial applications and had been pioneered in airline reservation systems.

Challenges and Constraints

Compatibility—Address Size. By far the greatest technical challenge was the achieving of strict (binary) upward and downward compatibility, while enabling each level of computer to compete in its own market against rifle-shot competitors. How to keep the smallest machine low-cost, without thereby overly constraining the supercomputer? How to enable the supercomputer to be super-fast without burdening the low-cost one? The principal problem was address size. The top of the line needed lots of address bits; could the bottom of the line (serially implemented) afford the memory bit investment and the performance hit of fetching lots of empty address bytes?

Compatibility—Operation Set. How to provide complex operations such as floating-point for scientific applications and character-string operations for business data without com-promising the cost objectives of the machines?

Broader Application Scope. A third major challenge was achieving the total systems diversity needed for new applications (especially communications and remote terminals), for compute-intensive systems, and for data-processing-intensive systems.

Conversion from Existing Systems. Conversion from second-generation systems was a nightmare that we didn't spend much effort thinking about during the first year of the design.

Most Significant Design Decisions

8-Bit Byte. The byte is 8 bits rather than the 6-bit byte that had characterized all first- and second-generation computers (except Stretch). This was the biggest and most hotly debated decision. It has many ramifications: floating-point precision argued for 48-bit words and 96-bit double words, hence 6-bit bytes. An instruction length of 24 bits was too small; 48, too large. What would be the demand for the lowercase alphabet, almost unknown in earlier computers?

The future application promise of the lowercase alphabet was convincing to me. We settled on 8-bit bytes, 32-bit data words and single-address instructions, and 32- and 64-bit floating-point words.

Failed Stack Architecture. We started with a stack architecture as an attack on the address-length problem. After pursuing this for six months, we found it worked fine for mid-range and up, but killed performance at the bottom of the line, where the stack had to be implemented in main memory, rather than in registers.

Design Competition. After the stack architecture failed, Amdahl proposed that we have an internal design competition. His idea worked brilliantly—Amdahl's team and Blaauw's team each independently came up with a base-register solution to the address-size problem. So we adopted that.

24-Bit Addresses. We reluctantly settled on this size, with addressing to the byte. We knew, and I publicly predicted in 1965, that we would at some point in the life of the architecture have to go to 32 bits, but we couldn't afford it for 1964 implementations.[4] Various wise provisions were made for that future jump, but unfortunately, the Branch and Link subroutine call instruction was inadvertently designed to use the upper 8 bits of address that should have been left untouched.

This is a clear example of the danger of team designs. I had failed to indoctrinate the whole team strongly enough with our vision for future expansion, and none of the reviews caught this mistake.

Standard I/O Interface. To enable a wide diversity of specialized application systems, we designed a standard logical, electrical, and mechanical interface for the attachment of all I/O devices, as Buchholz had first done on Stretch. This radically reduced configuration and software costs and simplified engineering development of I/O devices and control units.

Supervisory Control Provisions. A carefully thought-out set of supervisory capabilities was designed, so the systems could be controlled by an operating system without manual intervention. These included an interruption system, memory protection, a privileged instruction mode, and a timer.

Single-Error Detection. Complete end-to-end single-error detection was mandated for all S/360 implementations, in spite of no evident customer desire to pay for such. This substantially helped in achieving the stiff reliability and maintainability goals.

Commercial data-processing computers from all manufacturers had from the initial UNIVAC incorporated extensive checking. Scientific computers, from the initial Burks, Goldstine, and von Neumann paper, had not. This seems inverted; surely a hardware error in calculating an atomic explosion matters more than one in a utility bill. I think the difference is that the scientific community routinely incorporated global checks such as energy conservation in their programs.

We had observed that people were by 1961 *trusting* the answers from their computers, so as a matter of professional responsibility we incorporated the hardware checking and hoped the extra cost would not kill the market.

Decimal Arithmetic. In order to simplify conversion and user training for the huge data-processing market, we decided to incorporate decimal arithmetic as well as binary arithmetic. (All addressing was binary, in contrast to earlier 650, 1401, 1410, 7070, 7074, and 7080 systems.)

Providing a decimal datatype was probably a mistake; we should have instead seen to it that COBOL and other languages handled that problem by keeping money amounts in integral pennies, so there would be no fractional conversion error. How much omitting the decimal datatype would have hurt marketing, one can only speculate. The hardware cost was not substantial; the software cost and the added conceptual complexity were.

Multiprocessing. Provisions were made for multiple processors to be configured into a single system, with system control operating on whichever one was not failing.

Microprogrammed Implementation. We mandated, in the SPREAD report, microprogrammed implementation unless a particular engineering manager could show a 33 percent performance/cost advantage for conventional logic. This enabled the lower-end processors to include the fairly rich uniform operation set with the only cost being a little more control memory. Models 60 and 64 started development with conventional logic and switched during development to a single Model 65, with a microprogrammed implementation. Models 75 and 91 used conventional logic.

Emulation of Earlier Architectures. Stewart Tucker saw that the 32-bit-4-parity-bit memory and datapath word of the Model 65 implementation could gracefully accommodate the 36-bit-no-parity word of the 7090. He invented a microcoded 7090 emulator that used the Model 65 datapaths quite effectively. This breakthrough proved to be a major solution to the conversion problem for 7090, 7074, and 7080 customers.[5]

At a crucial point in January 1964, William Harms, Gerald Ottoway, and William Wright devised almost overnight a microprogrammed emulation of the 1401 on the Model 30. This mightily addressed the biggest single customer conversion problem.

No Virtual Memory.   During S/360 architecture definition, *virtual memory* was invented on the Cambridge Atlas, and operating systems using it were developed at Cambridge, MIT, and Michigan. We debated long and hard about whether to switch our design over. We decided not to, for performance reasons. This was a mistake, which was rectified in the first successor generation, System/370.

New Random-Access I/O Devices.   The project spent a lot of development effort on a new drum for operating system residence and new disk files. We saw this as fundamental for new applications and for diversity of system configurations. Similarly, new single-line and multiline communications controllers were developed.

Input-Output Channels.   I/O was handled by independently operating channels, essentially specialized stored-program units, some optimized for rapid block transfer and some for multiplexing up to 256 communication lines.

Milestone Events

Summer 1961.   Work starts in DSD on the architecture of the new product line. Amdahl, Boehm, and Cocke from IBM Research join Blaauw's architecture team from the 8000 series. Work begins on the stack approach.

January 1962.   A corporate-wide effort is organized.

Spring 1962.   The first performance evaluations show the stack architecture to be noncompetitive. A design competition leads to base-register addressing.

Summer 1962.   The byte-size debate is settled.

Fall 1962.   A first draft of the architecture manual is produced.

Fall 1963.   The architecture manual is frozen.

January 1964. There is a major product fight between S/360 Model 30 and GPD's 1401S, a six-times-faster 1401 successor pushed by Haanstra, now Division President of GPD. S/360 won by the invention of 1401 emulation on Model 30.

April 1964. The announcement is made of Models 30, 40, 50, 65, and 75, with a hint that Model 90 is coming.

February 1965. The first S/360 is shipped (Model 40).

August 1972. System/370 virtual memory is announced.

Early 1980. System/370 XA 31-bit architecture is announced.

2000. z-Series 64-bit architecture is announced.[6]

Assessment

Firmness

One definition of *firmness* for a computer architecture would be "durability." I predicted that the architecture would endure in various implementations for 25 years, with modifications to provide larger addresses.[4] It is now 45 years since the S/360 announcement, and the architecture endures as progressively augmented. One recent implementation is the IBM z/90, announced in March 2007. It is still backward-compatible; S/360 programs will still run. These so-called *mainframes* continue to do a large portion of the world's database work, running a descendant of MVS/360, VM/360, or, increasingly, Linux as the operating system.

Another definition of *firmness* would be "impact on the field." Gordon Bell, himself a great computer architect for DEC, recently identified the System/360 as the most influential computer in history, referring to intellectual influence, not market presence, where the PC would win handily.[7] The S/360's switch to the 8-bit byte changed computer architecture completely and permanently. Its heavy emphasis on disk-based input-output configurations also changed system design radically.[8]

Gene Amdahl licensed S/360 architecture and implemented it exactly in the highly successful Amdahl Corporation computer family. RCA licensed the architecture and used it in its Spectra 70 family. Although RCA faithfully implemented all the architecture affecting Problem Mode, its architects chose to do an idiosyncratic version of the Supervisory Mode architecture. RCA's version was licensed and extensively used by Siemens, Fujitsu, and Hitachi and was copied by the Soviets.

S/360 architecture clearly influenced DEC's VAX family and the PDP-11 computer family and its numerous microcomputer descendants such as the Motorola 6800, 68000.

Usefulness—Competitiveness, Market by Market

Commercially, the System/360 gamble was a big success. IBM annual reports show an average annual growth in revenue of 21 percent from 1964 to 1968, and an average growth of 20 percent in profit from 1964 to 1968.

Some 144 new products were announced on April 7, 1964. Many of these were various memory options. Most, however, were a stunning array of 8-bit input-output devices: multiple printers, some with variable character sets; multiple disks, some with replaceable cartridges; new tape systems; a spectrum of communications terminals and network devices; new card punches, readers, and printers; and miscellaneous devices such as check sorters and factory-data-input terminals. The richness of this collection, developed in many far-flung laboratories, enabled a near-infinite variety and scale of system configurations. The standard I/O interface and its software support meant that configuration growth and change were easy. CPU compatibility meant that the machine at the center of a configuration was often upgraded to a different model over a weekend, without changing the I/O configuration *or the software.*

All the models did well in their respective markets. The Model 30, with its disks and printer, was an instant success. The upward-compatible Model 20 did very well when it appeared soon after.

The Model 65 was a major success in applications previously performed on 7090, 7094, 7094 II, 7080, 7074, and other models. The new database techniques were well served by this model, and it and its descendant models dominated the field. It also did very well as the engineering computing workhorse. The serious competitors were mostly themselves computers with S/360 architecture, the so-called plug compatibles, usually running OS/360 software.

Models 75, 91, and others in that family were designed as scientific supercomputers. They split that market pretty evenly with the contemporary CDC and Cray machines, but the Cray descendants came to dominate it. Four Model 75s provided the ground-based computing for the *Apollo* program; hardened derivatives of System/360 served as the on-board computers.

Delight

The original architecture was rather clean, as was the careful conceptual separation of architecture, implementation, and technological realization.[9] The requirement of strict upward and downward compatibility imposed a strict discipline that protected the low end from functional deficiency and the high end from excess. (Similarly, any writer learns that a strict page limit often yields cleaner and more effective writing.) Blaauw left well-placed spaces in the operation-code list for future additions. And additions there certainly have been, with the result that the operation-code set is no longer as orderly as it was.

Our biggest mistake technically was the failure to adopt virtual memory at the outset. This was a case of expert designers going wrong in a big way (Chapter 14).

Our biggest mistake esthetically and conceptually was our failure to recognize that an I/O channel was just another computer. Cray's peripheral processors, introduced on the CDC 6600, are a superb embodiment of an elegant and powerful concept. Each of many concurrent I/O flows is controlled by an architecturally separate simple small binary computer, all implemented with one time-shared dataflow.

The ugliest thing in the original CPU architecture was the SS instruction format, which provided a base register but not a separate index register, as did all the other formats. As remarked above, Branch and Link uses high-order address bits that should have been reserved for the expansion to 32-bit addresses. Load Address cleared those same high-order bits.

A smaller mistake is that we initially failed to provide a guard digit in the definition of floating-point operations. We had to field-modify the first S/360 computers after delivery.

Perhaps the most telling esthetic critique of our effort would be a jeer that the S/360 was really three architectures under one cover: the basic 32-bit binary machine, the 64-bit floating-point machine with a different dataflow, and the byte-by-byte processor, with a quite different dataflow and even decimal arithmetic (chapter frontispiece, Figure 24-1, and Figure 24-2). In fact, when one adds selector channels and multiplex channels, there are really five architectures present. Microcoded implementations make it all work.

What was achieved by these multiple concurrent architectures was a truly general-purpose computer family, adaptable by suitable processor, memory, and especially I/O configurations, to all kinds of applications and performance needs.

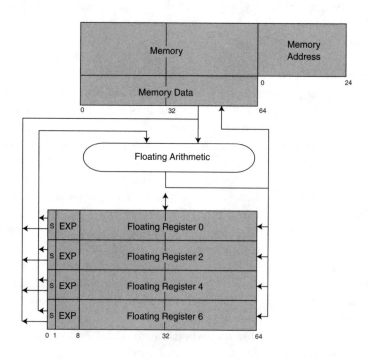

Figure 24-1   System/360 floating-point dataflow
Blaauw and Brooks [1997], *Computer Architecture*, Figure 12-79

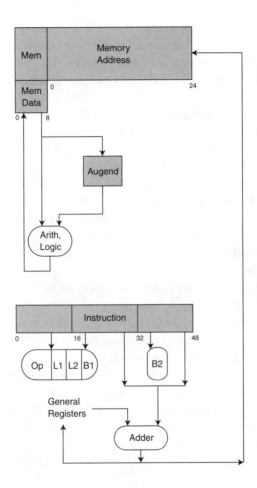

Figure 24-2   System/360 byte-by-byte dataflow
Blaauw and Brooks [1997], *Computer Architecture*, Figure 12-80

General Lessons Learned

1. Allow plenty of project time for design. It makes the product much better and useful longer, and it might even make delivery sooner by reducing rework.
2. Having multiple concurrent implementations of the same architecture strongly protects the architecture from bad compromises, when it is discovered that an implementation has (usually inadvertently) departed from the architecture. With

only one implementation, it is always easier, cheaper, and faster to change the manual rather than the machine. Chapter 6 of *The Mythical Man-Month* treats this and other methods of ensuring conformity of implementation to architecture (rather than the reverse) in some detail.

3. Amdahl's proposal for a *design competition* when our first design ran aground proved very fruitful. It produced great concurrence on many issues, and it quickly spotlighted the crucial differences. Moreover, it had a powerful positive effect on team morale. In 2008, I heard for the first time in over 40 years from Doug Baird, who had been a junior architect on the team. He still remembered appreciatively that his rather junior team had had a chance to put their design forward on the same basis as all the distinguished architects on the team.

4. For totally new designs, as opposed to follow-on products, from the beginning devote part of the design effort to establishing metrics for performance and other essential properties, and approximate cost surrogates (such as bits of register for third-generation computers).

5. Market forecasting methodology is designed for follow-on products, not radical innovations (a lesson elaborated in Chapter 19). Designers of totally new products should spend lots of early effort getting forecasters on board with the new concepts.

Notes and References

1. The most important treatments of the S/360 architecture rationale are

   - Amdahl [1964], "Architecture of the IBM System/360"
   - Blaauw and Brooks [1964], "Outline of the logical structure of System/360"
   - Blaauw and Brooks [1997], *Computer Architecture*, Section 12.4
   - Evans [1986], "System/360: A retrospective view"

- IBM Corp. [1961], "Processor products—final report of SPREAD Task Group, Dec. 28, 1961."
- IBM Corp. [1964ff], *IBM System/360 Principles of Operation, Form A22-6821-0*
- *IBM Systems Journal* 3, no. 2 (all)
- Pugh [1991], *IBM's 360 and Early 370 Systems*

2. IBM Corp. [1961], "Processor products—final report of SPREAD Task Group, Dec. 28, 1961."

3. Wise, "IBM's $5,000,000,000 gamble."

4. Brooks [1965], "The future of computer architecture."

5. Tucker [1965], "Emulation of large systems." In the event, he did not map one 7090 floating-point word to one S/360 word, but spread out the parts.

6. http://en.wikipedia.org/wiki/System_370 contains an excellent treatment of the evolution of the architecture and of the highlights of the basic architecture (accessed December 2008). So does http://www.answers.com/topic/ibm-system-360, as of August 2009.

7. Bell [2008], "IT vet Gordon Bell talks about the most influential computers."

8. Bell and Newell [1971], *Computer Structures*, Section 3, 561–637, gives another assessment and a quite detailed discussion.

9. Blaauw and Brooks [1997], *Computer Architecture*, treats this important three-way distinction in detail in Section 1.1.

25

Case Study: IBM Operating System/360

The central tension in the software process comes from the fact that we must go from an informally identified need that exists in-the-world to a formal model that operates in-the-computer.

BRUCE BLUM [1996], *BEYOND PROGRAMMING*

Peach and cherries, a metaphor for the OS/360 big control program and the several smaller and independent language compilers and utilities that complete the OS/360 support package

Highlights and Peculiarities[1]

Bold Decision.   Develop one software package: one operating system and set of compilers and utilities for an entire range of computers and I/O configurations. It can be generated to fit and exploit a variety of memory sizes and I/O configurations.

Bold Decision.   Mandate a random-access device for operating systems residence.

Bold Decision.   Do not require an operator. Design the operating system so that it can run the computer system without manual input or intervention. Operators serve as the computer's hands and feet for mounting disks, tapes, card decks, and printer paper. Alternatively, the same operating system can be configured to be fully controlled by a human operator.

Bold Decision.   Incorporate multitasking for the concurrent safe execution of jobs and programs not specifically designed to be run concurrently.

Device-Independent I/O.   Programs are written for abstract I/O datatypes, called *access methods*. I/O device types, specific devices, and space on them are automatically allocated when a job is scheduled for execution. The same merge-sort program, for example, can be run disk-to-disk for one run and tape-to-tape for another. Whether output is printed or stored can readily be changed at run time, without program alteration.

Industrial-Strength.   OS/360 was an industrial-strength operating system, designed to run 24/7, to log and restart automatically after failures. Through its generations this characteristic has been strengthened, so that its descendants are still widely used for 24/7 database systems.

Teleprocessing.   The system powerfully supports remote access for real-time database access and batch job execution.

Primitive Time-sharing.   The system is not designed for interactive terminal programming and debugging, so it supports it in less efficient ways.

Virtual Memory Added Somewhat Later.   As originally shipped, S/360 computers and the OS/360 package did not provide virtual memory. Both were changed in the first subsequent iteration, and all versions had virtual memory by 1970.

Assembler versus High-Level Languages.   Although by 1961 probably a majority of computer programming was done in the high-level languages Fortran, COBOL, and Report Program Generator, assembler-language thinking affects some parts of the OS/360 design. A powerful macro-assembler, reflecting the quite different macro use traditions of the scientific-computing and the commercial data-processing communities, was provided as one of the language packages. By 1966, measurements of some large installations showed that application programs written in assembler accounted for only about 1 percent of computer time.

Introduction and Context

From its inception in 1961 until mid-1965, I had the once-in-a-lifetime opportunity to manage the IBM System/360 Computer Family Project—first the hardware and then the Operating System/360 software package. This computer family, announced on April 7, 1964, and first shipped in February 1965, defined "third-generation" computers and introduced (semi)-integrated-circuit technology into off-the-shelf computer products.

Just as the first-generation operating systems were developed for second-generation computers, so OS/360 is the first of the second-generation software support packages, developed for the first of the third-generation computers. There were few precedents of integrated operating systems.

System/360's strict binary compatibility enabled us to design a single software support package that would support the whole product family and could be cost-shared across the entire family, with its large combined market forecast. This in turn enabled building a software support package of unprecedented richness and completeness. I shall describe the OS/360 software package in the present tense, since its linear descendants are still major players in the mainframe world.

The term *Operating System/360*, or *OS/360*, is used ambiguously to describe both an entire software support package—operating system proper, language compilers, and utilities—and, more narrowly, just the operating system itself. As the chapter frontispiece suggests, our team sometimes thought of the entire package as a big peach and a lot of smaller, distinct cherries. I shall usually use the term to describe only the operating system proper.

Besides the OS/360 support package, there was initially planned and delivered a Basic Tape Support package, including a Fortran compiler, for small-memory systems with no disk, and a Basic Punched Card Support Package. The OS/360 package was originally targeted for all systems with 16K of memory or more. We couldn't fit that size with even minimal function, so we raised our minimum memory requirement to 64K. Concern for small-system customers and OS/360 delays led the company to initiate an entire separate support package optimized for smaller memory sizes, known as *Disk Operating System/360*, or *DOS/360*.[2] It, too, evolved, and its descendants are alive today.

The System/360 Computer Family

Chapter 24 describes the market context for the computer family and gives its chief architectural properties. A radical conceptual innovation was that all of the models (except the cheapest, Model 20) would be logically identical, upward- *and downward-*compatible implementations of a single architecture. Blaauw and I define a *computer architecture* to be precisely the set of computer properties visible to the programmer, not including speed.[3] In software engineering terms, a computer architecture in our precisely restricted sense is equivalent to an abstract datatype. It defines the sets of valid data, their abstract representations, and the syntax and semantics of the set of operations proper to those datasets. Each computer implementation then is an instance of that type. So is each emulator, or each simulator. In practice, our first hardware implementations ranged from 8 to 64 bits wide in dataflow and had various memory and circuit speeds.

Software Context as of 1961

Operating Systems. First-generation operating systems were sharply differentiated as to whether they were designed for scientific computing or for commercial data processing. They were batch operating systems, designed to control the sequential processing of a stream of independent jobs.

Each had three components that had evolved separately. A *supervisor*, resident in memory all the time, had evolved from earlier interruption-handling routines. A *data-management* component had evolved into a standard library of input-output routines that were linked into the application program. A *scheduler*, typically resident on tape, was rolled into memory between jobs to specify the mounting of tape (and card) files and the disposition of the output produced. Operating systems provided for the use of disk files, but generally the operating system itself was resident on tape.

Late-first-generation IBM operating systems provided for Simultaneous Peripheral Operation On Line (SPOOL), so that at any given time a second-generation computer could be executing one main application and several card-to-tape/disk, tape/disk-to-card, tape/disk-to-printer utilities. These latter were "trusted programs," carefully written so as not to corrupt or intrude on the main application, which usually ran tape-to-tape or disk-to-disk. Thus a computer would be preparing tapes for the next job, running a main job, and printing output from the previous job, all at once.

Language Compilers. IBM customers were using a wide variety of high-level languages, and IBM was committed to providing compilers for those. Most popular were Fortran and COBOL. ALGOL was popular in Europe. At the lower end of the spectrum, Report Program Generator (RPG) was popular with those converting from punched-card installations.

The evolution of assembler programs was technically interesting. The classical two-pass assembler had sprouted two preliminary passes that constituted a macro-operation generator with rich compile-time capabilities, including branching and looping. Such macro assemblers were used in two quite different ways.

The scientific computing community typically used programmer-written macros as open subroutines for frequent higher-level operations, such as matrix operations. Macros gave not only coding ease but run-time speed, avoiding the overhead of subroutine calls.

In contrast, many business data-processing shops had evolved the practice of having a small group of gurus write a "house" macro library that essentially defined new datatypes, with data structures and operations defining a specialized programming language for that firm's business practices. The larger body of programmers just used this macro library, typically not creating any new macros of their own.

Utilities.   A variety of utilities, hardly noticed but necessary and nontrivial, completed each computer software package: sort program generators, media translators, format translators, debugging aids, memory dumps.

Free Software.   In those days, manufacturers gave away operating systems and compilers to stimulate the sale and use of hardware. Hence the cost of the software packages had to be built into the prices of the hardware.[4]

Challenges Accepted

The occasion to do an all-new software support package brought forward many challenges of what would constitute the "next step" in software support. Some were accepted, others rejected.

Universal Applicability.   Whereas previous-generation software support packages were sharply differentiated by application areas and performance level, the OS/360 package was designed to cover the entire spectrum of applications. The very name *System/360* had been chosen to indicate an "all-around computer system." It was also designed to cover a very large performance range, from a modest 64K-memory system to the most elaborate supercomputer system or massive database configuration.

The response to this challenge mostly affected the languages and their compilers. A new, general-purpose programming language, PL/I, was developed in cooperation with the scientific and commercial IBM user associations. Multiple compilers optimized for different memory sizes were built for each of Fortran, COBOL, Assembler, and PL/I. The teams responsible for the compilers or utilities assessed the ideas in their several user communities, and each incorporated advances over the previous-generation products. Here I will discuss only the most innovative component, the operating system proper.

Disk Residence. The new availability of an inexpensive disk drive, the IBM 2311, with its then-immense capacity of 7MB, meant that we could design the operating system to assume operating system residence on a "random-access" device rather than on magnetic tape. This made the biggest single difference in the design concepts. Operating system modules could be quickly rolled into memory as needed, and they could be made small and function-specific.

A new, word-parallel magnetic drum provided low-latency, high-data-rate operating systems residence for higher-performance computer systems.

Multiprogramming. OS/360 made the big leap to concurrent operation of independent, untrusted programs—a leap made possible by the hardware supervisory capabilities of the System/360 architecture. Early OS/360 versions supported multiple tasks of fixed size, for which memory allocation was straightforward. Within two years the MVS version supported multiprogramming in full generality. This proved much more difficult than we expected.

The OS, Not the Operator, in Control. A key new concept, now routine, is that the OS, not the operator, *controls* the computer. As late as 1987, some supercomputers such as the Control Data Corporation's spin-off ETA's ETA 10, were still running under manual operator control. A corollary of OS control, pioneered in Stretch, and routine today, is that the keyboard or console is just another I/O device, with very few buttons that directly *do* anything (for example, Power, Restart).

Teleprocessing, but Not Time-sharing. OS/360 was designed from the ground up as a teleprocessing system, but not really a terminal-based time-sharing system. This concept contrasts with that of the contemporary MIT Multics System. OS/360 was designed for industrial-strength scientific and data-processing applications of all sizes; Multics was designed as an exploratory system, primarily for program development.

24/7 Robust Operation. OS/360 is designed to provide check-point-restart points automatically, to sense hardware errors, and to restart after either a hardware or a software failure. When used in a multiprocessor configuration, diagnostics enable a well processor to sideline a sick one and to assume its workload. From the beginning, OS/360 was intended to be usable around the clock, although it took some evolutionary steps to get there.

Design Decisions[5]

System Structure

In OS/360, the three independent streams of control program evolution come together. The Supervisor evolved from early interrupt-handling routines; the Scheduler, from earlier tape-based job schedulers; the Data Management System, from earlier packages of I/O subroutines. The system structure mirrors this diverse ancestry.

The Supervisor. Whereas original supervisors handled only program interruptions, and thereby allocated the processor's instruction counter among tasks, a multiprogramming supervisor must allocate main memory space as well. The OS/360 Supervisor allocates memory blocks and computer cycles among tasks according to priority.

The OS/360 Supervisor keeps control of the computer by controlling the instruction counter. It lends that control to one program at a time. Any program fault, including attempted violation of any of the system protection mechanisms, causes an interruption, giving the instruction counter back to the Supervisor. Asynchronous event reports from I/O devices, such as operation completions, do the same. Moreover, the Supervisor controls a protected elapsed-time clock that interrupts, so it can seize control after any specified interval, thus stopping endless loops in buggy programs. Only the Supervisor can set the various memory and other protections and perform other privileged operations such as input-output control.

When an ordinary application program wants a service from the Supervisor, such as an additional memory block, it makes its request by a Supervisor Call hardware operation. This is an intentional interruption, with the instruction carrying parameters to the Supervisor. So the only access to the Supervisor is a humble access, on the Supervisor's terms.

The Supervisor also provides mechanisms for mutually unaware programs to communicate with each other at run time.

The Scheduler. The OS/360 Scheduler prepares the concurrent execution of independent "jobs" and then manages the sequential execution of "tasks" within each job, such as compilation, linking to libraries, execution, output transformation. When a job is ready to be scheduled, the Scheduler checks the job priority, allocates any needed I/O devices, gives operator instructions for the mounting of any off-line data volumes, and enqueues the job for execution. The Supervisor then allocates initial memory and initiates the first task. As output is produced, the Scheduler manages its disposition and the dismounting of any finished data volumes.

OS/360, more explicitly than any of its predecessors, recognizes scheduling time as a binding occasion distinct from compile time with its rigidities and run time with its overheads. Not only are separately compiled program modules bound to each other at scheduling time by a Linker, but dataset names are bound to particular datasets on particular devices only at scheduling time. This binding is specified by the Job Control Language, which is executed by the Scheduler.

Data Management. Although strict program compatibility was the most distinctive new *concept* of the System/360 computer family, the rich set of I/O devices was its most important system attribute in terms of application breadth, configuration flexibility, and performance enhancement. The single standard mechanical, electrical, and logical I/O interface radically reduced the engineering cost for new I/O devices, radically simplified system configuration, and radically eased configuration growth and change.

The crucial software innovation complementing and exploiting the standard hardware I/O interface was a standard software interface—a single system of I/O control and data management for all kinds of I/O devices. I consider it the most important innovation in OS/360.

A resulting new feature was *device-independent input-output*. The application programmer wrote in terms of dataset names. Bindings to particular datasets, to particular reels of tape, to tape versus disk, to disk versus communication line or printer, all were usually deferred to scheduling time.

Four access methods were designed especially for exploitation of the fleet of new disk types, across the range of disk applications. These embodied different trade-offs between dynamic flexibility and maximum-performance buffered or block transfer:

- Sequential access method—tape-like, buffered
  Example: for sorting (works for tapes, printers, and card decks, as well as for disks)
- Direct access method—pure random access to a record
  Example: for airline reservations
- Partitioned access method—fast fixed-block transfer
  Example: for operating system modules
- Indexed sequential access method—sequential, buffered, but rapidly handling random queries
  Example: for utility billing

Two other access methods were designed especially to provide full flexibility and ease of use for both terminals and high-speed telecommunications.

Of all the I/O devices, the check sorters alone, curiously enough, posed a rigid constraint on operating system performance—the time of a paper check's flight between the reading head and the sorter pocket is fixed and short. In banks' check-routing and check-processing facilities, these machines read the magnetic-ink numerals along the bottom of the check at a reading station and then route the check into one of some 24 pockets, at a rate of up to 40 checks/second.[6]

Assessment

The Successes

Full Function, Universal Applicability. OS/360 established a new baseline for operating system function. It did indeed support a surprisingly wide range of applications, system configurations, and performance.

Robustness. The level of robustness has become peerless. It is *the* industrial-strength operating system and has become a standard for the massive database applications that consume most mainframe cycles.

Data Management System. Device-independent input-output was a major simplification of the programming task and a major flexibility for data center operation and evolution. Weekend reconfigurations of processors and I/O devices are routinely performed. After such reconfigurations, most applications can still be run without recompilation.

Teleprocessing Support. OS/360 became the basis for wide networks of terminals for banking, retail, and most other industries.

Accommodated Virtual Memory. When IBM adopted virtual memory on the System/370 successor line, OS/360 served as the base for OS/360 Multiple Virtual Systems (MVS), an extension, but not a total rewrite.

Amdahl, Hitachi, and Fujitsu. Most manufacturers of S/360 plug-compatible computers did not undertake software systems but used the OS/360 package.

Weaknesses in the Design

The System. OS/360 is too rich. Systems residence on a disk removed the size constraint that had disciplined earlier OS designers—we put in many functional goodies of marginal usefulness.[7] Featuritis is even now not yet dead in the software community.

Two quite different debugging systems are provided, one conceived for interactive use from terminals with rapid recompilation, the other conceived for batch operation. It was the best *batch* debugging system ever designed, yet totally obsolete from birth.

The system-generation process of OS/360 is wondrously flexible and wondrously onerous. We should have configured a small number of standard packages to meet the needs of most users and offered these to supplement the fully flexible configuration process.

Control Blocks.   Communication among modules is by system-wide shared control blocks, each with a structured set of variables read by and written by the several modules. Every programmer had access to all the control blocks. Had we understood and adopted in 1963 the information-hiding strategy Parnas set forth in 1971, we would have avoided much grief in original construction and all subsequent maintenance. Object-oriented programming is today's embodiment of information hiding; we all recognize its superiority.

Virtual Memory.   As discussed in Chapter 24, we missed the early boat on virtual memory in the initial processors and had to retrofit it just a few years later. The required extension to OS/360 was more difficult and costly than if it had been originally designed in.

The Scheduler's Job Control Language.   The Job Control Language is the worst programming language ever designed by anybody anywhere—it was designed under my management. The very concept is wrong; we did not see it as a programming language but as "a few control cards to precede the job." I have elaborated on its flaws in Chapter 14.

Complexities in the Data Management System.   We should have cut loose from the key-count-data variable-length block structure established for IBM's earlier disks and designed for one or two sizes of fixed-length blocks on all random-access devices.

The I/O device-control unit-channel attachment tree is unnecessarily complex.[8] We should have specified one (probably virtual) channel per device and one (probably virtual) control unit per device.

I believe we could have invented one sequential disk access method that would have combined the optimizations of the three: SAM, PAM, ISAM.

Weaknesses in the Process

I have treated this topic at length in *The Mythical Man-Month*. Here I will highlight only two points.

I am firmly convinced that if we had built the whole thing in PL/I, the best high-level language available at the time, the OS would have been just as fast, far cleaner and more reliable, and built more swiftly. In fact, it was built in PLS, a syntactically sugared assembler language. Using PL/I (or any high-level language) would have indeed required careful training of our force in how to write *good* PL/I code, PL/I source that would compile to fast run-time code.

We should have maintained rigid architectural control over all the interfaces, insisting that all declarations of external variables be *included* from libraries, not crafted anew in each instance. Many bugs would have been prevented.

The Designers

About 1,000 people worked on the entire OS/360 software package. Here I identify both the teams and those individuals who contributed most to the conceptual structure.

Key Players

> Labs: Poughkeepsie, Endicott, San Jose, New York City, Hursley (UK), La Gaude (France)
>
> OS/360 Architect: Martin Belsky
>
> > Key: Bernie Witt, George Mealy, William Clark
>
> Control Program Manager: Scott Locken
>
> Compilers, Utilities Manager: Dick Case
>
> OS/360 Assistant Project Manager: Dick Case
>
> OS/360 Manager from 1965: Fritz Trapnell

The best single document is the *Concepts and Facilities* manual, written by Bernard Witt.[9,10]

General Lessons Learned

1. Give the system architect full authority over the design (Chapter 19). This "multimillion-dollar mistake" is more fully discussed in *The Mythical Man-Month,* pages 47ff.
2. Take the time necessary to do a sound design and prototyping, whatever the schedule pressures. The project will be completed sooner, not later, because of time so invested. Chapters 21–24 illustrate the benefits of enough design time; this one illustrates the opposite.

Notes and References

1. This essay is derived from Brooks [2002], "The history of IBM Operating System/360," in Broy and Denert [2002], *Software Pioneers.* The material is taken largely from *IBM Systems Journal* 5, no. 1 [1966].

2. http://en.wikipedia.org/wiki/DOS/360_and_successors, accessed August 2009.

3. Blaauw and Brooks [1997], *Computer Architecture*, Section 1.1.

4. Grad [2002], "A personal recollection," describes the 1969 unbundling of software and hardware.

5. Pugh [1991], *IBM's 360 and Early 370 Systems*, gives a detailed history of the OS/360 initial development.

6. More information and a photo of a successor machine is at http://www.thegalleryofoldiron.com/3890.HTM, accessed August 2009.

7. Brooks [1995], *The Mythical Man-Month*, Chapter 5.

8. Blaauw and Brooks [1997], *Computer Architecture*, Section 8.22.

9. IBM Corp. and Witt [1965], *IBM Operating System/360, Concepts and Facilities*, Form C28-6535-0.

10. Witt [1994], *Software Architecture and Design*, elaborates on the design concepts and approaches.

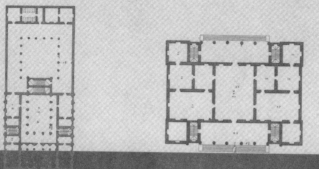

COMPUTER ARCHITECTURE

Concepts and Evolution

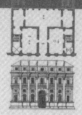

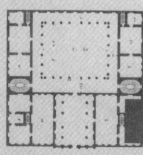

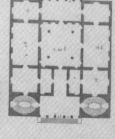

Gerrit A. Blaauw

Frederick P. Brooks, Jr.

26

Case Study: Book Design of Computer Architecture: Concepts and Evolution

Oh that my words were now written; oh that they were printed in a book!

JOB 19:23

Book writing has logarithmic convergence.

Dust jacket of Blaauw and Brooks [1997], *Computer Architecture*

Highlights and Peculiarities

Bold Decision.   Stick with a narrow but quite precise definition of *computer architecture* as the scope of the work. Although we first introduced the term in 1962, and a quite precise definition in 1964, it had come to be broadly used in a much looser sense. We carefully define and distinguish *architecture, implementation,* and *realization.* We treat only architecture, defined as exactly those properties of the computer that govern what programs will run and what results they will produce, and not how fast. This precision enables one to define *program compatibility.*

Bold Decision.   Incorporate a "zoo" of 30 computer architectures, described in a standardized format. The format includes a prose description of "highlights and peculiarities," a short description of the historical and technical context, a drawn programming model, enumeration of the design decisions, and precise drawn and APL descriptions of the data representations, formats, and significant operations.

Bold Decision.   Build, test, and publish executable simulators of the zoo computer architectures, all written in APL. Each zoo machine includes an executable APL program simulating the machine's instruction fetch, decode, and calling of the appropriate data-fetching and operation routines. The significant operations are also described with executable APL functions. Building these simulators forced our close scrutiny of the machines and that added great precision to these descriptions. It is not evident that many people have ever used the simulators.

Matrix Organization.   The design decisions constituting a computer architecture are treated twice, once systematically in order of the decision domains, and then again in the context of all the interrelated decisions in each specific machine.

Decision Trees.   We use *decision trees* as a formal tool for representing design choices. The 80-some trees are linked together into a single vast unified decision tree for computer architecture. This formalism, of course, treats design as problem solving by search of a well-defined space, which model I argue vigorously *against* in this book! My view of design has broadened and deepened since we did that book.

Computer Architecture Evolution: Divergence and Convergence. We cover the evolution of computer architecture from the very beginning (Babbage) up through 1985, showing the wide experimental divergence and the subsequent convergence to a surprisingly standard architecture. This brings together documentation of many early computers, as well as modern ones.

Research Monograph as Well. Our work on System/360 and on the book itself yielded many research results that were not piecemeal publishable. Hence the book contains many newly published results, enumerated in its Preface. This is peculiar for what looks like merely a text for practitioners and students.

Comprehensive Reference. Terms are carefully defined. An extensive subject index leads especially to those definitions and their substantial treatments, as well as all occurrences. There are separate person-name and machine-name indexes. The bibliography contains over 500 items. The book may be useful as a reference long after the didactic material is useful for teaching.

Introduction and Context

Authors:

Gerrit A. Blaauw and Frederick Brooks

Dates:

~1971–1997

Context

Both of us had left the practice of computer architecture and were teaching courses in the subject. The book grew as we needed course material. After about two course administrations apiece, we undertook to design a book, not principally as a text for students, but as a systematic treatment for practitioners. We did include extensive exercises, designed for both class use and self-study.

Objectives

From the Preface to *Computer Architecture*:

"Our aim in this book is to give a thorough treatment of the art of computer architecture. This work is not intended primarily as a textbook, but rather as a guide and reference for the practicing architect and as a research monograph setting forth a new conceptual framework for computer architecture. We have given enough of the historical evolution that one can see not only what present practice is, but how it came to be so, as well as what has been already tried and discarded. Our goal is to display unfamiliar design alternatives, and to analyze and systematize familiar ones.

"It seems useful to provide a compendium of the issues arising in the design of computer architecture, and to discuss the factors pro and con on the various known solutions to design problems. Each architect will then be able to provide his own set of weightings to these factors as dictated by his application, his technology, and his taste and ingenuity."

Opportunities

Because we had worked closely together for eight years at IBM, communication was easy and thought patterns familiar. This made our telecollaboration easy, as described in Chapter 7.

We had worked together on the design of three computer architectures, and each of us had participated in the design of others. These projects had occasioned our studying the designs of our predecessors, and teaching had solidified our understanding of those works and their significance. We owned programming manuals for most of those machines.

The design of System/360 architecture was not hurried, because its semi-integrated circuit technology would not be ready before 1964. Hence those design decisions were thoroughly debated, and we had studied the pros and cons of many architecture issues in that context.

Book preparation time and effort budget were essentially unlimited. Or so we thought. This was a major mistake. In the event, the book was too late to be of maximum influence and use.

Constraints

Each of us had active research programs and teaching schedules, as well as growing children. After starting this book, each of us published a related book. So this book often languished.

Design Decisions

Sequence. In any expository writing, sequence is the hardest single design decision. The general graph of interrelated concepts must be cut to a tree structure, so it can be mapped onto the linear structure of the text.

We saw two major possible orders, each very important. So we incorporated both orders, with much cross-referencing. Part I treats design decisions systematically in conceptual order. But each real decision must be made in the context of all the other decisions for that computer. So we illustrate the design decisions in the contexts of the several computer specimens in Part II, "A computer zoo."

The "Highlights and peculiarities" section above enumerates other major design decisions that need no further elaboration.

Assessment

Firmness. As measured by permanence, the design is firm. After 13 years, its usefulness is not diminished nor its treatments obsoleted, although it must be supplemented by material describing more recent developments.

Commodity. The book came out too late for some of its potential uses. For a textbook for one or two architecture courses, one would use Hennessy and Patterson's superb and continually updated *Computer Architecture: A Quantitative Approach* instead.

The professional computer architect needs to be familiar with our work, both for familiarity with his predecessors' works and as a guide and reference. It has a small but devoted following, mostly among computer architects.

Delight. Others must assess that.

Lessons Learned

1. Probably a less ambitious work sooner would have been more useful to the profession. When I now teach a single course from *Computer Architecture*, I feature the zoo and its specimens, treating design decisions as they are encountered in vivid examples, rather than systematically. Perhaps we should have written and published that part of the book separately, first, and more quickly. That would not have been easy; much of the zoo discussion assumes the concepts introduced and expounded in Part I, "Design decisions."

2. Book writing has logarithmic convergence. Checking the last few uncertain facts, fixing the last few glitched figures, verifying the last few obscure references—these tasks take inordinate proportions of the total effort. The hardest little tasks get put off until the end.

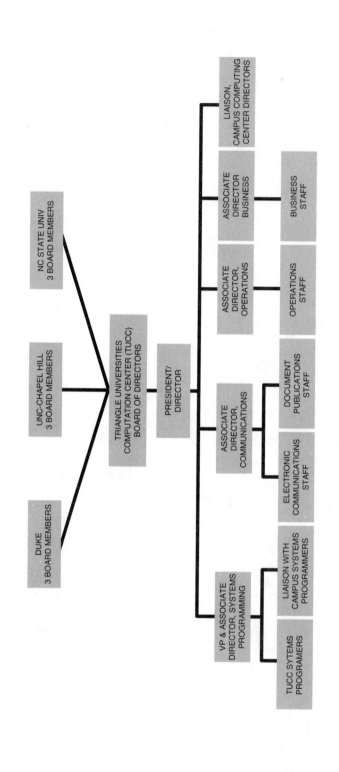

27

Case Study: A Joint Computer Center Organization: Triangle Universities Computation Center

The purpose of computing is insight, not numbers.

RICHARD W. HAMMING [1962], *NUMERICAL METHODS FOR SCIENTISTS AND ENGINEERS*

Triangle Universities Computation Center (TUCC) organization chart as of 1980

Highlights and Peculiarities

Bold Decision. Establish this as a joint center. Three universities would pool their resources, co-own, and operate a single high-performance computation center.

Pooling Resources. To exploit the quadratic performance/price curve, resources would be pooled. At the time, and for many years, spending n times as much typically bought at least n^2 times as much computing capability. This fact provided a strong economic incentive to overcome the real and foreseen difficulties in co-owning a center.

No Organizational Models. The concept of a joint academic computation center was unexplored, so far as we knew, so there were no models for the organization.

Decision-Making Power. The budgeted commodity in the design was power. How to protect individual owners' distinct interests, while enabling efficient decision making?

Diverse Applications. Some of the owners used the center for both academic and administrative computing; others, for academic computing only.

Neutral Site. A building was acquired in the Research Triangle Park, about equidistant from each campus.

Telecomputing Crucial but Not Sufficient. The IBM System/360 equipment acquired was designed and software-supported for remote job entry and interactive computing. It was initially used in remote-job-entry mode, but with a priority system that emphasized quick turnaround for small jobs. A courier service hauled tapes and disk packs back and forth in a station wagon to provide "high-bandwidth" transmission of large datasets.

Statewide Influence. In 1964, few higher-education institutions in North Carolina (other than the TUCC owners) had any computing capability or know-how. A separate organization, the North Carolina Computer Orientation Project under the North

Carolina Board of Higher Education, rented TUCC capacity and offered other North Carolina universities and colleges

- A year of free computer time at 100 jobs per month
- A year's free use of a teletype machine installed on their campus
- The free services of "circuit riders" who introduced computing by visiting campuses, teaching teachers, holding workshops, providing telephonic consultation, and troubleshooting

Some 100 institutions took advantage of this service, many continuing their TUCC use at their own expense for years.

Durability. The TUCC organization proved effective for 18 years, even as the relative needs of the three co-owners diverged. It was made obsolete by the minicomputer revolution, although the institutions operated a joint supercomputer center specialized for scientific applications for many years thereafter, under a different organizational model.

Introduction and Context

Location:

Research Triangle Park, NC

Owners:

Duke University, a private university (Durham, NC)

North Carolina State University (Raleigh, NC)

University of North Carolina at Chapel Hill

Organization Designers:

TUCC Board of Directors

Dates:

1964–1992

Context

Duke University, North Carolina State University, and the University of North Carolina at Chapel Hill each had first-generation computers, operated by centralized computer centers. Each needed to upgrade in capacity and capability. Each wanted more computer than it could afford.

The three universities decided to pool their resources and operate a single modern high-performance facility (more than they could collectively afford without help).

The National Science Foundation made a substantial grant, partly to fund exploration of the novel organizational model for providing academic computing service for research.

IBM, having located a new product development and manufacturing facility in Research Triangle Park, helped quite substantially with funding for the first three years, by renting a night shift.

The design problem was how to organize the joint facility administratively.

Objectives[1]

Primary Goals

Primary Goal of the Center. Deliver a prompt, high-quality computing service to clients with a wide variety of applications and a wide range of sophistication.

Primary Goal of the Organization Design. Develop a smooth-running governance plan for a joint computer center owned equally by three different institutions with different needs and objectives.

Other Objectives

- Maintain the financial stability of the center.
- Ensure that decisions are made efficiently and expeditiously.
- Ensure that each owner's users get a fair share of all resources.

- Ensure that each owner's financial investment is protected.
- Ensure that no owner loses on an issue of critical self-interest.
- Enable the center to operate as a single center, not three partitions, for economies of scale—one staff, one set of equipment, one job stream.
- Enable owners to change their contributions to the joint center and thereby get more or less service.

Opportunities

Economies of Scale. At the time of design, the economies of scale of running one big center instead of three little ones were substantial. They consisted of staff savings—especially important for 24-hour operation—and computer rental savings, since computers, memory, disks, and other I/O devices all followed square-law performance/price curves.

Teleoperation Possible. New technologies available with the new third-generation computers for the first time made it possible to submit and receive computing jobs remotely and to hold interactive computing sessions remotely.

National Prototype. By moving swiftly, TUCC could pioneer a model of a joint regional computing center. A big center would be nationally visible and add to the visibility of North Carolina's relatively new Research Triangle. A new prototypical organization would reinforce an existing reputation for innovation and for uncommon local cooperation among universities.

Attract Government Support. The economies of scale could attract extra U.S. government support because the novel concept offered increased value for money to funding agencies. Moreover, the pioneering nature of the model would also attract the attention of funders.

Attract Industrial Support. The scale and national visibility of a joint center would make it a likely candidate for substantial support from industry.

Constraints

Speed of Operating Decisions. Daily operations had to be managed crisply and efficiently.

Frequent Capacity Upgrades Necessary. Both demand and funding were expected to increase rapidly, so configuration changes would have to be made routinely and responsively.

Protection of Owners' Different Vital Interests. Duke, as the smallest of the institutions, had to be sure it wouldn't be called on to contribute more than it could afford. NCSU, as the heaviest user, had to be sure it could count on needed capacity. Duke had to be sure the two state-owned branches of the UNC system would not vote together to private-institution Duke's disadvantage.

TUCC Budget Stability. TUCC itself must make moderately long-term commitments (leases, officer contracts), so it had to be assured of budgetary stability.

Owners' Budget Stability. The owners' own budgetary processes required long lead times for any increase in TUCC's funding.

University CEOs with a Lot at Stake. Each owning university's CEO stood to benefit by enhancement of the Research Triangle. Each was responsible for the self-interests of his own institution.

University CEOs with Little Time to Participate, but Authority Not Delegated. Not all campuses had chief information officers with authority to commit the campus, so decisions might be slow.

Some Fractious and/or Stubborn Individuals. Some of the players had reputations of being strong-willed and stubborn.

Design Decisions

Careful Separation of Policy and Operations. Policy was to be determined by a board of directors, meeting monthly; operating decisions were to be made by a staff under a CEO, the Director of TUCC.

Board Composition. The board had to be small enough to work, but big enough to represent various segments of each campus. We ended with ten members—three chosen by and from each owning campus, plus the TUCC Director. The Director of the North Carolina Computer Orientation Project also had a seat at the table. Since NCCOP was housed in the TUCC building, its Director had substantial informal influence on what happened.

Voting Alternatives Considered for the Board

- Unanimous consent of members
- Simple majority of members
- Unanimous consent of institutions, each institution vote decided by a majority of its board members
- Majority of institutions

Unanimous Consent Not Required. We decided early on that the unanimous consent of members would make it too hard to get decisions. Avoiding the requirement of consensus greatly eased decision making.

Majority of Members Rather than Majority of Institutions. We decided that we wanted to encourage the board to think as a unit, and to discourage division according to institutional affiliation. Hence we specified that normal decisions would be made by a simple majority of the directors present and voting.

"Issues of Fundamental Importance." These were explicitly recognized as requiring more than normal consensus and were spelled out in the By-Laws:

- Selection or discharge of a TUCC Director
- An annual budget increase of more than 10 percent
- Modifying the Articles of Incorporation or the By-Laws

A unanimous vote by the owning institutions was required for Issues of Fundamental Importance. Note that this did not require all members of the board to agree even in such a case. Two-thirds of any owner's delegation decided its vote.

Escape Hatch.   Any owner institution could declare any issue to be an Issue of Fundamental Importance, requiring unanimity by institutions. This procedure was made suitably onerous—the institution's representatives could table an issue for a month. Then the institution's CEO could by letter elevate the matter to Issue of Fundamental Importance status. So any institution could, with deliberate effort, stop any action it deemed inimical to its vital interests.

Rotating Chairmanship.   The chairmanship of the TUCC board rotated, with two-year terms, among the owners.

Rationing Power

In all of these decisions, thought had to be given to the rationing of power:

- Between staff and board
- Between majority and minority, by institutions and fractious individuals
- Between academic users and administrative users

Assessment

Firmness

Durability.   The TUCC organization worked through 18 years, two Directors, three generations of computer mainframes, and substantial shifts away from the three-equal-owner-users model.

Escape Hatch.   It was never used, as I recall. Its presence was a great psychological comfort and, I think, avoided sessions in which any group felt trapped and forced to fight for its life.

Operation as a Single Entity.   The staff, as expected, operated as a single enterprise. So did the board, a gratifying outcome. Only rarely did divisions occur along institutional lines. Differences of opinion more often divided the board along faculty/administrator or bold/conservative lines.

Usefulness

Model Flexibility. As NCSU's usage increased, various ad hoc arrangements were adopted whereby it put in more money for specific capacity enhancements (for example, more memory) in return for an increased usage share of the whole resource. Such devices long preserved the form, if not the substance, of the three-equal-owners premise under which TUCC was begun. After the minicomputer revolution, Duke usage declined. Much computing service at Duke went to departmentally managed minicomputers.

Finally, the notion of unequal shares was formalized. The sticky point was equal versus proportional representation on the board. This was resolved by defining a use-fraction that would trigger another representative.

Tension between On-Campus and TUCC Computing Capacity. From the beginning, each TUCC owner had also a campus computing center with a staff to help its users, and hardware for entering input and printing output from TUCC. This hardware also (unavoidably) had the capacity to run some of the campus's jobs.

Each campus center director therefore faced continual decisions as to how much of his budget to put into TUCC capacity and how much into the on-campus facility.

NCSU tended to meet most user needs at TUCC, satisfying its growth requirements by buying an ever-larger share of the growing TUCC resource. Duke tended to meet most of its needs with its declining share of TUCC—that one-third initial share was a big fraction of the Duke computing budget. UNC continued to use its third of the growing TUCC resource, but it tended to meet its excess growth requirements by building up the on-campus installation rather than by enlarging its share of TUCC.

Lessons Learned

1. Careful and explicit identification at the beginning of the vital interests of each of the three university partners and of the central facility's director was a big help in arriving quickly at agreed-upon organization mechanics.

2. Providing an ultimate appeal procedure, though not easy to invoke, assured each participant that it wouldn't be trodden upon.

3. Recognizing that there were differing interests within each partner, and hence getting their representation in each partner's delegation, paid off. To a surprising degree, divisions of opinion on many issues were by area of responsibility, rather than by school: the finance-house representatives from all three of the schools often voted together, as did the three campus-computer-center representatives, and the three faculty-user representatives.

   I do not remember that any steps were taken to ensure that each campus delegation would represent these several interests, but the several administrators who appointed each delegation were wise enough to get it right.

4. It is easy for a governing board for such an enterprise to become just a rubber stamp for the management. We found it necessary to meet monthly to avoid this hazard.

5. Some CEOs tend to fill board meetings with presentations, rather than discussions of real issues. Perhaps CEOs overestimate the untoward consequences of being overridden if a CEO takes a real issue to the board.

   Nor, in my experience, do many CEOs use their board members severally, as advisers in their areas of expertise. I think this a real loss.

Notes and References

1. The By-Laws of the Triangle Universities Computation Center are posted on the Web at http://www.cs.unc.edu/~brooks/DesignofDesign.

28
Recommended Reading

The Bibliography includes complete citations for all the references in the text, plus other relevant and high-quality items on the design process. I here point to certain of these works that I find exceptionally valuable for those interested in the design process as such. They are in alphabetical order by author, with brief comments.

Blaauw, G. A., and F. P. Brooks, Jr. [1997]. *Computer Architecture: Concepts and Evolution*.

Section 1.1 distinguishes *architecture, implementation,* and *realization*. Section 1.2 gives an overview of the design of computer architectures. It also formalizes and illustrates the concept of a design tree of individual design decisions. Section 1.4 undertakes to define and characterize what makes an architecture good.

Boehm, B. [2007]. *Software Engineering: Barry Boehm's Lifetime Contributions to Software Development, Management and Research*.

An indispensable set of papers covering many aspects of software design.

Brooks, F. P., Jr. [1975, 1995]. *The Mythical Man-Month: Essays on Software Engineering*, Anniversary edition.

Chapter 16, "No silver bullet," separates design problems into the essential and the accidental (or *incidental*, if you prefer). Chapter 19 gives a 1975-to-1995 retrospective.

Burks, A. W., H. H. Goldstine, and J. von Neumann [1946]. "Preliminary discussion of the logical design of an electronic computing instrument."

The most important computer paper ever written. Stunningly comprehensive. Available on line.

Cross, N., K. Dorst, et al., eds. [1992]. *Research in Design Thinking.*

Contains Cross's devastating critique of Simon: real designers don't do it that way, and here are the studies that show it. Other papers in the book are also valuable.

DeMarco, T., and T. Lister [1987]. *Peopleware: Productive Projects and Teams*, 2nd edition.

Important research results and insights on the nontechnical factors affecting design quality.

Hales, C. [1987, 1991]. *An Analysis of the Engineering Design Process in an Industrial Context.*

Probably the most complete published documentation of a real, substantial design process, done by a co-designer who also served simultaneously as a scholarly observer. Originally Hales's Cambridge PhD dissertation.

Hennessy, J., and D. A. Patterson [1990, 2006]. *Computer Architecture: A Quantitative Approach*, 4th edition.

The definitive text on the design of computer architectures. Dramatically shows the convergence to a standard architecture.

Hoffman, D., and D. Weiss, eds. [2001]. *Software Fundamentals: Collected Papers by David L. Parnas.*

The other indispensable set of papers covering many aspects of software design.

Mills, H. D. [1971]. "Top-down programming in large systems." In *Debugging Techniques in Large Systems*, ed. R. Rustin.

Teaches and argues for incremental design and programming.

Royce, W. [1970]. "Managing the development of large software systems." *Proceedings of IEEE Wescon.*

The classic paper describing and decrying the Waterfall Model. It advocates an alternative model.

Schön, D. [1983]. *The Reflective Practitioner.*

Simon, H. A. [1969, 1996]. *The Sciences of the Artificial*, 3rd edition.

The most influential and articulate proposal of the Rational Model for design.

Winograd, T., et al., eds.[1996]. *Bringing Design to Software.*

A very helpful collection, including important papers.

Wozniak, S. [2006]. *iWoz: From Computer Geek to Cult Icon: How I Invented the Personal Computer, Co-Founded Apple, and Had Fun Doing It.*

An illuminating autobiography from an engineer's engineer, giving many insights into design.

Acknowledgments

Name	Design Domain	Most Relevant Affiliations
Conversations and Interviews		
David Andrews	Naval architecture	Royal Corps of Naval Constructors, University College London
Marco Aurisicchio	Software—design rationale, DRed	University of Cambridge
Rui Bastos	Graphic chip architecure	nVidia
Gerrit Blaauw	Computer hardware, book design	IBM, University of Twente
Barry Boehm	Software—ROCKET orbit calculator	RAND, TRW Systems, University of Southern California
Robert Bracewell	Software—design rationale, DRed	University of Cambridge
John Clarkson	Training simulators	PA Consulting Group, University of Cambridge
Sir David Davies	Railroad safety	Ministry of Defense, Royal Academy of Engineering
Neil Dodgson	Computer science curriculum	University of Cambridge

Name	Design Domain	Most Relevant Affiliations
Sir John Fairclough	Computer hardware	IBM, UK Chief Scientific Advisor
Ken Fast	Naval architecture—nuclear submarine	General Dynamics Electric Boat
Steve Furber	Computer hardware—BBC Microcomputer, ARM	Acorn Computers Ltd., University of Manchester
Gordon Glegg	Mechanical engineering	University of Cambridge
Donald Greenberg	Architecture—house design, design automation	Cornell University
Bill Hillier	Urban planning—space syntax	University College London
Jeffrey Jupp	Aircraft—Airbus 380, distributed development	Airbus UK of British Aerospace
Julie Jupp	Design-build financing models	University of Cambridge
Joe Lohde	Theme park attractions	Disney Entertainment
Janet McDonnell	Design studies—design practices, collaboration	Central St. Martins College of Art and Design
Craig Mudge	Integrated circuits	Digital, PARC, Pacific Challenge
Sir Alan Muir Woods	Tunnels—Channel Tunnel early studies	William Halcrow and Partners
Bradford Parkinson	Systems engineering—GPS	U.S. Air Force, Stanford University
David Patterson	Computer hardware—RISC, RAID	University of California–Berkeley

Name	Design Domain	Most Relevant Affiliations
Sharif Razzaque	Design methodology— prototypes, rework	Lockheed Martin, University of N.C., InnerOptic Technology
Richard Riesenfeld	Software—geometric design, numerical control	University of Utah
James Robertson	Software— requirements process	Atlantic Systems Guild
Suzanne Robertson	Software— requirements process	Atlantic Systems Guild
Donald Schön	Architecture, design theory	Massachusetts Institute of Technology
Albert Segars	Technology innovation	University of North Carolina
Mary Shaw	Software engineering—value-based SE	Carnegie-Mellon University
Herbert Simon	Design theory, artificial intelligence	Carnegie-Mellon University
Malcolm Simon	Software—tesselation	AVEVA, University of Cambridge
William Swarthout	Software—self-explaining program	Institute for Creative Technologies
Ken Wallace	Design studies	University of Cambridge
Mary Whitton	Computer hardware—Ikonas; software—virtual environments	Ikonas Graphics, Trancept, University of North Carolina

Name	Design Domain	Most Relevant Affiliations
Sir Maurice Wilkes	Computer hardware—EDSAC	University of Cambridge
Martin Williams	Plant engineering—VEs in oil platform design	Kellogg Brown & Root
Steve Wozniak	Computer hardware—Apple II	Apple Computer, Inc.
Reviews		
Anonymous		
Gordon Bell	Computer hardware	DEC, Microsoft
Gerrit Blaauw	Computer hardware	IBM, University of Twente
Grady Booch	Software	Rational Software Corp., IBM Rational
Kenneth Brooks	Software	DEC, Sparklight.com
Roger Brooks	Law	Cravath, Swaine & Moore
Richard Case	Computer hardware, operating systems	IBM
Mary Shaw	Software	Carnegie-Mellon University
Ivan Sutherland	Computer hardware	Evans and Sutherland, Sun Microsystems, Oregon State University
Eoin Woods	Software	Artechra, Barclays Global Investors
William Wright	Computer hardware	IBM, University of North Carolina

Bibliography

Aiken, Howard H. [1937]. "Proposed automatic calculating machine." In *Perspectives on the Computer Revolution* [1989], eds. Z. W. Pylyshyn and L. J. Bannon. Norwood, NJ: Ablex Publishing Corp., 29–37.

Air Force Studies Board, Committee on Pre-Milestone A Systems Engineering, and Paul Kaminsky, Chairman [2008]. *Pre-Milestone A and Early-Phase Systems Engineering.* Washington, DC: National Research Council.

Akin, Omer [1988]. "Expertise of the architect." In *Expert Systems for Engineering Design*, ed. M. D. Rychener. New York: Academic Press, 173–196.

——— [2008]. "Variants and invariants of design cognition." In *Design Thinking Research Symposium 7*, eds. J. McDonnell and P. Lloyd. London.

Alexander, Christopher [1964]. *Notes on the Synthesis of Form.* Cambridge, MA: Harvard University Press.

——— [1979]. *The Timeless Way of Building.* New York: Oxford University Press.

Alexander, Christopher, Sara Ishikawa, and Murray Silverstein [1977]. *A Pattern Language: Towns, Buildings, Construction.* New York: Oxford University Press.

Allen, Frances, and John Cocke [1971]. *Design and Optimization of Compilers.* Englewood Cliffs, NJ: Prentice Hall.

——— [1972]. "A catalog of optimizing transformations." In *Design and Optimization of Compilers*, ed. R. Rustin. Englewood Cliffs, NJ: Prentice Hall.

Amdahl, Gene M., Gerrit A. Blaauw, and F. P. Brooks, Jr. [1964]. "Architecture of the IBM System/360." *IBM Journal of Research and Development* 8 (2): 87–101.

Arden, Bruce W., Bernard A. Galler, T. C. O'Brien, et al. [1966]. "Program and addressing structure in a time-sharing environment." *Journal of the ACM* 13 (1): 1–16.

Arthur, K., T. Preston, R. M. Taylor II, et al. [1998]. "Designing and building the PIT: A head-tracked stereo workspace for two users." In *Proceedings of the 2nd International Immersive Projection Technology Workshop*, eds. B. Frölich, J. Deisinger, H.-J. Bullinger, et al. Vienna: Springer Computer Science.

Aurisicchio, M., M. Gourtovaia, R. H. Bracewell, et al. [2007]. "Evaluation of how DRed design rationale is interpreted." In *Proceedings of the 16th International Conference on Engineering Design (ICED '07)*, ed. J.-C. Bocquet. Glasgow: The Design Society, 63–64.

Bacon, Sir Francis [1605]. *The Two Books of the Proficience and Advancement of Learning*.

Barkstrom, Bruce R. [2004, updated Jan. 29, 2004]. "The standard Waterfall Model for systems development." Retrieved April 11, 2008, from http://web.archive.org/web/20050310133243/http:// asd-www.larc.nasa.gov/barkstrom/public/The_Standard_ Waterfall_Model_For_Systems_Development.htm.

Bell, C. Gordon [2008]. "Q & A: IT vet Gordon Bell talks about the most influential computers." *ComputerWorld*, April 29.

Bell, C. Gordon, J. Craig Mudge, and John E. McNamara [1978]. *Computer Engineering: A DEC View of Hardware Systems Design*. Maynard, MA: Digital Press.

Bell, C. Gordon, and Allen Newell [1971]. *Computer Structures: Readings and Examples*. New York: McGraw-Hill.

Bergin, Thomas J., and Richard G. Gibson, eds. [1996]. *History of Programming Languages*, vol. 2. Reading, MA: Addison-Wesley (ACM Press).

Billington, David P. [2003]. *The Art of Structural Design: A Swiss Legacy*. Princeton, NJ: Princeton University Art Museum.

Blaauw, G. A. [1965]. "Door de vingers zien." Inaugural address at Twente Technical University. Enschede, Netherlands: Technische Hogeschool Twente.

———— [1970]. "Hardware requirement for the Fourth Generation." In *Fourth Generation Computers*, ed. F. Gruenberger. Englewood Cliffs, NJ: Prentice Hall, 155–168.

Blaauw, Gerrit A., and Frederick P. Brooks, Jr. [1964]. "Outline of the logical structure of System/360." *IBM Systems Journal* 3 (2): 119–135.

—— [1997]. *Computer Architecture: Concepts and Evolution.* Reading, MA: Addison-Wesley.

Blum, Bruce I. [1996]. *Beyond Programming.* Oxford: Oxford University Press.

Bødker, S., P., J. Ehn, M. Kammersgaard, et al. [1987]. "A utopian experience: On design of powerful computer-based tools for skilled graphic workers." In *Computers and Democracy: A Scandinavian Challenge,* eds. G. Bjerknes, P. Ehn, M. Kyng, et al. Avebury, UK: Aldershot, 251–278.

Boehm, Barry [1988]. "A spiral model of software development and enhancement." *Computer* 21 (5): 61–72.

—— [2007]. *Software Engineering: Barry Boehm's Lifetime Contributions to Software Development, Management and Research,* ed. R. Selby. New York: John Wiley/IEEE Press.

Boehm, Barry W., Terence E. Gray, and Thomas Seewaldt [1984]. "Prototyping versus specifying: A multiproject experiment." *IEEE Transactions on Software Engineering* SE-10 (3): 290–303.

Booch, Grady [2009]. "Handbook of software architecture." Retrieved July 22, 2009, from http://www.handbookofsoftwarearchitecture.com/index.jsp?page=Main.

Bracewell, R. H., and K. M. Wallace [2003]. "A tool for capturing design rationale." *Proceedings of the 14th International Conference on Engineering Design (ICED '03).* Stockholm: The Design Society.

Britton, Edward, James S. Lipscomb, Michael Pique, et al. [1981]. *The GRIP-75 Man-Machine Interface.* Invited videotape presented at 1981 SIGGRAPH conference. ACM SIGGRAPH.

Brooks, F. P., Jr. [1956]. "The analytic design of automatic data processing systems." PhD dissertation, Harvard University Computation Laboratory, Cambridge, MA.

—— [1964]. *"NPL Announcement Sprint": Letters to W. C. Hume, B. O. Evans, H .D. Ross, Jr.* Poughkeepsie, NY: IBM Processor Office.

—— [1965]. "The future of computer architecture." In *Proceedings of IFIPS Congress '65.* Amsterdam: Elsevier North Holland.

—— [1972]. "Brooks beach house design." From http://www.cs.ucl.ac.uk/staff/S.Stumpf/DR.html.

—— [1975, 1995]. *The Mythical Man-Month: Essays on Software Engineering*. Reading, MA: Addison-Wesley.

—— [1977]. "The computer 'scientist' as toolsmith: Studies in interactive computer graphics." *Proceedings of International Federation of Information Processing Congress '77*, ed. B. Gilchrist. Amsterdam: Elsevier North Holland.

—— [1986]. "No silver bullet: Essence and accident in software engineering" (reprinted in Brooks [1995]). In *Information Processing 1986, Proceedings of the IFIPS Tenth World Computer Conference*, ed. H.-J. Kugler. Amsterdam: Elsevier Science, 1069–1076.

—— [1996]. "Keynote address: Language design as design." In *History of Programming Languages*, vol. 2, eds. T. J. Bergin and R. G. Gibson. Boston: Addison-Wesley (ACM Press), 4–16.

—— [1996]. "The computer scientist as toolsmith II." (Keynote/Newell Award address at SIGGRAPH 94.) *Communications of the ACM* 39 (3): 61–68.

—— [1999]. "What's real about virtual reality?" *IEEE Computer Graphics and Applications* 19 (6): 16–27.

—— [2002]. "The history of IBM Operating System/360." In *Software Pioneers: Contributions to Software Engineering*, eds. M. Broy and E. Denert. Berlin: Springer, 170–178.

Brooks, F. P., Jr., and Kenneth E. Iverson [1969]. *Automatic Data Processing: System/360 Edition*. New York: John Wiley.

Brooks, F. P., Jr., and Michael Pique [1985]. "Computer graphics for molecular studies." In *Molecular Dynamics and Protein Structure*, ed. J. Hermans. Chapel Hill, NC: University of North Carolina (distributed by Polycrystal Book Service), 109.

Brooks, Kenneth P. [1988]. "A two-view document editor with user-definable document structure." PhD dissertation, Stanford University, Palo Alto, CA.

—— [1991]. "A two-view document editor." *Computer* 24 (6): 7–19.

Broy, M., and Ernst Denert, eds. [2002]. *Software Pioneers: Contributions to Software Engineering*. Berlin: Springer.

Buchholz, Werner, ed. [1962]. *Planning a Computer System: Project Stretch*. Hightstown, NJ: McGraw-Hill.

Burge, J., and D. C. Brown [2008]. "Software engineering using RATionale." *Journal of Systems and Software* 81 (3): 395–413.

Burks, Arthur W., Herman H. Goldstine, and John von Neumann [1946]. "Preliminary discussion of the logical design of an electronic computing instrument." In *Collected Works of John von Neumann* [1963], vol. 5, ed. A. H. Taub. New York: Macmillan, 5: 34–79. Also at http://research.microsoft.com/en-us/um/people/gbell/Computer_Structures_Readings_and_Examples/00000112.html.

Buschmann, Frank, Regine Meunier, Hans Rohnert, et al. [1996]. *Pattern-Oriented Software Architecture: A System of Patterns*. New York: John Wiley.

Bush, Vannevar [1945]. "That we may think." *Atlantic Monthly* 176 (1): 101–108.

Buxton, William, and B. Myers [1986]. "A study in two-handed input." *Proceedings of the SIGCHI Conference on Human Factors in Computing Systems*. New York: ACM, 321–326.

Chen, Kuohsiang, and Charles L. Owen [1997]. "Form language and style description." *Design Studies* 18 (3): 249–274.

Chesterfield, Lord [1774]. *Lord Chesterfield's Letters*.

Clark, Nicola [2006]. "The Airbus saga: Hubris and haste snarled the A380." *International Herald Tribune*, December 11.

Clarkson, John, and Mari Huhtala, eds. [2005]. *Engineering Design: Theory and Practice—A Symposium in Honour of Ken Wallace*. Cambridge, UK: University of Cambridge Engineering Design Centre.

Cockburn, Alistair [2000]. *Writing Effective Use Cases*. Boston: Addison-Wesley.

Cockburn, Alistair, and Laurie Williams [2001]. "The costs and benefits of pair programming." In *Extreme Programming Examined*, eds. G. Succi and M. Marchesi. Boston: Addison-Wesley, 223–248.

Cocke, John, and Harwood Kolsky [1959]. "The virtual memory in the STRETCH computer." In *AFIPS Eastern Joint Computer Conference*. New York: ACM, 16: 82–93.

Cocke, John, and Jacob T. Schwartz [1970]. *Programming Languages and Their Compilers: Preliminary Notes*. New York: Courant Institute of Mathematical Sciences.

Codd, E. F., E. S. Lowry, E. McDonough, et al. [1959]. "Multiprogramming STRETCH: feasibility considerations." *Communications of the ACM* 2 (11): 13–17.

Conklin, J., and M. L. Begeman [1988]. "gIBIS: A hypertext tool for exploratory policy discussion." *ACM Transactions on Information Systems* 6 (4): 303–331.

Conner, Brookshire D., Scott S. Snibbe, Kenneth P. Herndon, et al. [1992]. "Three-dimensional widgets." In *Proceedings of the 1992 Symposium on Interactive 3D Graphics*. Cambridge, MA: ACM, 183–188.

Cross, Nigel [1962]. "Research in design thinking." In *Research in Design Thinking*, eds. N. Cross, K. Dorst, and N. Roozenburg. Delft: Delft University Press.

———, ed. [1984]. *Developments in Design Methodology*. Chichester, UK: John Wiley.

——— [1989, 1994, 2000]. *Engineering Design Methods: Strategies for Product Design*. Chichester, UK: John Wiley.

——— [2006]. *Designerly Ways of Knowing*. London: Springer.

Cross, Nigel, K. Christiaans, and K. Dorst, eds. [1996a]. *Analysing Design Activity*. Chichester, UK: John Wiley.

Cross, Nigel, and Anita Clayburn Cross [1996b]. "Winning by design: The methods of Gordon Murray, racing car designer." *Design Studies* 17 (1): 91–107.

Cross, Nigel, and Kees Dorst [1999]. "Co-evolution of problem and solution spaces in creative design." In *Computational Models of Creative Design*, vol. 4, eds. J. S. Gero and M. L. Maher. Sydney: Key Centre of Design Computing and Cognition, University of Sydney, 243–262.

Cross, Nigel, Kees Dorst, and Norbert Roozenburg, eds. [1962b]. *Research in Design Thinking*. Delft: Delft University Press.

Davies, Sir David [2000]. *Automatic Train Protection for the Railway Network in Britain: A Study; Report to the Deputy Prime Minister*. London: Royal Academy of Engineering.

DeMarco, Tom, Peter Hruschka, Tim Lister, et al. [2008]. *Adrenaline Junkies and Template Zombies: Understanding Patterns of Project Behavior*. New York: Dorset House.

DeMarco, Tom, and Tim Lister [1987, 1999]. *Peopleware: Productive Projects and Teams*. New York: Dorset House.

Denning, Peter, and Pamela Dargan [1996]. "Action-centered design." In *Bringing Design to Software*, ed. T. Winograd. Reading, MA: Addison-Wesley, 110–120.

Dennis, Jack B. [1965]. "Segmentation and the design of multiprogrammed computer systems." *Journal of the ACM* 12 (4): 589–602.

Descartes, René [1628]. "Rules for the direction of the mind." In *Philosophical Writings*. London: Thomas Nelson and Sons Ltd., 153–180.

Dijkstra, Edsger W. [1968]. "A constructive approach to the problem of program correctness." *BIT* 8: 174–186.

—— [1982]. *Selected Writings on Computing: A Personal Perspective*. Berlin: Springer-Verlag.

Dornburg, Courtney C., S. M. Stevens, S. M. L. Hendrickson, et al. [2007]. *Improving Human Effectiveness for Extreme-Scale Problem Solving— Final Report (Assessing the Effectiveness of Electronic Brainstorming in an Industrial Setting)*. Albuquerque, NM: Sandia National Laboratories.

Dorst, Kees [2006]. "Design problems and design paradoxes." *Design Issues* 22: 4–17.

Dorst, Kees, and Nigel Cross [2001]. "Creativity in the design process: Coevolution of problem–solution." *Design Studies* 22 (5): 425–437.

Dorst, Kees, and Judith Dijkhuis [1995]. "Comparing paradigms for describing design activity." *Design Studies* 16 (2): 261–274.

Eastman, Charles [1997]. [Review of] "Analyzing Design Activity." *Design Studies*, 18 (4): 475–476.

Economist [2009]. "Grounded—the airlines and business travel." Economist.com.

—— [2009]. "Harvest moon: Artificial satellites are helping farmers boost crop yields." *Economist*, November 5.

Ettlinger, Steve [2007]. *Twinkie, Deconstructed*. New York: Hudson Street Press.

Evans, Bob O. [1986]. "System/360: A retrospective view." *Annals of the History of Computing* 8 (2): 155–179.

Ferguson, Eugene S. [1992]. *Engineering and the Mind's Eye*. Cambridge, MA: MIT Press.

Fowler, H. W. [1926, 1944]. *A Dictionary of Modern English Usage*. Oxford: Oxford University Press.

Galle, Per, and Lásló Béla Kovács [1992]. "Introspective observations of sketch design." *Design Studies* 13 (3): 229–272.

Gamma, Erich, Richard Helm, Ralph Johnson, et al. [1995]. *Design Patterns: Elements of Reusable Object-Oriented Software*. Reading, MA: Addison-Wesley.

Garner, Steve [2001]. "Comparing graphic actions between remote and proximal design teams." *Design Studies* 22 (4): 365–376.

———— [2005]. "Revealing design complexity: Lessons from the Open University." *CoDesign* 1 (4): 267–276.

Gelernter, David H. [1998]. *Machine Beauty: Elegance and the Heart of Technology*. New York: Basic Books.

Gerstner, Louis V., Jr. [2002]. *Who Says Elephants Can't Dance? Inside IBM's Historic Turnaround*. New York: Harper Business.

Ghemawat, Pankaj [2007]. *Redefining Global Strategy: Crossing Borders in a World Where Differences Still Matter*. Cambridge, MA: Harvard Business School Press.

Glegg, Gordon L. [1969]. *The Design of Design*. Cambridge, UK: Cambridge University Press.

Goel, Vinod [1991]. "Sketches of thought: A study of the role of sketching in design problem-solving and its implications for the computational theory of the mind." PhD dissertation, University of California at Berkeley, Berkeley, CA.

———— [1995]. *Sketches of Thought*. Cambridge, MA: MIT Press.

Goldschmidt, Gabriela [1995]. "The designer as a team of one." *Design Studies* 16 (2): 189–210.

Gould, John D., and Clayton Lewis [1985]. "Designing for usability: Key principles and what designers think." *Communications of the ACM* 28 (3): 300–311.

Grad, B. [2002]. "A personal recollection: IBM's unbundling of software and services." *IEEE Annals of the History of Computing* 24 (1): 64–71.

Greenbaum, Joan, and Morten Kyng, eds. [1991]. *Design at Work: Cooperative Design of Computer Systems*. Hillsdale, NJ: Lawrence Erlbaum Associates.

Hales, Crispin [1991]. *An Analysis of the Engineering Design Process in an Industrial Context*. Eastleigh, UK: Gants Hill.

Hamming, Richard W. [1963, 1973]. *Numerical Methods for Scientists and Engineers*. New York: McGraw-Hill.

Heath, Tom [1989]. "Lessons from Vitruvius." *Design Studies* 10 (3): 246–253.

Hennessy, John L., and David A. Patterson [1990, 1996, 2002, 2006]. *Computer Architecture: A Quantitative Approach.* San Mateo, CA: Morgan Kaufmann.

Herbsleb, James D., Audris Mockus, Thomas A. Finholt, et al. [2000]. "Distance, dependencies, and delay in a global collaboration." In *CSCW '00: Proceedings of the 2000 ACM Conference on Computer-Supported Collaborative Work.* Philadelphia, PA: ACM, 319–328.

Hickling, Allen [1982]. "Beyond a linear iterative process?" In *Changing Design*, eds. B. Evans, J. A. Powell, et al. Chichester, UK: John Wiley, 275–293.

Highet, Gilbert [1950]. *The Art of Teaching.* New York: Vintage.

Hillier, Bill, and Alan Penn [1995]. "Can there be a domain-independent theory of design?—a comment." Short comment on accepting the *Design Studies* best paper award. They doubt that there can be such a theory.

Hinds, P., and S. Kiesler, eds. [2002]. *Distributed Work.* Cambridge, MA: MIT Press.

Hoff, Marcian E. (Ted) [1972]. "The one-chip CPU—computer or component?" In *Proceedings of the Computer Systems Design Conference [WESCON]* 16.

Hoffman, Daniel M., and David M. Weiss, eds. [2001]. *Software Fundamentals: Collected Papers by David L. Parnas.* Boston: Addison-Wesley.

Holson, Laura M. [2009]. "Putting a bolder face on Google." *New York Times*, February 28.

Holt, J. E., D. F. Radcliffe, and D. Schoorl [1985]. "Design or problem solving—a critical choice for the engineering profession." *Design Studies* 6 (2): 107–110.

Howard, Hugh [2006]. *Dr. Kimball and Mr. Jefferson: Rediscovering the Founding Fathers of American Architecture.* New York: Bloomsbury USA.

IBM Corp. [1965]. *IBM Operating System/360, Job Control Language.* Form C28-6539-0. Armonk, NY: IBM Corp.

IBM Corp., Gerrit Blaauw, and Andris Padegs [1964]. *IBM System/360 Principles of Operation. Poughkeepsie, NY, Form A22-6821-0.* Armonk, NY: IBM Corp.

IBM Corp., John W. Haanstra, and SPREAD Task Force [1961]. "Processor products—final report of SPREAD Task Group, Dec. 28, 1961." Reprinted in *IEEE Annals of the History of Computing* 5 (January 1983): 6–26.

IBM Corp. and Bernard Witt [1965]. *IBM Operating System/360, Concepts and Facilities, Form C28-6535-0.* Armonk, NY: IBM Corporation.

Insko, Brent [2001]. "Passive haptics significantly enhances virtual environments." PhD dissertation, University of North Carolina at Chapel Hill, Chapel Hill, NC.

Janlert, Lars-Erik, and Erik Stolterman [1997]. "The character of things." *Design Studies* 18 (3): 297–314.

Jupp, Julie R., and C. M. Eckert [2007]. "A unified framework for analysing decision-making in design: A multi-perspective approach." In *Proceedings of the Conference on Knowledge and Information Management.* New York: ACM.

Klein, Gerwin [2009a]. "Operating system verification—an overview." *Sadhana (India)* 34 (1): 27–69.

Klein, Gerwin , Kevin Elphinstone, Gernot Heiser, et al. [2009b]. "seL4: Formal verification of an OS kernel." In *Proceedings of the 22nd ACM Symposium on Operating Systems Principles.* New York: ACM.

Kruchten, Philippe [1999]. "The software architect and the software architecture team." In *Software Architecture*, ed. P. Donohoe. Dordrecht, Netherlands: Kluwer Academic Publications, 565–583.

Lansdown, John [1987]. "The creative aspects of CAD: A possible approach." *Design Studies* 8 (2): 76–81.

Lee, Jintai [1993]. "The 1992 workshop on design rationale capture and use." *AI Magazine* 14: 24–26.

——— [1997]. "Design rationale systems: Understanding the issues." *IEEE Intelligent Systems* 12 (3): 78–85.

Lehman, Manny M., and Laszlo A. Belady [1971]. "Programming system dynamics." In *ACM SIGOPS Third Symposium on Operating System Principles.* New York: ACM.

——— [1976]. "A model of large program development." *IBM Systems Journal* 3: 225–252.

Leverett, B. W., R. G. G. Cattell, S. O. Hobbs, et al. [1980]. "An overview of the production-quality compiler-compiler project." *Computer* 13 (8): 38–49.

Lewis, C. S. [1947]. *Miracles: A Preliminary Study*. San Francisco: Harper Collins.

——— [1961]. *An Experiment in Criticism*. Cambridge, UK: Cambridge University Press.

Locke, John [1690]. *An Essay Concerning Human Understanding*. Oxford: Oxford University Press.

Lohr, Steve [2009]. "The crowd is wise (when it's focused)." *New York Times*, July 19.

Luck, Rachael [2009]. "Does this compromise your design? Socially producing a design concept in talk-in-interaction." Reprinted in McDonnell [2009]. *CoDesign* 5 (1): 21–34.

MacLean, A., R. M. Young, and T. P. Moran [1989]. "Designing rationale: The argument behind the artifact." In *Proceedings of CHI'89 Conference on Human Factors in Computing Systems*. New York: ACM, 247–252.

Madison, James [1787]. *Notes on the Debates in the Federal Convention of 1787*.

Maher, Mary L., J. Poon, and S. Boulanger [1996]. "Formalising design exploration as co-evolution: A combined gene approach." In *Advances in Formal Design Methods for CAD*, eds. J. S. Gero and F. Sudeweks. London: Chapman and Hall.

Maher, Mary Lou, and Hsien-Hui Tang [2003]. "Co-evolution as a computational and cognitive model of design." *Research in Engineering Design* 14 (1): 47–63.

Margolin, Victor, and Richard Buchanan, eds. [1995]. *The Idea of Design*. Cambridge, MA: MIT Press.

McDonnell, Janet, and Peter Lloyd, eds. [2008]. *About Designing: Analysing Design Meetings*. Leiden: CRC Press/Balkema.

McManus, John, and Trevor Wood-Harper [2003]. *Information Systems Project Management: Methods, Tools and Techniques*. London: Financial Times Management.

Meehan, Michael, Brent Insko, Mary C. Whitton, et al. [2002]. "Physiological measures of presence in stressful virtual environments." *ACM Transactions on Graphics, Proceedings of ACM SIGGRAPH 2002* 21 (3): 645–652.

Menn, Christian [1996]. "The place of aesthetics in bridge design." *Structural Engineering International* 6 (2): 93–95.

Mills, Harlan D. [1971]. "Top-down programming in large systems." In *Debugging Techniques in Large Systems,* ed. R. Rustin. Englewood Cliffs, NJ: Prentice Hall.

Mills, Harlan D., M. Dyer, and R. Linger [1987]. "Cleanroom software engineering." *IEEE Software* 4 (5): 19–25.

Moran, Thomas P., and John M. Carroll, eds. [1996]. *Design Rationale: Concepts, Techniques, and Use.* Mahwah, NJ: Lawrence Erlbaum Associates.

Mosteller, Frederick, and D. L. Wallace [1964]. *Inference and Disputed Authorship: Federalist Papers.* Reading, MA: Addison-Wesley.

Muir Wood, Sir Alan [2007]. "Strategy for risk management." In *Tunneling 2007.*

Murray, Charles J. [1997]. *The Supermen: The Story of Seymour Cray and the Technical Wizards Behind the Supercomputer.* New York: John Wiley.

Naur, Peter, and Brian Randell [1968]. "Software engineering: Report of a conference sponsored by the NATO Science Committee." NATO Software Engineering Conference, Garmisch, DE. Scientific Affairs Division, NATO.

Noble, Douglas, and Horst W. J. Rittel [1988]. "Issue-based information systems for design." In *Proceedings of the ACADIA '88 Conference.* Ann Arbor, MI: Association for Computer Aided Design in Architecture.

Osborn, Alexander F. [1963]. *Applied Imagination: Principles and Procedures of Creative Problem Solving.* New York: Charles Scribner's Sons.

Pahl, Gerhardt [2005]. "VADEMECUM—recommendations for developing and applying design methodologies." In *Engineering Design: Theory and Practice—A Symposium in Honour of Ken Wallace,* eds. J. Clarkson and M. Huhtala. Cambridge, UK: University of Cambridge Engineering Design Centre, 126–135.

Pahl, G., and W. Beitz [1984, 1996, 2007]. *Engineering Design: A Systematic Approach.* Berlin: Springer-Verlag.

Parnas, David L. [1979]. "Designing software for ease of extension and contraction." *IEEE Transactions on Software Engineering* 5 (2): 128–138.

—— [2001]. *Software Fundamentals: Collected Papers by David L. Parnas*, eds. D. Hoffman and D. Weiss. Boston: Addison-Wesley.

Patterson, David [1981]. "RISC I: A reduced instruction set architecture." *Computer Architecture News* 9 (3): 443–458.

Paulk, Mark C. [1995]. "The evolution of the SEI's capability maturity model for software." *Software Process: Improvement and Practice* pilot issue (1): 3–15.

Petroski, Henry [2008]. *Success through Failure: The Paradox of Design*. Princeton: Princeton University Press.

Pique, Michael, Jane S. Richardson, and F. P. Brooks, Jr. [1982]. *What Does a Protein Look Like?* Invited videotape presented at 1982 SIGGRAPH Conference.

Pugh, Emerson W., Lyle R. Johnson, and John H. Palmer [1991]. *IBM's 360 and Early 370 Systems*. Cambridge, MA: MIT Press.

Radin, George [1982]. "The 801 minicomputer." *ACM SIGPLAN Notices* 17 (4): 39–47.

—— [1983]. "The IBM 801 minicomputer." *IBM Journal of Research and Development* 27 (3): 237–246.

Raskar, R., G. Welch, M. Cutts, et al. [1998]. "The office of the future: A unified approach to image-based modeling and spatially immersive displays." In *SIGGRAPH '98: The Twenty-fifth Annual Conference on Computer Graphics and Interactive Techniques*. New York: ACM, 179–188.

Raymond, Eric S. [2001]. "The golden cauldron." In *The Cathedral and the Bazaar: Musings on Linux and Open Source by an Accidental Revolutionary*. Sebastopol, CA: O'Reilly Media.

—— [2001]. *The Cathedral and the Bazaar: Musings on Linux and Open Source by an Accidental Revolutionary*. Sebastopol, CA: O'Reilly Media.

Risen, Isadore L. [1970]. "A theory on meetings." *Public Administration Review* 30 (1): 90–92.

Rittel, Horst, and Melvin Webber [1973]. "Dilemmas in a general theory of planning." *Policy Sciences* 4: 155–169.

Robertson, Suzanne, and James Robertson [2005]. *Requirements-Led Project Management: Discovering David's Slingshot*. Boston: Addison-Wesley.

————— [2006]. *Mastering the Requirements Process.* Boston: Addison-Wesley.

Royce, Winston [1970]. "Managing the development of large software systems." In *Proceedings of IEEE Wescon.* New York: IEEE Press.

Rybczynski, Witold [1989]. *The Most Beautiful House in the World.* New York: Penguin Group.

Salton, Gerald [1958]. "An automatic data processing system for public utility revenue accounting." PhD dissertation, Harvard University Computation Laboratory, Cambridge, MA.

Sammet, Jean E. [1969]. *Programming Languages: History and Fundamentals.* Englewood Cliffs, NJ: Prentice Hall.

Sayers, Dorothy [1941]. *The Mind of the Maker.* New York: Harcourt Brace Jovanovich.

Schön, Donald [1984]. *The Reflective Practitioner: How Professionals Think in Action.* New York: Basic Books.

————— [1986]. *Educating the Reflective Practitioner.* San Francisco: Jossey-Bass.

Schön, Donald A., and Glenn Wiggins [1992]. "Kinds of seeing and their functions in designing." *Design Studies* 13 (2): 135–156.

Selby, Richard, ed. [2007]. *Software Engineering: Barry Boehm's Lifetime Contributions to Software Development, Management and Research.* New York: John Wiley/IEEE Press.

Shannon, Claude, and Warren Weaver [1949]. *The Mathematical Theory of Communication.* Urbana, IL: University of Illinois at Urbana.

Shum, Simon J. B., Albert M. Selvin, Maarten Sierhuis, et al. [2006]. "Hypermedia support for argumentation-based rationale: 15 years on from gIBIS and QOC." In *Rationale Management in Software Engineering*, eds. A. H. Dutoit, R. McCall, I. Mistrik, et al. Berlin: Springer-Verlag.

Sibly, P. G., and A. C. Walker [1977]. "Structural accidents and their causes." *Proceedings of the Institution of Civil Engineers, Part 1,* 62: 191–208.

Simon, H. A. [1969, 1981, 1996]. *The Sciences of the Artificial.* Cambridge, MA: MIT Press.

Smethurst, Canon A. F. [1967]. *The Pictorial History of Salisbury Cathedral.* London: Pitkin Pictorials.

Sonnenwald, Diane H., Mary C. Whitton, and Kelly L. Maglaughlin [2003]. "Evaluating a scientific collaboratory: Results of a controlled experiment." *ACM Transactions on Computer-Human Interaction* 10 (2): 150–176.

Squires, Arthur [1986]. *The Tender Ship: Governmental Management of Technological Change*. Boston: Birkhauser.

Stillinger, Jack [1991]. *Multiple Authorship and the Myth of Solitary Genius*. New York: Oxford University Press.

Stoakley, Richard, Matthew Conway, and Randy Pausch [1995]. "Virtual reality on a WIM: Interactive worlds in miniature." In *SIGCHI Conference on Human Factors in Computing Systems*. Denver, CO: ACM Press/Addison-Wesley, 265–272.

Strassen, Volker [1969]. "Gaussian elimination is not optimal." *Numerische Mathematik* 13: 354–356.

Sullivan, William G., Pui-Mun Lee, James T. Luxhoj, et al. [1994]. "Survey of engineering design literature: Methodology, education, economics, and management aspects." *Engineering Economist* 40 (1): 7–40.

Sumner, F. H., G. Haley, and E. C. Y. Chen [1962]. "The central control unit of the 'Atlas' computer." In *Information Processing 1962, Proceedings of the IFIP Congress '62*. Amsterdam: Elsevier North Holland.

Svensson, U. P., and U. R. Kristiansen [2002]. "Computational modelling and simulation of acoustic spaces." In *Proceedings of the AES 22nd International Conference: Virtual, Synthetic, and Entertainment Audio*. New York: Audio Engineering Society, 1–20.

Teasley, S., L. Covi, M. S. Krishnan, and Judith S. Olson [2000]. "How does radical collocation help a team succeed?" In *CSCW '00: Proceedings of the ACM 2000 Conference on Computer Supported Cooperative Work*. New York: ACM, 339–346.

Thornton, J. E. [1964]. *Design of a Computer—The CDC 6600*. Glenview, IL: Scott, Foresman.

Tolkien, John R. R. [1964]. "On fairy-stories." In *Tree and Leaf*. London: George, Allen & Unwin, Ltd., 3–84.

Torrance, E. Paul [1970]. "Dyadic interaction as a facilitator of gifted performance." *Gifted Child Quarterly* 14 (3): 139–143.

Tovey, Sir Donald [1950]. "Johann Sebastian Bach." *Encyclopedia Britannica*, vol. 2. Chicago: Encyclopedia Britannica, 868–875.

Towles, Herman, Wei-Chao Chen, Ruigang Yang, et al. [2002]. "3D tele-collaboration over Internet2." In *Proceedings of the International Workshop on Immersive Telepresence (ITP2002)*. New York: ACM.

Tucker, Stewart G. [1965]. "Emulation of large systems." *Communications of the ACM* 8 (12): 753–761.

Tyree, Jeff, and Art Akerman [2005]. "Architecture decisions: Demystifying architecture." *IEEE Software* 22 (2): 19–27.

Ullman, David G. [1962]. "The foundations of the modern design environment: An imaginary retrospective." In *Research in Design Thinking*, eds. N. Cross, K. Dorst, and N. Roozenburg. Delft: Delft University Press.

van der Poel, W. L. [1959]. "ZEBRA, a simple binary computer." Reprinted in Bell and Newell [1971], 200–204. In *Proceedings of ICIP*. Paris: UNESCO, 361–365.

———— [1962]. *The Logical Principles of Some Simple Computers*. Amsterdam: Excelsior.

VDI, Verein Deutscher Ingenieure [1986, 1987]. *VDI-2221: Systematic Approach to the Design of Technical Systems and Products*. Düsseldorf, DE: VDI Verlag.

Vincenti, Walter G. [1990]. *What Engineers Know and How They Know It: Analytical Studies from Aeronautical Engineering*. Baltimore, MD: Johns Hopkins University Press.

Visser, Willemien [2006]. *The Cognitive Artifacts of Designing*. Mahwah, NJ: Lawrence Erlbaum Associates.

Vitruvius, Marcus Vitruvius Pollo [22 BC, 1960]. *De Architectura (The Ten Books on Architecture)*. Rome: Dover.

Waldron, Manjula B., and Kenneth J. Waldron [1988]. "A time sequence study of a complex mechanical system design." *Design Studies* 9 (2): 95–106.

Weisberg, R. W. [1986]. *Creativity: Genius and Other Myths*. New York: Freeman.

Wexelblat, Richard L., ed. [1981]. *History of Programming Languages*. New York: Academic Press (ACM Monograph Series).

Whitton, Mary C., Benjamin Lok, Brent Insko, et al. [2005]. "Integrating real and virtual objects in virtual environments." In *Proceedings of HCI International 2005*. Berlin: Springer-Verlag, 9.

Wilkes, Maurice V. [1985]. *Memoirs of a Computer Pioneer*. Cambridge, MA: MIT Press.

Wilkes, Maurice V., and W. Renwick [1949]. "The EDSAC." In *Report of a Conference on High Speed Automatic Calculating Machines*. Cambridge, UK: University Mathematics Laboratory, 9–12.

Williams, F. C., and T. Kilburn [1948]. "Electronic digital computers." *Nature* 162: 487.

Williams, Laurie, Robert R. Kessler, Ward Cunningham, et al. [2000]. "Strengthening the case for pair-programming." *IEEE Software* 17 (4): 19–25.

Winograd, Terry, John Bennett, Laura De Young, et al., eds. [1996]. *Bringing Design to Software*. New York: ACM Press.

Wise, T. A. [1966]. "I.B.M.'s $5,000,000,000 Gamble." *Fortune* 74 (September): 118–123, 224–228; (October): 138–143, 199–212.

Witt, Bernard I., F. Terry Baker, and Everett W. Merritt [1994]. *Software Architecture and Design: Principles, Models, and Methods*. New York: Van Nostrand Reinhold.

Wolff, Christoff [2000]. *Johann Sebastian Bach: The Learned Musician*. New York: W. W. Norton.

Wozniak, Steve, and Gina Smith [2006]. *iWoz: From Computer Geek to Cult Icon: How I Invented the Personal Computer, Co-Founded Apple, and Had Fun Doing It*. New York: W. W. Norton.

Ziman, John M., ed. [2000]. *Technological Innovation as an Evolutionary Process*. Cambridge, UK: Cambridge University Press.

People Index

Adair, Paul N. (Red), 90
Adam, Robert, 136, 253
Aiken, Howard H., xiv, 164, 375
Akerman, Art, 390
Akin, Omer, 18, 146, 375
Alexander, Christopher, 9, 150,
    194, 217, 295, 306, 311, 375
Allen, Frances E. (Fran), 249, 255,
    375
Amdahl, Gene M., 76, 92, 121,
    158, 314, 319, 322, 323, 328,
    375
Andrews, David, 371
Arden, Bruce W., 159, 376
Arthur, Kevin, 217, 376
Aurisicchio, Marco, 198, 200, 371,
    376

Bach, Johann Sebastian, 65, 128,
    135, 147, 148, 153, 154, 207,
    245
Bacon, Sir Francis, 3, 4, 113, 376
Baird, Douglas, 328
Baker, F. Terry, 391
Bannon, L. J., 375
Barkstrom, Bruce R., 376
Baruch, Bernard, 63, 83
Bastos, Rui, 371
Begeman, M. L., 380
Beitz, Wolfgang, xiv, 9, 11, 16, 18,
    30, 32, 33, 34, 39, 58, 386
Belady, Laszlo, 156, 240, 384
Bell, Alexander Graham, 233

Bell, Gordon C., 147, 151, 159,
    160, 313, 323, 329, 374, 376
Belsky, Martin, 343
Bennett, John, 391
Bergin, Thomas J., 164, 376, 378
Billington, David P., 84, 376
Bjerknes, G., 377
Blaauw, Gerrit A. (Gerry), 7, 9,
    11, 15, 34, 70, 84, 95, 123, 124,
    141, 142, 143, 145, 147, 149,
    150, 151, 157, 158, 160, 189,
    254, 256, 313, 314, 319, 322,
    325, 326, 327, 328, 344, 347,
    367, 371, 374, 375, 376, 377,
    383
Blum, Bruce I., 331, 377
Bocquet, J.-C., 376
Boehm, Barry W., 21, 48, 51, 57,
    58, 59, 367, 371, 377, 388
Boehm, Elaine, 322
Booch, Grady, 161, 164, 181, 374,
    377
Boulanger, S., 53, 385
Bourbaki Seminar, 106
Bracewell, Robert H. (Rob), 198,
    199, 200, 371, 376, 377
Bragg, Sir William Henry, 106
Bragg, William Lawrence, 106
Britton, Edward, 216, 377
Brooks, Kenneth P., xiii, 226, 261,
    282, 374, 378
Brooks, Nancy G., xiii, 26, 186,
    261, 281, 282, 298, 308, 309
Brooks, Octavia, 261

Subject Index

Note: Boldface page references indicate definitions or the beginning point of a substantial treatment. Page numbers in those scopes are not separately listed under that term.

FROM THE AUTHOR OF *THE MYTHICAL MAN-MONTH*

THE DESIGN OF DESIGN

ESSAYS FROM A COMPUTER SCIENTIST

FREDERICK P. BROOKS, JR.

FREE Online Edition

Your purchase of *The Design of Design* includes access to a free online edition for 45 days through the Safari Books Online subscription service. Nearly every Addison-Wesley Professional book is available online through Safari Books Online, along with more than 5,000 other technical books and videos from publishers such as Cisco Press, Exam Cram, IBM Press, O'Reilly, Prentice Hall, Que, and Sams.

SAFARI BOOKS ONLINE allows you to search for a specific answer, cut and paste code, download chapters, and stay current with emerging technologies.

Activate your FREE Online Edition at
www.informit.com/safarifree

> **STEP 1:**   Enter the coupon code: RNTJZAA.

> **STEP 2:**   New Safari users, complete the brief registration form.
>   Safari subscribers, just log in.

If you have difficulty registering on Safari or accessing the online edition, please e-mail customer-service@safaribooksonline.com

Safari
Books Online